Dugout Days

Dugout Days

Untold Tales and Leadership Lessons from the Extraordinary Career of Billy Martin

Michael DeMarco

AMACOM

American Management Association

New York • Atlanta • Boston • Chicago • Kansas City • San Francisco • Washington, D. C.
Brussels • Mexico City • Tokyo • Toronto

Special discounts on bulk quantities of AMACOM books are available to corporations, professional associations, and other organizations. For details, contact Special Sales Department, AMACOM, a division of American Management Association, 1601 Broadway, New York, NY 10019.
Tel.: 212-903-8316. Fax: 212-903-8083.
Web site: www.amacombooks.org

This publication is designed to provide accurate and authoritative information in regard to the subject matter covered. It is sold with the understanding that the publisher is not engaged in rendering legal, accounting, or other professional service. If legal advice or other expert assistance is required, the services of a competent professional person should be sought.

Grateful acknowledgment is made to the following sources for permission to reprint, reference, and/or quote from their works:

Billyball by Billy Martin and Phil Pepe, copyright © 1987 by Billy Martin and Phil Pepe. Used by permission of Doubleday, a division of Random House, Inc.
The Last Yankee by David Falkner, copyright © by David Falkner. Reprinted with the permission of Simon & Schuster.
The Patton Mind by Roger H. Nye, copyright © 1993 by Roger H. Nye. Used by permission of Avery Publishing, a division of Penguin Putnam, Inc.

Library of Congress Cataloging-in-Publication Data

DeMarco, Michael.
    Dugout days : untold tales and leadership lessons from the extraordinary career of Billy Martin / Michael DeMarco.
        p.   cm.
    Includes bibliographical references and index.
    ISBN 0-8144-0561-4
    1. Martin, Billy   2. Baseball managers—United States—Biography.   3. Leadership.   I. Title.
GV865.M35 D46   2001
796.357'092—dc21   2001016051

Printing number

10 9 8 7 6 5 4 3 2 1

To Kinger

Contents

Foreword

I'm sure that there's a lot of you out there who have a hard time seeing my dad as a leader because of things you've read. People see him as the battler, the scrapper, the argumentative guy that he was, in one sense.

But in this book, I think you'll see a lot more of what dad was all about. Sure, you'll read stories about my dad in full uniform standing under running showers yelling and screaming at one of his players. You'll also read about a couple of my dad's postgame locker room outbursts. That's the Billy Martin who sold a lot of newspapers, and that's probably the Billy Martin a lot of you feel like you know, in a way. And that *was* my dad.

But there's also the Billy Martin who picked up the phone and called Dave Righetti's parents after Rags threw his famous July 4, 1983 no-hitter against the Red Sox. There's the Billy Martin who helped a young, pressing Mike Pagliarulo to relax a little just by taking him out alone for a couple of beers and some baseball talk. And there's the Billy Martin who restored the confidence of Paul Blair, maybe the greatest defensive center fielder ever, by leaving the bat in his hands in so many clutch batting situations during that World Championship season of 1977.

Dad had the ability to push people's buttons, and he was unique in his ability to read people, to find out what made them click, and to get different guys to perform and to play with confidence. He would take one guy who needed to be built up and tell him, "Hey, you're my guy. I don't care about last year. I don't care how you start this year. I don't care what happens. I'm sticking by you, kid." Then he could take another guy who wasn't playing the way he had in previous years and say to him, "Look here, I don't care what you've done in the past. You're going to have to come out here and bust your ass for me. And if you do, you're going to be all right. But if you don't, hit the road." It all depended on the particulars of each ballplayer.

Dad was an expert in building up guys' confidence levels. Baseball, like most of life, is a very mental game. I think dad looked at his ballplayers from a mental standpoint and said, "What can I get away with this guy mentally, before he loses faith in himself?" If certain guys are overexposed, not only does everyone else see their weaknesses but the players themselves start to believe in those weaknesses. Dad didn't want that to happen. He wanted to protect players from their weaknesses, even if they had a lot of them.

When I think about dad managing, I immediately think about the Oakland A's. In my mind, those were probably the happiest days for him in his career as a manager. He was the show there. It was Billyball. Those guys believed in him and in that whole situation, and they went out and did well.

My dad loved the kids on that team, and I think he got a major rush out of taking what everybody would define as a subpar team and *winning*. I think he loved to squeeze every ounce of ability out of lesser players, and I think then he felt he was best doing his job. I think he lived for saying, "Let's go! You guys run through a wall for me, and I can turn you into winners." And guys wanted to win for dad. And that's what I think your job as a leader in baseball, or business, or anything is. You need to find a way to make people believe in themselves and want to perform their best. And that's what dad was all about.

In one of the books that has come out on dad since his accident, the author ends by creating a picture of my dad in the late 1980s, riding through the streets of New York City in the back of his stretch limo.

I guess the limo kind of represents both the success my father had achieved in baseball and at the same time the excesses of his lifestyle. Coming from next to nothing, he enjoyed the luxuries that his success enabled him to afford, and he earned them. But I think it's more important with dad to remember the succeeding itself.

So I'd like to give you another picture of my dad that I think better captures what his life was about. It's my dad in Scottsdale, Arizona in the spring of 1980. He'd been fired twice as Yankee manager, and his reputation in the game of baseball was on the line. To reestablish that reputation, he took over an A's team that in 1979 had lost 108 games and attracted only 300,000 fans.

But in comes dad with his whole crew of coaches. I can see dad leaning up against the batting cage, his eyes darting around the diamond, watching the personnel he's got. And instead of seeing nothing, he sees something. And he builds these guys up, he gives them pride, and he teaches them the game. He's out there on the field, not buried in some office. He's instructing, preaching, screaming, and leading.

And these guys go out and win for him. It's aggressive, it's wild, it's Billyball. The A's become winners, the fans came out in record numbers, and the whole baseball world has to stand up and take notice. He made them into a winning, marketable club. By early 1981, dad's on the cover of *Time* magazine, and by the end of that season, the A's are playing the New York Yankees for a chance to go to the World Series!

His bottom line was winning. And he didn't care how people felt about him, which is still hard for me to swallow. He used to say to me, "Partner, I don't care if they love me or hate me, as long as I can find a way to make those guys win."

Other people get quoted for this, but this is dad's line: "If it's just about how we play the game, why the hell do we keep score?" And he meant that. In baseball, as in probably all business, there's a bottom line. And in baseball, the bottom line is winning. Billy Martin won everywhere he went. He is synonymous with winning. Did he ever make mistakes? Of course. Would there be things that he would retract if he had a chance to do them over? I feel certain of that. But when it came to the bottom line of baseball, you'll be hard pressed to find any other manager in the history of the game that was any more of a winner than he was. I don't care what a reporter or anybody else says, there's no refuting that. So there's definitely something to learn from what my dad did on the field.

I think the quality that most personifies what my father was about is loyalty. Whether it be with his coaches or his players, he wanted to be surrounded with loyalty. I know it's kind of funny in a way, because of the way he seemed to battle management all the time. You look at it from an outsider's view, and you say, "Well, he expected this loyalty from his guys, and in turn, he was loyal to them, but he always seemed to have his troubles with management. Where was his loyalty to them?" But even there, I don't think he ever felt like he was *disloyal* to management. I just think he felt like he had to do his job his way. He always said, "I'm not a yes man. If they wanted a yes man, they should've hired a yes man." Sometimes that was a weakness in my dad's business sense, there's no doubt about it. I don't like to say my dad had any weaknesses, but I'm realistic. That was one of his flaws. At some level, it was part of who he was, but there were times when he should have bitten his tongue. It pains me to say that, but he wasn't perfect. Who is?

And while we're on the topic of my dad's imperfections, we have to talk about the New York Yankees. His blessing and his curse were that he so badly wanted to be a Yankee. The first time he became Yankee manager was great, and the team played great. In 1976 they made their first trip to the World Series since 1964, and they won their first World Championship in 15 years the following season. But you probably know everything that went on then with my dad and George Steinbrenner for the Yankees to get to those achievements. Had it been up to me, he'd have never gone back there.

But in his mind he was a Yankee, and that was where he belonged. That was it for him. That was where he lived his best years. That was where he and Mickey Mantle and Whitey Ford owned the world. That was where they won World Series and were walking demigods. Still, to me, except for the 1950s and the World Series in 1977, New York was a shame for dad, because I think there are so many negative connotations that he's associated with there, with the continuing "George and Billy" show. But this is how my dad wanted it to be.

I hope this book can open some eyes and make people think about dad and about how he was a leader and a damn good one. You may not agree with some of the things he did and some of the approaches he used to get a player or a club moving. That's OK. He could be very tough, and he could be outrageous. But I think these things can be considered in a thoughtful manner, not just sensationalized.

I really miss my dad, of course, and I think baseball misses him too. I hope that in these pages, you will understand why he's missed.

Billy Martin, Jr.
Arlington, Texas
June 2000

Acknowledgments

The main inspiration for this book is, of course, Billy Martin himself. I first became very interested in baseball at the age of seven in 1976, the same year that Billy led the Yankees back to the World Series for the first time since 1964. For the next several years, I was as devoted a fan of the Yankees and of Billy Martin as a young kid could be. I collected baseball cards. I watched the games on WPIX. I was thrilled to get Billy's autograph one night at Fenway Park in 1978, and only weeks later I was saddened when Billy resigned his job under fire. Days after that, I was of course joyous again when Billy's future rehiring was announced before an Old-Timers' Day crowd at Yankee Stadium. And a few years later, I was as excited as the rest of the country by Billyball, the exciting brand of baseball Billy's Oakland A's played in 1980 and 1981. These memories remain very vivid these many years later, and it has been a thrill to think back to these times in the writing of this book.

Four people in particular helped to turn this book from an idea into reality, and I will always appreciate the faith that each of them showed in me. Judge Eddie Sapir, Billy Martin's agent and friend, started the ball rolling simply by showing some belief in me, by encouraging me to move forward, and by putting me in touch with Billy Martin, Jr. Billy, Jr.

picked up where Judge Sapir left off, and he helped me to see this project through during a very busy time in his life. Next is my agent Marty Appel, who believed enough in my early drafts to take me on as a client and to sell my idea to a publisher. Finally, I thank my editor Ellen Kadin, who liked my ideas and who has always been there to help me throughout the writing process.

I am, of course, greatly indebted to the many players, personnel, and friends who were around Billy during his career and who agreed to take time from their schedules to speak with me. I think you will see in the following pages that they often went beyond the call of duty in helping me create this book. A few people in baseball front offices put in great effort to help me, and they include Amy Abramczyk of the Milwaukee Brewers, Jim Duquette of the New York Mets, and Debbie Gallas of the Oakland A's. Also, the staff of the Baseball Hall of Fame Library were of great help in the early days of my efforts.

Finally, I'd also like to thank family and friends for their support and encouragement. They include most of all Jen, Benjamin, Mom, Dad, Summer, Mark, Blair, the Sportos, the Shermans, the Munzers, the Kings, and the McCauleys. I'd also like to thank some of the leaders who have influenced me over the years: Hank and Steve Tomkowicz, Frank Zoltek, Jim St. Denis, Ed Noel, Peter Willmott, Paul Lawrence, Bill Takis, and David Treworgy. Their lessons and influence are greatly appreciated.

Who's Who in *Dugout Days*

▶ **Marty Appel:** *Marty was the director of public relations for the New York Yankees when Billy Martin was first hired to manage the team in 1975. He currently runs Marty Appel Public Relations, which provides PR assistance to the sports world.*

▶ **Paul Blair:** *A speedy center fielder who won eight Gold Gloves and played in six World Series with the Orioles and Yankees, Blair was an important member of Billy Martin's 1977 World Champion Yankees, winning several games with clutch hitting and fielding. For his career, Blair hit .250 with 134 HRs and 620 RBIs. Today, he is the coach of the Coppin State College baseball team in Baltimore.*

▶ **Jackie Brown:** *Jackie Brown pitched for the Senators, Rangers, Indians, and Expos between 1970 and 1977. His best season came in 1974, when Billy Martin gave him an opportunity to pitch in his starting rota-*

tion. That year, Brown was 13–12, with a 3.57 ERA and 134 strikeouts. He later was the Rangers' pitching coach for several seasons.

▶ **Rod Carew:** *The Hall of Famer came to the big leagues in 1967 and learned to play second base under coach Billy Martin's tutelage. In 1969, with Billy making his managerial debut, Carew won the first of his seven batting championships and tied a record by stealing home seven times. He had 3,053 hits for his 19-year career and was an All-Star 17 times. In his 1977 MVP season, Carew's .388 batting average was 50 points higher than that of NL champ Dave Parker, the largest margin in baseball history. Carew honored Billy by having him serve as his daughter Stephanie's godfather. Rod is currently the Milwaukee Brewers' hitting coach.*

▶ **Tom Grieve:** *Tom Grieve played for the Senators, Rangers, Mets, and Cardinals from 1970 to 1979. He emerged as a valuable role player under Billy Martin, hitting .276 with 14 home runs and 61 RBIs for the 1975 Rangers. In 1976, he had a career-best year, batting .255 with 20 home runs and 81 RBIs. After his playing career ended, Grieve became the general manager of the Rangers. Currently, he is a broadcaster for the club. His son, Ben Grieve, is one of baseball's brightest young stars and the winner of the 1998 AL Rookie of the Year Award.*

▶ **Toby Harrah:** *A four-time All-Star who played 17 years in the big leagues, Harrah's career took off under Billy Martin. In 1974, Toby hit .260 with 21 HRs and 74 RBIs, and in 1975, the numbers climbed to .293, 20, and 93, with a .406 on-base percentage. He was a rangy shortstop and a gritty player. For his career, Harrah had 1,954 hits, 195 HRs, 1,115 runs scored, 919 RBIs, and 238 stolen bases. He hit 20 or more HRs five times, scored 90 or more runs four times, and played in 155 games or more five times. Harrah managed the Rangers briefly in 1992 and has been a coaching fixture since his career ended in 1986. He currently is a member of Buddy Bell's Colorado Rockies staff.*

▶ **Ron Hassey:** *Ron Hassey played for Billy Martin's 1985 New York Yankee club. He became known to Yankee fans as "Babe" for several mas-*

*sive, clutch home runs during the stretch drive. That season, Hassey hit
.296 with 13 home runs and 42 RBIs. He later played on Tony LaRussa's
A's, traveling to the World Series in 1988, 1989, and 1990. Hassey is
currently an assistant general manager of the Arizona Diamondbacks.*

▶ **Mike Heath:** *Mike Heath came up to the majors to fill in for an injured
Thurman Munson on Billy Martin's 1978 Yankees. He later was Billy's
catcher in Oakland from 1980 to 1982. Heath played in the big leagues
from 1978 to 1991, compiling a lifetime average of .252, with 1,061
career hits, 86 home runs, and 469 RBIs. Teammate Matt Keough said
of Heath, "Mike Heath was the best throwing catcher in the American
League at that time, by far. He was the most athletic, best-throwing
catcher in the American League. We never had to worry about the running game, because Mike just eliminated it. Or the bunting game,
because he was so fast getting out from behind home plate."*

▶ **Willie Horton:** *A four-time All-Star who was a member of the 1968
World Champion Tigers, Horton played for Billy Martin on the
1971–1973 Detroit club, including the 1972 AL East champs. Horton
drove in 100 or more runs three times in his career, and he hit 36 HRs in
1968. He credits Billy with sparking the desire in him to play as long as
he did; for his career, Horton played in 2,028 games, had 1,993 hits,
slugged 325 HRs, and drove home 1,163 runs. He later was a coach for
Billy with the 1985 Yankees.*

▶ **Matt Keough:** *Originally signed as an infielder by Charlie Finley, Keough
became a pitcher in the minors in 1976. By 1978, he was pitching in the
All-Star Game, where he first met Billy Martin. In 1979, Keough lost his
first 14 decisions and ended up the season at 2–17, only to turn it
around with Billy in 1980, when he won 16 games and had a 2.92 ERA.
Matt pitched a brilliant game against Dave Righetti and the Yanks in the
1981 AL Championship Series, leaving after eight-plus innings down
1–0. He is currently a scout in the Tampa Bay organization.*

▶ **Mickey Klutts:** *Like Heath, Klutts played for Billy Martin in New York,
debuting in 1976 and also appearing briefly with the 1977 and 1978*

World Championship clubs. Klutts went to the A's in 1979 and was a pla-tooning third baseman on Billy's Billyball clubs of 1980–1982. Injury-plagued throughout his career, Klutts hit .269 with 4 home runs and 21 RBIs in 75 games for the 1980 A's, and .370 with 5 home runs and 11 RBIs in only 15 games with the AL West Champion 1981 A's.

▶ **Tony LaRussa:** One of the most successful managers of the era, LaRussa has piloted the White Sox, A's, and Cardinals into postseason play since first taking the reigns in 1979. LaRussa learned a great deal about his craft as a young skipper by going up against Billy Martin's Yankee and A's clubs. LaRussa's 1988 A's, led by "Bash Brothers" Jose Canseco and Mark McGwire, went 104–58 and traveled to the World Series for the first of three straight times. The club won the Series in 1989. LaRussa later led the Cardinals to the 1996 NL Central title and enjoyed Mark McGwire's home run assaults in 1998 and 1999 from his dugout vantage point. LaRussa's Cardinals in 2000 took the NL Central Division, swept the Braves in the division series, but then fell to the Mets in the NL Championship Series.

▶ **Frank Lucchesi:** A coach with Billy Martin's Texas Rangers in 1974 and 1975, Lucchesi had managed in the minors, winning seven pennants in 19 years, before becoming the manager of the Philadelphia Phillies in 1970. Lucchesi later piloted the Rangers and the Cubs, compiling a 316–399 record in seven seasons. Lucchesi, raised "four blocks from my baseball idol, Joe DiMaggio, right near Fisherman's Wharf in the Ital-ian area" of San Francisco, played semipro ball with Billy Martin as kids in the Bay Area, and later in the minor leagues.

▶ **Gil McDougald:** A teammate of Billy's on four World Championship Yan-kees clubs, Gil McDougald was a five-time All-Star, and the AL Rookie of the Year in 1951. Gil played in eight World Series for the Yankees. He once drove in six runs in one inning, and as a rookie, he hit a World Series grand slam home run. He hit .276 for his ten-year career, with 1,291 hits and 112 HRs. He played in 53 World Series games, fourth on the all-time list, and he ranks in the top ten in at-bats, hits, HRs, runs, RBIs, walks, and strikeouts for Fall Classic play.

▶ **Charlie Manuel:** *The manager of the Cleveland Indians, Charlie played his rookie season in the big leagues for Billy Martin with the 1969 Twins. He played 19 years in the minors, the majors, and Japan, and has coached and managed in the minors and majors since retiring as an active player. Charlie was the first American to be named MVP in Japan, after hitting .324 with 37 homers and 97 RBIs there in 1979. He hit 192 homers in six seasons in Japan, including 48 in 1980.*

▶ **Bobby Meacham:** *Bobby Meacham played for Billy Martin during each of Billy's stints with the Yankees in the 1980s—1983, 1985, and 1988. He was the Yankees' regular shortstop in 1984 and 1985, enjoying his best season with Billy in 1985. That year he hit only .218, but he drove in 47 runs and played in 156 games. Since retiring, Meacham has coached and managed in the minor leagues and is currently a roving minor league instructor with the Pittsburgh Pirates organization.*

▶ **Sam Mele:** *Sam Mele played against Billy Martin in a career that began with the Red Sox in 1947 and ended with the Indians in 1956. As a Red Sox rookie in 1947, Mele hit .302 with 12 home runs and 73 RBIs. In 1951, while playing for the Washington Senators, Mele drove in 94 runs on the strength of only 5 homers. From 1961 through 1968, Mele managed the Minnesota Twins. While managing the Twins, Mele brought Billy Martin onto the field for his first coaching experience. He took them to the 1965 World Series against the Los Angeles Dodgers. After his managerial career ended, Mele spent many years as a scout for the Red Sox and remained close with Billy Martin until Billy died in 1989.*

▶ **George Mitterwald:** *A rookie catcher for Billy Martin with the 1969 Twins, George Mitterwald was a career .236 hitter with 76 HRs and 301 RBIs. In 1973, he hit .259 with 16 HRs and 64 RBIs for the Cubs, and a year later, he hit 3 homers in a game against the Pirates. Mitterwald coached for Billy with the A's from 1980 to 1982 and the Yankees in 1988.*

▶ **Jackie Moore:** *Although Jackie Moore played only 21 games in the big leagues, all with the 1965 Detroit Tigers, he has been a fixture in the* game for decades. Moore coached with Billy Martin with the Texas Rangers and Oakland A's and later managed the A's for three seasons. While Moore was managing the A's, such stars as Jose Canseco and Mark McGwire first came to the big leagues. Moore is currently the manager of the AA Round Rock Express, an Astros farm team owned by Nolan Ryan.

▶ **Mickey Morabito:** *Mickey Morabito was one of Billy Martin's best friends, and he had an up-close view of Billy's top years in the dugout, first as the Yankees' publicity director from 1977 through 1979, and later as Billy's publicity director and traveling secretary with the Oakland A's of 1980–1982. Morabito has remained Oakland's traveling secretary to this day and enjoyed the glory days of LaRussa, McGwire, and Canseco almost as much as the Billyball years.*

▶ **Ray Negron:** *A man who has given his life to baseball, Negron is currently part of the Cleveland Indians front office. Negron came out of New York City as a shortstop and played in the Pittsburgh Pirates chain in the early 1970s. After his playing days ended, he worked in the Yankee clubhouse where he grew very close to both Billy Martin and Reggie Jackson. Later, he served as a baseball agent representing players such as Juan Beniquez and Jose Uribe and worked in the Yankee front office.*

▶ **Mike Norris:** *The leader of Billy Martin's amazing Oakland pitching staff, Norris went 22–9 with a 2.54 ERA in 1980 after struggling to get a chance with the club for the five previous seasons. He was an All-Star that season and also won two Gold Glove awards for his fielding. He went 12–9 with a 3.75 ERA in 1981, helping the A's to the AL Championship Series in the strike-shortened season. For his career, Norris was 57–59 with a 3.91 ERA.*

▶ **Mike Pagliarulo:** *Pags played for the Yankees from 1984 through 1989. He also played for the Padres, Twins, Orioles, and Rangers before retiring in 1995. Pagliarulo came to the big leagues under Yogi Berra in 1984, and he blossomed under Billy Martin in 1985, batting .239 with 19 homers and 62 RBIs. Nicknamed Rambo for his no-holds-barred style* *of play, he had career highs of 32 homers and 87 RBIs with the 1987 Yankees and played a key role in the Twins' 1991 World Series championship. Pags retired with 134 home runs.*

▶ **Phil Pepe:** *Phil Pepe is a well-known and longtime New York sportswriter who currently hosts a radio show called* The Pep Talk *on New York's CBS-FM. He also organizes the annual Baseball Writers of America Awards Dinner. During Billy Martin's years at the helm of the Yankees, Pepe was the Yankee beat writer for* The New York Daily News. *Over the years, Phil has written numerous books about baseball and famous ballplayers, including one each with the "Three Musketeers" of the New York Yankees: Billy Martin, Mickey Mantle, and Whitey Ford.*

▶ **Lenny Randle:** *A football and baseball standout at Arizona State University, Randle blossomed as a major leaguer under Billy Martin in 1974. Never having had more than 249 at-bats or having hit more than .219 for managers Ted Williams and Whitey Herzog, Randle exploded to a .302 season with Billy. He smacked 157 hits, scored 65 runs, drove in 49 more, and swiped 26 bases. Interestingly enough, he played regularly for Billy at two new positions that year, third base (89 games) and outfield (21 games), as well as 40 games at his accustomed second base. Randle also played for the Mets, Cubs, Yankees, and Mariners in a career that lasted through 1982. He is a fixture on baseball "bloopers" shows for a well-known play in which he got down on all fours in an effort to literally blow a bunt foul while playing for the Mariners. Today, he conducts baseball clinics for children all over the world.*

▶ **Bill Reedy:** *One of Billy Martin's best friends, Bill Reedy was a Detroit tavern owner and city council aide throughout Billy's entire managerial career. His bar, Reedy's, was in the shadows of Tiger Stadium and one of Billy's favorite haunts during his years there.*

▶ **Rich Reese:** *A fine-fielding first baseman, Rich Reese got 419 at-bats with Billy Martin's 1969 Twins and responded by hitting .322 with 16 HRs and 69 RBIs, helping the club to the AL Championship Series. He had three pinch-hit grand slams for the Twins and compiled a .253 bat-*

ting average with 52 HRs and 245 RBIs over parts of ten big league seasons.

▶ **Bobby Richardson:** *The man who replaced Billy Martin as the Yankees' second baseman in 1957, Bobby Richardson played for the Bombers from 1955 through 1966, appearing in seven World Series along the way. Richardson was the MVP of the 1960 Fall Classic, batting .367. For his career, Richardson hit .266 with 1,432 hits, won five Gold Gloves, and was a seven-time All-Star. He later went on to coach the Carolina Coastal and South Carolina baseball teams and even ran for Congress. A devout Baptist and true teammate, Richardson was the minister for Mickey Mantle's funeral in 1995.*

▶ **Dave Righetti:** *One of the greatest relief pitchers in Yankee history, and the owner of a July 4, 1983 no-hitter against arch-rival Boston, Rags played for Billy Martin in 1979, 1983, 1985, and 1988. Martin managed Righetti as both a starter and a reliever. On July 3, 1983, while partying with Willie Nelson, Waylon Jennings, Goose Gossage, Bobby Murcer, and others, Billy sent 24-year-old Righetti home to get some rest. The rest, as they say, is history. Righetti retired with 252 saves, including a then all-time best of 46 in 1986. He is currently the pitching coach for the San Francisco Giants, and his role in the Giants' trip to the 2000 Division Series has been much heralded.*

▶ **Mickey Rivers:** *The man who jump-started Billy Martin's 1976–1978 Yankee World Series clubs from the leadoff spot, Mick the Quick is a memorable baseball character from the era. Famous for his wacky quotes, for calling people "Gozzlehead," "Warplehead," and even "Mailboxhead," and for his fondness of the ponies, Rivers was above all else an intimidating slasher at the plate who could run like the wind. Rivers hit .312 for the 1976 Yanks with 95 runs scored, 67 RBIs, and 43 steals. He hit .326 for the 1977 club with 79 runs scored, 69 driven in, 12 HRs, and 22 steals. In 1980, he hit .333 for Texas with 210 hits, 96 runs scored, 60 RBIs, and 18 steals. For his career, Rivers had a .295 average, with 1,660 hits and 267 steals.*

▶ **Buck Showalter:** *Most recently the manager of the Arizona Diamondbacks, Buck led the D-Backs to a 100-win season and the NL West title in only their second year of existence in 1999. Buck came to know Billy Martin as a young manager in the Yankees' minor-league system in the early-to-mid 1980s. Showalter climbed the ranks rapidly, and in 1989, while piloting AA Albany to a 97–46 record, he was named* Baseball America's *Minor League Manager of the Year. By 1991, he was at the helm of a big league club, where along with general manager Gene "Stick" Michael, he helped to restore the Yankees to respectability. They reached first place in the AL East before the 1994 strike wiped out the rest of the season, and earned a wild card bid in 1995 that brought the team into the postseason for the first time since 1981. Showalter is known as a hard-working, extremely disciplined, baseball traditionalist who knows the game extremely well.*

▶ **Charlie Silvera:** *A backup catcher who played on seven Yankee pennant winners from 1948 to 1956, Charlie Silvera hit .282 for his career. In the famed pennant race with Boston in 1949, Silvera played in 58 games and batted 130 times, hitting .315 with a .403 on-base percentage. Silvera met Billy Martin in the mid-1940s around the Pacific Coast League parks, played with Billy on the Yankee Dynasty teams, and in 1969 joined Billy's staff as a coach with the Twins. He later coached with Billy in Detroit and Texas as well. Charlie remains active in the game, and currently is a scout for the Tampa Bay Devil Rays.*

▶ **Fred "Chicken" Stanley:** *A pivotal member of the Yankees' World Series teams of 1976, 1977, and 1978, Chicken Stanley was a slick-fielding shortstop and versatile batsman. He got his first chance to play regularly for Billy Martin's 1976 Yankees, and later was the shortstop for Billy's 1981 and 1982 A's teams. Stanley has been a successful baseball executive since his career ended in 1982 and has enjoyed stints as director of player personnel for the Astros and Brewers and assistant general manager for the Brewers. Currently, Chicken is a manager in the San Francisco Giants system.*

About Billy Martin

The man who would grow up to be Yankee #1 was born in Berkeley, California, on May 16, 1928 as Alfred Manuel Martin, and was raised by his strong-willed mother and his grandmother. A small and ungainly child, "Billy" Martin nonetheless learned to excel in sports of all kinds, with nearby Kenney Park his home away from home throughout his adolescent years. A high school standout in baseball and basketball, Martin caught the attention of Red Adams, the trainer of the Oakland Oaks club in the then-prominent Pacific Coast League. During a tryout session, Adams pointed out Martin to then–Oaks manager Casey Stengel. The childless Stengel fell in love with Billy's energy, aggressiveness, and love for the game, and would come to see the boy as the son he never had. Likewise, Billy would see Stengel as the father he lacked.

Billy spent 1946 and 1947 playing for Oaks farm teams before joining Stengel in Oakland for the 1948 season. Together, the two helped spark the Oaks to a championship, earning Stengel—a failure in previous stints as a major league manager—a ticket to manage the mighty New York Yankees. More important, Stengel encouraged Billy to fully release his aggressive fury on the field.

By 1950, Billy was playing for Stengel under the bright lights of Yankee Stadium. Never the star ballplayer that his two great friends Mickey Mantle and Whitey Ford were, Billy was nonetheless a fine second baseman who did the little things to win a game—a sacrifice, a hard slide to break up a double play, getting hit by a pitch—and he seemingly always came through in the clutch. He is well remembered for his game-saving catch of a windblown pop-up off the bat of Jackie Robinson in the seventh and final game of the 1952 World Series, a play described in these pages by Billy's friend and teammate Gil McDougald. And in the Yankees-Dodgers World Series of 1953, Billy earned MVP honors by hitting .500 with 12 hits, including the game-winner in the bottom of the ninth of the finale. 1953 was also Billy's best offensive season in the game, as he hit .257 with 15 homers and 75 runs batted in.

Martin is also remembered for his pugilistic tendencies, which Stengel encouraged him to use as a means of sparking the club. During his years with the Yankees, Billy had celebrated fights with Clint Courtney, Jimmy Piersall, and Tommy Lasorda among others.

All tolled, Billy played for Yankee World Champions in 1950, 1951, 1952, 1953, and 1956, and played in the Bronx Bombers' losing effort to the Brooklyn Dodgers in 1955. Playing for the Yankees gave Martin a sense of pride that he had never achieved otherwise in life, and he literally lived for being part of the team. Billy's teammates, especially his hard-partying partners Mantle and Ford, but also others like Charlie Silvera, Yogi Berra, and Phil Rizzuto, were like brothers to him.

In mid-1957, at a Copacabana celebration for the birthdays of Billy and Yogi, a fight broke out among several Yankees and some members of a local bowling team. Although Billy was innocent in this instance, the Yankees' general manager took advantage of the opportunity to rid himself of a player whom he considered to be a bad influence on others, especially Mantle. Deeply saddened and embittered by the trade, Martin did not speak to Stengel—whom he felt did not protect him—for years, and his playing career went into decline. Martin played his final season for the Minnesota Twins in 1961.

Following his release in spring training of 1962, Martin was retained by the Twins as a scout, a position he held for three seasons. In

1965, Twins manager Sam Mele installed Martin as his third base coach, and in part due to the aggressive running game Billy inspired, the Twins traveled to the World Series, only to lose to a Sandy Koufax–led Los Angeles Dodgers team. Martin remained the third base coach until 1968, when he was asked by Twins ownership to take over as the manager of the Denver farm team, which was floundering desperately at the time. In the first of what would be many shocking turnarounds, Martin converted the Bears into immediate winners, stirring up a great deal of fanfare in the process. Martin installed the same type of aggressive, in-your-face brand of baseball that would characterize his entire managerial career.

By 1969, Billy was managing the Twins, sparking the team to an AL West first-place 97–65 record during the first year of divisional play. His performance was particularly notable because the Twins had finished in seventh place the year before, winning only 79 games against 83 losses. However, when Billy interceded in a midseason bar fight between pitcher Dave Boswell and outfielder Bobby Allison and proceeded to beat up Boswell badly, he lost points with owner Calvin Griffith, and following a loss to the Baltimore Orioles in the AL playoffs, Martin was fired.

Billy reemerged in Detroit in 1971, taking over an aging Tiger team, which had gone 79–83 in 1970 for a fourth-place finish in the AL East. Martin led the Tigers to second in 1971 (91–72, .562) and first place in 1972 (86–70, .551), only to be fired in late 1973 after repeated disagreements with club general manager Jim Campbell. Days after his firing, Billy was hired to manage the last-place Texas Rangers by team owner and old friend Bob Short.

In 1974, Billy brought true big league baseball to Texas for the first time, as the Rangers improved from the previous season's 57–105, .352 record to an amazing 84–76, .525 mark and a second-place finish. But when Short sold the team to Brad Corbett, an owner who took a more hands-on approach with personnel decisions, Billy's days in Texas were numbered.

Late 1975 saw Billy arriving in New York for his first stint as Yankee manager. The Yankees had not been to the World Series since 1964, and owner George Steinbrenner, who had bought the club in 1973 promising results, made the decision to install Martin in the managerial seat of his protégé Casey Stengel, who would pass away later that year. In his first full season at the helm of the Yankees, Billy recast the Yankees in his image and led the aggressive club to a first-place finish and victory over the Royals in the AL Championship Series on the strength of Chris Chambliss's bottom-of-the-ninth homer off Mark Littel. However, when the Reds of Johnny Bench, Pete Rose, Joe Morgan, and Tony Perez swept the Yanks in the World Series, Steinbrenner stepped in, signing the flamboyant slugger Reggie Jackson to the team. The world would never be the same.

In 1977, Martin's Yankees fought and snarled their way to a difficult World Championship, as tensions between Billy and Reggie simmered all season. On a nationally televised game versus the Boston Red Sox on a hot July afternoon, the two men nearly came to blows in the Fenway Park dugout. All was forgiven, at least temporarily, when Reggie's three homers versus the Dodgers in the sixth game of the World Series brought the Yankees their first title since 1962.

In 1978, with the team struggling to maintain the hot pace of the Boston Red Sox, the tensions between Billy, Reggie, and George ultimately contributed to an O'Hare Airport outburst from Billy ("One's a born liar, the other's convicted") that led to his forced resignation. Billy was gone, but he had restored the team to what he saw as its rightful location in the standings—number 1. He returned to the club in mid-1979, only to suffer along with the rest of the team when the team captain, and his favorite player, Thurman Munson, was killed in a tragic plane crash. Billy lost his Yankee managerial job for the second time when he was fired in the off-season following his fight with a marshmallow salesman.

Next, from 1980 to 1982, came Billyball, the swashbuckling brand of bare-knuckled baseball that Billy brought to his hometown Oakland A's. In 1979, the A's were the laughing stock of baseball, losing 108 games for a miserable .333 winning percentage. But Billy turned the team around, using the suicide squeeze, the steal of home, double steals, hit and runs, and every other trick that he had learned in his 35 years in professional baseball. In 1980, the team jumped to second place, winning 83 games against 79 losses for a .512 winning percentage. Billyball captured the imagination of baseball fans not only in Oakland, but nationwide. His 1981 team came out of the gate at 11 wins and 0 losses, landing Billy on the cover of *Time* magazine, and helping secure the AL West title for the A's, with a strike-shortened 64–45 record and a .587 winning percentage. Professional and personal troubles throughout 1982, as well as an inkling that the Yankees job might once more be his, led to a rapid diminution of his dream job in Oakland, and in 1983, Billy was back in pinstripes.

The 1980s saw Billy pilot the Bombers three times—1983, 1985, and 1988—all with very strong results, but no first-place finishes. In 1986, his beloved #1 was retired by the Yankees, and a plaque of Billy was hung in Yankee Stadium's hallowed Monument Park. At the ceremony, Billy told the capacity crowd, "I may not have been the greatest Yankee ever to put on the pinstripes, but I am the proudest." For his 16-year managerial career, Billy won 1,253 games versus 1,013 losses, good for a .553 winning percentage. Billy's winning percentage remains in the top 20 all-time, but the mark is all the greater considering his many turnarounds, particularly of the Rangers and A's. Billy remains the only manager to manage two 100-loss teams to winning campaigns the next season.

Billy Martin died in a one-car accident on Christmas Day, 1989, at the age of 61. While Billy's life was plagued by troubles and controversies both on and off the field and both in and out of bars, he was a bright, often charming, and very passionate man. While his life is in many ways tragic, he nonetheless lived life fully, picking up loyal friends and sworn enemies along the way, and his success on the diamond remains a testimony to the will of the underdog.

Dugout Days

Introduction

Billy Martin. More than ten years after his death, the name still comes roaring at sports fans like a high and tight fastball. Without thinking, a barrage of instant, high-speed images of Billy come flooding to the mind: Billy screaming wildly at an umpire while dusting him with dirt. Billy attempting to attack Reggie Jackson in the Fenway Park dugout. Billy, the Boss, and innumerable hirings and firings. Billy and a blur of brawls with a range of characters—from opponents, to teammates, to reporters, to the legendary Minnesota marshmallow salesman.

Certainly this was part of Billy, but only part. For all of the sensationalist back-page copy that was generated by and around Billy Martin for some 40 years, there was also an ambitious individual pursuing and achieving great success, while enduring and overcoming significant disappointment. There was a leader, a man who understood his business well, and who could motivate, teach, and guide his followers to achieve.

Billy Martin as a Leader

As Billy's career came to a close in 1988, his unshifting focus on winning no longer seemed to resonate with our society. At the same time, the United States was growing increasingly intolerant of the boys-will-be-boys lifestyle that Billy and many other athletes from the 1950s, 1960s, and 1970s enjoyed. Eventually, the elbow-bending escapades and periodic brawls that were always part of Billy's folklore were cast in an almost totally negative light.

But at right about the same time Billy managed his last baseball game, corporate America was embracing his values. To win in an increasingly competitive global marketplace, American business leaders had to get tough and face facts—fast. In 1987, General Electric's now legendary chief executive officer, Jack Welch, told a group of his company's managers, "The world of the 1990s and beyond . . . will belong to passionate, driven leaders—people who not only have enormous amounts of energy but who can energize those whom they lead."[1]

Welch easily could have been describing Billy during his dugout heyday—passionate, driven, possessed of energy, and energizing. Indeed, today, America's bosses and America's global competitors think more like Billy than they ever did before, though they may not know it. Through this book, you will come to know Billy the leader as never before. Much of it may surprise you, especially if your image of Billy is that of the wild, mean, alcoholic boor.

Amid the barrage of articles focusing on the brawls, booze, and firings written at the time of Billy's Christmas 1989 death, Thomas Boswell of *The Washington Post* wrote, "With time . . . perhaps we will be able to take a slightly longer view and . . . remember Martin the player, the manager, the teacher."[2] To date, that longer view has not been taken. Biographers David Falkner, author of *The Last Yankee* (Simon & Schuster, 1992), and Peter Golenbock, author of *Wild, High and Tight* (St. Martin's Press, 1994), both have written broad presentations of Martin focusing extensively on his off-field adventures as well as his career as a baseball player and manager. While both authors present a chronology of ups and downs, statistics, and costars from Billy's career, they fail to satisfactorily deconstruct and analyze the leader. Yet it is Martin the leader—the passionate, driven, energetic, and energizing skipper—who remains important today to both the game of baseball and to the broader study of leadership.

The Two Sides of Billy Martin

Why is it that when we think of Billy Martin, we think of the battler and not the leader? Clearly, because his outrageous personality and constant contretemps attracted a lot of attention. Tom Grieve, one of Billy's players who is featured in this book, says, "If you're just taking it from the perspective of how he managed a baseball team and how his teams seemed to be a lot better with him as the manager, there's a lot to talk about there. I don't think any of it's coincidence. I think a lot of it had to do with him and what he brought to the party." But Grieve also admits, "I don't think you can write a book and have credibility if you don't at least acknowledge the other side. You don't have to dwell on it, but you kind of have to acknowledge it."

And Grieve is right. Billy was by no means a saint. He found trouble in a lot of places throughout his life, and he also brought a lot of trouble onto himself. The gunslinger attitude he adopted in the dugout conspired against him outside the lines. That same confidence and swagger that enabled him to infuse ballclubs with an aggressive fury to beat and embarrass an opponent made it difficult for him to avoid confrontations, whether in bars, parking lots, or office suites.

Baseball executive Mickey Morabito, one of Billy's close friends, says that without that other side, "It's not Billy. It's part of his aura, it's part of his character, it's part of what people loved about him, and there's no doubt about that. But it shouldn't just totally gloss over what he did as a manager. And unfortunately, the way the media covers him today, and in the books that have come out on him, that is the main focal point, when it should be just part of the equation."

Martin also helped a lot of people. As a leader, he was in a position to help people whom he cared about—and he often went well above and beyond the call of duty in this regard. Veteran baseball coach and manager Jackie Moore, who coached with Billy for many seasons in both Texas and Oakland, says,

> "I just hope that people get to know the other side of Billy—
> what a genuinely good person he was, how many people he
> helped, and little things that you don't hear enough about.

You hear about Billy kicking dirt on the umpires, or Billy getting thrown out of a ballgame, or Billy in a brawl. And sure, all of this happened, but that was the nature of the business. But there was also this guy that a lot of people came to. I've seen Billy reach into his pocket for a mother that had two little kids with her walking down the street. You could tell that they didn't have any money and were hungry. And he'd give 'em a $20 bill. And to see the look in their eyes and to see the impression he left—he didn't do it just to get recognized or anything. He did it because he had a feel for that. He loved kids, and he wanted to give something to them. He wanted to make them feel better."

This book is not a biography of Billy Martin and makes no attempt to present a complete picture of his life and times. Instead, this book takes the "longer view" Boswell suggested days after Billy's death. These pages present a thorough study of the traits that enabled Billy to organize, lead, and motivate teams in the words of the men who played for him and thrived on his methods.

He was a unique man. He placed great value in winning, yet he learned from a lifetime of losses and setbacks. He gained enormous individual fame, yet he gained it through devotion to the team concept, even as big dollars and greed changed the landscape of his sport. He used his experiences to teach and inspire hundreds of young players to earn their own successes, and he never forgot them after their on-field relationship ended.

To most of his players, Billy was a teacher and a winner, and the lessons he taught to them are timeless and basically without boundaries. Regardless of the problems that plagued his own life, self-inflicted or otherwise, Billy deserves this longer view. As gritty Yankee catcher Ron Hassey says, "No question, on the field he was a leader. Now all the things you hear about him, I'm sure a lot of it did happen, but that's not what I looked at Billy Martin as. I looked at him as manager of the New York Yankees who I played for when the game started and when it ended."

The Contents of This Book

In the pages that follow, that's whom we will look at as well. This book is largely made up of quotes based on interviews with many men who played for and played alongside Billy Martin, as well as many men who coached with him, managed him, and worked with him. As such, it analyzes and assesses Billy Martin as a leader: how he got where he did, why he was so good at what he did, and what we can learn and apply to our own lives as leaders from his life and career.

Throughout the chapters of this book, we will often refer to Paul Stoltz, who is president of PEAK Learning Incorporated and holds a doctorate in organizational communication and development. Stoltz—whose clients have included Deloitte & Touche LLP, Motorola, Abbott Labs, and US West, and who conducts seminars and workshops around the country—is the author of the book *Adversity Quotient*, which presents the thesis that an individual's ability to prevail in the face of adversity is the most important indicator for sustained success. Stoltz provides a valuable perspective on the life and leadership qualities of Billy Martin.

The book ends with an appendix on Billy's "turnarounds"—the way he improved baseball teams' records when he took over as manager.

Notes

1. Noel M. Tichy and Stratford Sherman, *Control Your Destiny or Someone Else Will* (New York: HarperBusiness, 1994), p. 182.
2. Thomas Boswell, *Game Day* (New York: Penguin Books, 1992), p. 353.

Get to the Top Billy-Style

"It was like the first or second day he was down on the field and he had this sense that he could see everything," Bill Kane, a longtime Yankee executive who knew Billy Martin for many years, once said. "If this was done or that was done, you could win a game. Move this way, one thing happened; move that way, another thing did. He said he just saw it all at once, all so clear."[1]

Kane presents a picture of Billy Martin as a baseball wizard, eerie and awe-inspiring, a man with a unique second sight enabling him to perform in a way in which most of us can only dream about. There's Billy in the dugout, his wiry body perched on the dugout steps, his piercing eyes rapidly scanning majestic Yankee Stadium for opportunity, his face tight with concentration, his chin jutting out defiantly, his mind five steps ahead of the opposing manager. He is baseball's warrior general. He is in his element—a natural.

Make no mistake about it, by the time Billy Martin took over the Yankees as manager in 1975, he had a feel for baseball that enabled him to conduct a game from the dugout like a baton-wielding maestro. Just as Mozart seemed to magically write symphonies or George Soros magically guesses the direction of the financial markets, Billy just knew what was going to happen next on the diamond.

Of course, Billy as born manager ultimately rings false. As with other so-called naturals, a closer examination reveals years of dedicated training, study, and preparation that eventually enabled Billy to manage a ballgame with such finely honed skills and insight as to appear almost magical.

Billy's Early Life

Before studying Billy as a manager and leader, it's appropriate to take a quick look at the early years of his life to understand the qualities, influences, and experiences that shaped him. The young Billy Martin was a passionate, driven, optimistic person who slowly but surely achieved very ambitious goals against difficult odds. The young Billy Martin applied time-honored traits of hard work, desire, self-sacrifice, and commitment to make it in baseball. And the bottom line is that Billy Martin earned the equivalent of a baseball Ph.D. and became the leader that he did through a long education in which ideas were formed, evolved, and finally crystallized into a daring leadership style.

Most achievers achieve because they work for it. It's not luck, natural gifts, or better connections that generate sustained success. Sure, "breaks" happen from time to time. But hard work and dedication sustain long-term success. That's what Billy was all about from the time he was a little kid in Berkeley, California. Ultimately, Billy controlled baseball games from the top step of the Yankee dugout in the 1970s and 1980s as well as he did because of qualities he developed over a lifetime of true devotion to his craft, and not because of any mystical gifts from above.

Setting Goals

Billy Martin didn't play baseball just for fun or for gaining standing in his social group. Baseball captured his imagination fully. He loved the game, and from an early age, he instinctively sought to align his passion with his life, establishing the challenging goals of becoming a professional baseball player and a New York Yankee. According to boyhood friend Rube DeAlba, "He used to tell me all the time, 'Rube, I'm going to the Yankees.' This is in tenth grade. I'd tell him, 'Yeah, sure, Billy.' He'd say, 'You watch me, Ruben, I'm going to the Yankees.'"[2]

Because Martin was small as a child and teen, and because he was not an extraordinary natural athlete, the odds were decidedly against him. Said Eddie Leishman, an Oakland area scout who initially passed on Billy for the minor league team he represented, "I liked him, but I didn't think he was strong enough. All I saw was a skinny kid who wanted to play. It didn't seem enough . . . the big leagues? That's something else."[3]

Billy had other disadvantages in life, including relative poverty compared with the nearby Berkeley college crowd, a lack of social status ensured by his West Berkeley residence, a large nose that garnered a lot of attention and teasing, and the knowledge that his father had walked out on his family before he was born. He lashed out at the teasing and his frustrations with a feistiness that he would brandish for his entire life. But when he learned to play ball—and excelled—he began to see self-worth in himself, and he began to gain positive recognition from others. Naturally, he wanted more, so that he could extinguish the insecurities his various adversities created inside. It would be a lifetime quest.

Paul Stoltz looks at adversities, such as those Billy faced, as:

"our defining moments. We are just beginning to understand the full impact of our childhood experiences upon our adult reality. Unfortunately, many children learn early lessons of hopelessness, which may be reinforced by their parents, teachers, relatives, friends, or anyone significant in their lives. Some get dealt even monstrous adversity that they somehow overcome. Once this authentic empowerment is unearthed and confirmed with a couple or more experiences, these individuals become bulletproof against adversity. They become immunized against helplessness. Many of the great athletes and leaders have stories of overcoming adversity. I have yet to hear of or meet someone people consider great who has not faced and overcome significant adversity along the way. As the saying goes, 'It is in the flames of adversity that our character is forged.'"

Billy certainly faced adversity when he was young, but through baseball, he found a way to fortify himself against the harsh world, and he found something he truly loved. Going to the Yankees was his own self-established measurement for success, and Billy pursued his goal with heart, soul, and vision—regardless of the skeptics—because his motive was genuine. Billy once told sportswriter Maury Allen, "I just knew I could do it . . . I didn't care what other people said. I think you can do anything you want to if you care enough."[4] Billy cared enough, and it helped to empower him.

▶ **Phil Pepe:** *If there was a chip on his shoulder, it was put there by the fact that people kept telling him he was too small to play professional baseball. He wasn't good enough. He wasn't big enough. He couldn't make it. He couldn't do this. He couldn't do that. And that made him more determined to disprove that. He had such a drive to prove them wrong, a drive to succeed. He just overachieved constantly. I'm not a psychologist, but I think a psychologist would probably tell you that it's all the result of his upbringing, coming from the other side of the tracks, so to speak. No money. Poverty. He fought all the time as a kid.*

▶ **Charlie Silvera:** *He was a sort of deprived kid. He grew up during the war in the gang area around Berkeley. He had a tough bringing up, but he hung around the Oakland ballpark with Red Adams, who was the trainer there, and Red helped formulate Billy. He sure had to take a lot of abuse, because he had that big nose before he got it fixed. He took a lot of kidding, but he wouldn't back down. He had to fight, because he was a funny looking little guy. He had to be competitive. He was smaller, and he had to do a lot of little things that a bigger guy didn't have to do. But he was tough, and he wanted to succeed.*

Dedication to the Game

Billy's words often echo those of the late Dr. Norman Vincent Peale, the well-known religious leader and positive thinker. Peale wrote in his classic book *The Power of Positive Thinking*, "A major key to success in this life, to attaining that which you deeply desire, is to be completely released and throw all there is of yourself into your job or any project in which you are engaged . . . Hold nothing back."[5] As anyone who ever saw Billy Martin on a baseball field can very well tell you, Billy never held anything back. He was totally dedicated and gave everything he had in life to the game.

▶ **Gil McDougald:** *Billy all the time was thinking about baseball, because baseball was his love. That's it. I mean, I could never say I was in love with baseball. Baseball to me was a game, that's strictly all it was. To Billy, it was more than a game. It was his life. He loved it. It was like he worshiped the game.*

▶ **Jackie Moore:** *It was his life. It was his marriage. It was everything to Billy. Baseball was religion to Billy. He lived and breathed it, talked about it. His love. There was no misunderstanding at all that baseball was his life. He just loved it. He loved every aspect about it. He couldn't wait to win this ballgame today, then get in to play the one tomorrow. The different excitement, the different strategy, it would bring a different challenge to him. He loved to compete.*

Billy's passion is memorable to his friends because it was so sincere, and it fueled his success. Many of us establish goals for the wrong reasons—money, parental approval, peer approval, and so on. But our goals must be meaningful to us, and must be aimed at providing us with real fulfillment, if they are to have value for us. It was that way with Billy and baseball. As a kid, Billy instinctively placed his love for baseball over every other aspect of his life, and he dreamed of the Yankees not for the money that he could earn but for the fulfillment that it would bring him. He achieved his goals, and ultimately money followed his success.

The Importance of Mentors

Billy played ball every chance he could, and in addition, he took full advantage of a perk that growing up in California allowed him—the exposure to several neighborhood big leaguers home for the winter, most notably Augie Galan. Galan, friendly with Billy's brother Tudo, took an interest in the undersized, overly ambitious kid, and gave him a unique tutorial few kids had. In essence, he became Billy's mentor.

▶ **Phil Pepe:** *Did you ever see the piece I did for* The New York Daily News Magazine *on going back with Billy to his old neighborhood? It was very interesting to see his old neighborhood. It was a neighborhood where a lot of professional ballplayers had grown up. He talked about a guy by the name of Augie Galan, who was one of his heroes and role models. There were about a handful of players who played in the major leagues, who were older than Billy, who were neighborhood guys, and Billy kind of looked at them and wanted to be like them.*

Billy was lucky to be surrounded by people who could teach him, but he also had the willingness to tirelessly pick their brains. And with the obvious love of the game that radiated from him, he had a magnetic pull on older guys who shared his passion. Across every field, energetic people who have "made the journey" often will go far out of their way to fan the flames in a youngster just getting started, especially one as eager as Billy.

According to Galan, Billy's first mentor, Billy "kind of took a shine to me . . . he'd come over and carry my grip for me down to the park."[6] Galan taught Billy baseball fundamentals on the one hand and mental strength on the other. Augie noted that, "I explained to him that . . . if you have the determination nobody can stop you. I don't care how big you are, how small you are, what you look like, if you got it, you can make it . . . I tried to insert that into him—just never give up, bear down all the time."[7]

Augie encouraged in Billy traits he definitely possessed, and he encouraged him to follow his dreams. Billy recalled, "I was just getting into baseball and I was at an impressionable age when Augie was playing in the big leagues and I guess he influenced me as much as anyone. When he came home during the off-season, he would work with me and help me . . . I admired Augie so much . . ."[8]

Later, after Billy made it to the minor leagues, many established baseball people came to admire his love of and dedication to the game—people like legendary managers Casey Stengel and Charlie Dressen and numerous ex-big leaguers such as Cookie Lavagetto and Ernie Lombardi. They also became mentors to the young Billy. In 1948, Stengel—managing Billy with the minor league Oakland Oaks—roomed the young player with ex-Dodger Lavagetto, who was just months removed from breaking up Yankee Bill Bevens's no-hitter in the ninth inning of the World Series. According to Cookie, "The first thing I noticed was how serious he was about the game . . . He was a smart kid, even then, you could tell he was going far."[9]

Like Galan before him, Lavagetto fanned the competitive drive already burning in Billy. Billy recalled, "I'll never forget what he said to me one night. He said, 'There are a lot of fellows in the minor leagues who have the ability to play in the majors, but they will never make it because they have no guts.'"[10]

Martin had guts, and he was learning along each step of the way that the qualities that he did possess—smarts, courage, heart—could get him to his goal as much as raw physical skill. His mentors added fuel to his fire and gave him direction and opportunities. Billy took full advantage.

Of course, Stengel was the most important mentor to Billy. As previously mentioned, Stengel managed Martin with the minor league Oakland Oaks in 1948, just a year before he took over as manager of the Yankees. He came to love the brash, skinny kid as a winner and as a son.

▶ **Charlie Silvera:** *I had met Billy right after the war when we used to go work out in the Oakland ballpark. Billy was always hanging around the Oakland ballpark there. He had a great teacher in Stengel. He emulated him. He was Casey's guy. He just wanted to win. He wanted to emulate Casey Stengel, and he picked up a lot of things from Casey Stengel. But he was Billy Martin.*

Stengel had the clout to make things happen in Martin's career, and he did. Whatever weaknesses others saw in Martin, Stengel saw heart, guts, and a boisterousness that could help keep a team on its toes. In 1949, Stengel left Oakland for the New York Yankees, and in

1950, he called for Billy, not because he was a great ballplayer, but because he was a winning ballplayer.

▶ **Gil McDougald:** *I tell ya, there were so many ballplayers that would have made it on any other ballclub, and been a real fine ballplayer, but they didn't play for our ballclub. But Billy was so aggressive in his own way, the way he played ball. Everything was from the heart with Billy. This is what he believed. He certainly believed he was the best ballplayer, that's for sure. He proved in certain situations like World Series time how valuable he was. And to see Billy do well in the World Series never surprised me, because he knew that he had the guts to challenge anybody. And what the hell, that's what it takes.*

▶ **Bobby Richardson:** *He wasn't as smooth as Jerry Coleman on the double play, but he played over Jerry because he'd knock the ball down, pick it up, and throw him out. He'd break up the double play. He'd do the things that would win the ballgame. So he in essence really was a winner. He was the guy that spurred all the others on. You know, you had a quiet [Phil] Rizzuto at shortstop, and you had Andy Carey at third base, who didn't say anything. But Billy was the one that would get on whoever it was. He'd give a little, "C'mon, run that ball out!" "Break up that double play!" "C'mon, we gotta go now!" And Stengel loved him—he was Stengel's type ballplayer.*

▶ **Charlie Silvera:** *Casey would prod him and say, "Go get 'em!" One night in the early '50s we were struggling. We were ahead in the standings, but we couldn't pull away, and it was later in the season. In Philly, Stengel says, "I'll give anybody $100 that gets hit with a pitched ball." Well, Billy got hit twice that night . . . So he did little things like that. Anything to win.*

Years later, coaches and players alike would come to understand the gratitude Billy felt toward his mentor Stengel for seeing something in him and giving him the chance to achieve his dreams.

▶ **Jackie Moore:** *You didn't have to be around Billy Martin too long to listen to him talk about Casey. It was a father-son relationship, and there* *was just such a love there. And to hear him tell stories, I knew Billy well enough to know that Casey left some kind of impression on him. I could feel how Billy appreciated it, and I saw how he tried to carry that on and pass it on to his players.*

▶ **Charlie Manuel:** *He used to talk about Casey Stengel all the time, and his way of talking about Casey was how much he really respected him and liked him. He would say things sometimes about Casey sort of in a derogatory way, but at the same time, if you could listen to him, you got the feeling that Casey had a lot of influence on him and helped make him into the player that he was.*

As much as Stengel loved Billy, he only used him in ways that were best for the team—an important lesson Billy would remember when he became a manager himself. Favorite or not, Billy played in only 34 games in 1950 and 51 games in 1951. Jerry Coleman started instead at second base. In 1952, with Coleman in the service, Billy became a semi-regular in Casey's platoon system, playing 107 games at second base as part of a three-man, two-position rotation. Gil McDougald played 38 games at second and another 117 at third, while Bobby Brown appeared in 24 at third base.

▶ **Gil McDougald:** *When Billy came up, Casey said, "You're my second baseman with Jerry Coleman." And then Jerry went into the service. Then Casey's idea was, "I like the way Gil swings the bat, I want him to play. When there's a left-handed pitcher, Gil plays third, Billy'll play second. If there's a right-handed pitcher, Brownie'll play third, Gil'll play second." Billy was caught in between, but he played his part. He never moaned or groaned. It wouldn't have done him any good with Casey. And the guys on the ballclub wouldn't have enjoyed it, either.*

Your boss and your coworkers don't want to hear you whine.

▶ **Charlie Silvera:** *If you talk to the guys that played for Casey—and I did for eight years—Casey, he didn't care what you thought of him. He platooned [Hank] Bauer and [Gene] Woodling, and [Cliff] Mapes and*

[Johnny] Lindell, and [Bobby] Brown and Billy Johnson. And they'd say, "I'll show that crooked-legged bastard." And Casey knew that. You gotta be a bit of a prick in order to be a good manager. You can't let other people influence you. Casey would say, "You guys don't like me too much. Now, when you get your World Series check, you like me a little better." You talk to the guys then—"Jeez, he's unfair." But now you talk to a lot of guys that played for him—"He was a pretty smart old man, wasn't he?" But when you're in your 20s, you know every damned thing there is.

So at the same time that Martin benefited from the individual relationship that he had with Stengel, he also saw his mentor at work, mixing the talents of 25 Yankees to form a unit that won five consecutive World Series championships from 1949 to 1953. Like the other players, Billy played his role and saw the team win again and again and again. The Old Man was in charge, and when things were done his way, the team won. For Billy, Stengel was a great mentor who could both help Billy with his playing career and at the same time show him his future as a manager.

Learning about Winning

Most baseball fans know that Billy's fame as a player was earned as the second baseman for the great Yankee teams of the 1950s. Billy was part of Yankee championship teams in 1950, 1951, 1952, 1953, and 1956 that were all business on the field.

▶ **Charlie Silvera:** *Thinking back now, when you went to the Yankees you had guys like Snuffy Stirnweiss, John Lindell, Tommy Henrich, and Billy Johnson, and the first thing they'd tell you when you got there, "OK, kid. You don't 'f—' with our money. We're here to win. We don't get 'em tomorrow, we get 'em today." And Billy understood, so later, when he got to play regularly, he was one of the guys who'd call a meeting and point fingers at some of the young kids and say, "Hey, you were out late, and here we're in a pennant drive. You guys better bear down, because we have to win it."*

▶ **Gil McDougald:** *Let me tell ya, for the Yankees, I never heard one guy ever say, "Have fun." It was always, "Get serious, we gotta win the game." But you read this all the time, the players saying it. I gotta laugh, because it's not fun. It's not fun to make errors. It's not fun to strike out with the bases loaded. I don't think many guys on our ballclub ever thought in the terms "fun." After the game, it was fun. We won. But never on the ballfield did we ever go out and say "have fun."*

Billy thrived within this serious on-field environment. In 1952 and 1953, his clutch fielding and hitting were especially vital to the Yankee championships. In the 1952 World Series, for example, he made his famous catch of a two-out, windblown, bases-loaded pop-up off the bat of Jackie Robinson that would have cleared the bases and spelled disaster for the Yankees. Other players remember it to this day.

▶ **Gil McDougald:** *Well, what happened was, Robinson hit the pop-up, and Jackie's a pull hitter. I'm playing deep at third, and the wind was blowing in and toward right field, coming across from third base to first base. So as soon as the ball went up, I started to run. And Billy was running. And Joe Collins was the closest to the ball, but he lost the ball because the sun field was on the right side of the diamond at that time. And Billy kept going, and when I reached the mound, I seen Billy coming. And Billy just made a helluva catch. He got there and just caught it at his knees. So how do you evaluate ballplayers? See, that was a real take-charge situation at that time, and Billy did the job. That's what saved the game and the Series. He showed he could perform under pressure. I tell ya, that was a helluva play.*

And in the 1953 Series, Billy had 12 hits in 24 at-bats to take the Series MVP award. Opponents like Sam Mele, an outfielder for such teams as the Red Sox, Orioles, and Senators in the 1940s and 1950s, were well aware of what Billy brought to the table.

▶ **Sam Mele:** *He knew the game. He knew how to win, he did things to win, and he did win. Made the big play when he had to make it, like that World Series pop fly. Or getting 12 hits in a Series one time. He did the* *things to help win the game. He'd steal a base, knock somebody on his ass breaking up a double play, and the next guy would get a base hit to win the game.*

And whether it was Billy, Mickey Mantle, Yogi Berra, Gil Mc-Dougald, Whitey Ford, or Phil Rizzuto starring in any particular game, it was always a Yankee team effort. As a Yankee, Martin absorbed the culture of an organization committed to success. The Yankees played as a team and played to win. And because they did win, role players like Billy earned individual fame greater than that of many stars on losing teams. Players like Billy, Andy Carey, Bobby Brown, and Joe Collins are more famous today than many others from their era who had higher averages, more home runs, and fancier gloves, because they were Yankees, and they won.

▶ **Bobby Richardson:** *I think my first reaction when I would just hear the name "Billy Martin" would be a member of those winning ballclubs when they won all those pennants in a row. I think he really valued the [Yankee] pinstripes. It was his life. He was the spark plug of that club. Encouraging, in his own way, the others to really go out and play together as a team.*

Teamwork—for the true Yankees, the culture ran deep, well beyond shallow sloganism. When Mickey Mantle, the greatest Yankee of the era, was approaching death, he told his friends and the media how he wanted to be remembered—not as the greatest switch-hitter of all time or an All-American hero, but simply as "a great teammate." Said Billy, "It was the Yankee way of doing things, teammates helping team-mates."[11] The feelings of kinship Billy felt with his teammates, and the pride that the Yankee uniform awakened in him, formed a grip that never let up throughout his life. Billy gave his heart and soul to his teammates, even ones who might be playing ahead of him on a given day such as McDougald, Coleman, or Richardson.

▶ **Gil McDougald:** *I think we were very close as a team. Casey liked the pla-toon system, and that you would think would have made it difficult. But it's* *a funny thing, when you're a ballplayer, especially when the game's on the line and you might be coming up, you like to hear the guy that is trying to win the same position that you play yelling, "Come on, Gil!" Well, Billy, I think, was the first one I'd listen to. Sure enough, he's rooting for you.*

In fact, even when the Yankees traded Billy during the summer of 1957, he took the time to sit down with Richardson, his successor, to pass the torch like a true teammate. Richardson recalled the incident.

▶ **Bobby Richardson:** *I remember very well when he was traded. We were in Kansas City and after the ballgame, we all got on our bus to go back to the hotel. And everybody was there except Casey Stengel and Billy Martin. And word sort of filtered through the bus that Casey and Billy were having a meeting inside and there was a possibility that Billy had been traded. And we waited for about an hour. I mean, it really took a long time. Finally, when he came out and got on the bus, he walked right to my seat and sat down by me. He said, "OK, kid, it's all yours now. I've been traded." And I'll never forget those words. He sat down by me and said, "OK, kid, it's all yours."*

Over time, Billy came to believe that what he brought to the table during his years with the team was a big reason why the Yankees were winning. Billy's five full seasons with the Yankees as a player—1950, 1951, 1952, 1953, and 1956—all resulted in World Series Championships. In 1954, Billy was in the service, and the Yankees did not make it to the World Series. In 1955, Billy spent most of the season in the service, returning to play the month of September and in the World Series; the Yankees did not win the Series. In 1957, Billy was traded to the Kansas City Athletics midseason, and the Yankees did not win the World Series. True, he was just a .257 career hitter. But he had a greater worth to the team than just reflected in his batting average.

▶ **Phil Pepe:** *If you look at his record, the years that he was with the Yankees they won, and the years he wasn't with them, they lost. When he went into the service, they lost. The year they traded him, they lost. It always seemed that when he was around, they had a tendency to* *win. He would be the first to tell you that he was the reason, or one of the reasons.*

As a player with the Yankees, Billy learned the lessons of winning—lessons he would pass on to his players when he became a manager.

The Devastation of Being Traded

A big factor in Martin's eventual managerial success came from the heartache he experienced in his 1957 trade from the Yankees to the Kansas City Athletics, and the erosion of his playing career from that day forward. As we have seen, as a true Yankee, Billy helped Bobby Richardson, his successor at second. But it took him years to recover from the shock and the hurt of the trade, and he didn't speak with his mentor Stengel for some eight years while his wounds healed.

Because his identity was that of Billy Martin, Yankee ballplayer—not just Billy Martin, winning ballplayer, or Billy Martin, hustling ballplayer—the trade was particularly devastating to him.

▶ **Billy Martin, Jr.:** *As a player, from the day he left there, he was never the same. He never played with the same confidence and bravado that he did as a Yankee, and he became a journeyman after that, because in the back of his mind it crushed him. It hurt him so bad. "How could they get rid of me? After what I'd done for them?" I think it skewed his judgment. There's no doubt about it.*

Paul Stoltz speaks of the goals we set as Mountains, and of the efforts we expend in Climbing our Mountains. Stoltz notes that our Mountains must be significant. He says of Billy's devastation at being traded, "This is a classic case of why it is so important that our Mountain be something greater than ourselves. It needs to be rooted in contribution, legacy, and a higher cause. Being a Yankee, while wildly ambitious, was a limited Mountain, like making money. Had I been Billy's friend, I would have asked, 'Why do you want to be a Yankee?' And I would have kept asking why until I unearthed the grander purpose for his life. This Mountain is not team dependent. If he had discovered that his drive was for 'helping other players play their best,' he could have Climbed that Mountain with undying passion until his final breath."

In a way, the trade was a blessing in disguise for Billy because, as a journeyman ballplayer on other teams, he was able to see, compare, and be part of several organizational styles that differed from the Yankee way he had accepted as his own. During stints with Kansas City, Detroit, Cleveland, Cincinnati, Milwaukee, and Minnesota, Martin played for nonchampionship-caliber squads.

His sad odyssey thus allowed Billy to observe and digest organizational differences between Yankee "winners," where as a role player he could be a star and a winner, and the second-division "losers," where he floundered without purpose.

▶ **Sam Mele:** *I think he knew—being with the Yankees—what it took to win. And when he went to those other lesser clubs, he could say, "Hey, I should be doin' it the way we did it with New York." Because it was winning, winning, winning, and they all participated. I do my part, you do your part, and he does his part.*

▶ **Charlie Silvera:** *He knew what it was to win, and what it took to win. You had to give up yourself. You had to go the other way. When he got traded, he saw the other side of it. You find out what it is to lose.*

Even worse than losing was the inevitable end of his career. In early 1962, the Twins released Billy as an active player. Sam Mele, the manager who had to let Billy go, played a significant role in launching Billy's own career as a manager by fighting to keep him in the Twins organization.

▶ **Sam Mele:** *That spring, [team owner Calvin] Griffith wants to let him go, and I have to release him. Everybody's gone, and I'm sitting in the clubhouse with him, and we're both crying like two little kids—this is no kidding. We'd struck up such a great friendship. It'd started when he was with the Yankees and I was with Boston . . . And I had to tell him he's released. But I said, "Damn it, I want you in the organization." And I talked to Calvin, I said, "He's got to be in the organization, Calvin." So they made him a scout.*

Waiting for a Break

The scouting job, which Billy occupied for the 1962, 1963, and 1964 seasons, was a return to the very lowest rungs of the baseball profession, but Billy wanted the job because he wanted to stay in the game he loved. Billy had received a lucrative offer to play professionally in Japan, where he was both known and popular from a few Yankee barnstorming trips, but he turned down the offer to stay in American baseball.

There is a lesson to be learned from Billy's actions: Oftentimes, just hanging in there until a break arrives can be critical. His playing career over, Billy hung in and developed additional skills through seven years of job assignments including scout, coach, and minor league manager, all for the Twins organization. By all accounts, these were happy years for Billy, and each of his roles with the Twins broadened his perspective as a baseball man and better prepared him for his role as manager.

In 1969, 12 years after his trade from the Yanks, he was back in the spotlight, this time with a new goal. No longer was he obsessed with being a Yankee (though probably the idea of assuming Stengel's seat in the Yankee dugout was somewhere in the back of his mind). Now, first and foremost, he wanted to prove that he wasn't Billy the Kid, baseball's incorrigible brat. He wanted to prove that he was a leader, and he got the chance as the new manager of the Minnesota Twins.

Paul Stoltz writes not only about Climbing our Mountains but also about what he calls the Adversity Quotient, or AQ. People with high AQs are demanding in a good sense of the word. To Stoltz, Billy was someone with a high AQ. And to Stoltz, being traded by the Yankees helped Billy clarify his goals—his Mountain. Stoltz notes, "Sometimes we Climb the wrong Mountain or we Climb the right Mountain for the wrong reasons. It often takes a fall to reach clarity and get back on the right path. His fall was a blessing. It gave him the clarity he needed to know it wasn't about being a Yankee. It was about something more. A fall can also reawaken us to the hard work and diligence it takes to continue our ascent. My guess is Billy was a high AQ guy who got confused about the Mountain, got some clarity, and got back on his path."

From 1962 to 1968, before becoming a manager, Billy was definitely not a man going through the motions and playing out the string in a dead-end job. He was dedicated to his work, and he enjoyed it.

▶ **Rich Reese:** *I first met Billy in 1963 when I was drafted by the Minnesota Twins from the Detroit Tigers. He spent endless hours throwing me balls at batting practice in Fernandina Beach, Florida. He was a very dedicated baseball man with his ultimate goal to be a manager in the major leagues. Obviously, he succeeded and did a tremendous job.*

▶ **Charlie Manuel:** *He'd come down and work out with us, and talk to us, and just kind of play baseball with us. He'd get out at second base, take ground balls, show guys how to turn double plays. For some reason, Billy took a liking to Graig Nettles and me and [Rick] Renick. As a matter of fact, we used to play with him all the time. We used to wrestle him, and hit him. I mean hard, too! He used to hit us back. He loved to play with you. He loved to mess around with you if you were that kind of person. If you were kind of loose and had fun, those were the kinds of people Billy liked. He was lively, very lively. He liked to laugh, he liked to joke. He liked all those aspects of the game. He loved being around the team. As far as being positive, he was always in a positive mood.*

Reese's recollection of "endless" hours spent with Billy shows how Martin was again applying the passion and dedication to his game that had enabled him to make the Yankees as a kid. And Manuel's recollections suggest a man who was having fun.

With a good attitude and a new focus on the game and his career, Martin was able to get a lot out of his scouting job, noting, "I really enjoyed the scouting job . . . I was close to the game I loved . . . Later, I would realize that my scouting job helped me as a manager because it honed my ability to evaluate players."[12]

His attitude and skill also scored him points with higher-ranking Twins management. His old friend Mele watched Billy run tryout camps during his scouting stint and liked what he saw. After three years as a scout, Billy inched his way closer to the manager's office by becoming Mele's third base coach.

▶ **Sam Mele:** *When he had the tryout camps at Metropolitan Stadium, I used to watch him work the kids in the infield and you could just see how good he was, and how he got along with the kids. He was scouting for us at the time, but I wanted him down here all the time to work with the infielders. He knew the game very well, and he had a way of getting it across so that people liked to work with him. And he got results. I finally talked to Calvin [Griffith]. I went right to the owner, and I said, "I want Billy down there working with my infielders."*

After becoming a coach, Billy's development continued. He had an excellent rapport with the players and with Mele. Billy coached third base for Sam for three seasons, and he contributed greatly to a 1965 trip to the World Series by sparking an aggressive running game in the club that had been lacking in 1964.

Then, in 1968, he was given the opportunity to take over the Twins' top minor league club, which had gotten off to a horrible start with a record of 7 wins and 22 losses. With the Denver Bears, Billy put the finishing touches on his managerial résumé.

▶ **George Mitterwald:** *When we were in Denver, we had a pretty good ballclub, but we started out real bad. So they gave Billy a chance to go there and manage, though he had never managed before. They told him that if he went there, he'd have a chance to really get his feet wet, get a chance to manage, and see what it was all about. Of course, he went there, and we had a tremendous year after he got there. Things just turned around.*

Billy guided the Bears to 58 wins against 28 losses over the rest of the season, good for a .674 winning percentage. With that, Billy was given the managerial reigns of the Twins, a much better-rounded baseball man than he had been when he and Sam Mele sat in the locker room and cried during the spring of 1962.

In your life and your work, you have to hang in there, because a break will come—especially if you are building your skills set and your knowledge during times when opportunities appear to be lacking. The change you're looking for won't necessarily occur overnight, but you always have to believe that you are going to get there, and always remind yourself of where you are and where you're going. More than 20 years after his decision to stay in the game as a scout, Billy would say, "You gotta know that life is mountains and valleys. Ups and downs. That's my strength. I know nothing is ever going to always go smooth."[13]

Ready to Become a Leader

When Billy became the Twins' manager in 1969, he took a team that had come in seventh the year before to a rousing first-place finish, and he became an "overnight" sensation. But of course, significant success is never an overnight proposition, and it wasn't for Billy. People who attach words like "luck" to another person's success are most likely naive, jealous, or just unaware of the true sacrifices made by people to achieve their success.

Billy was anything but lucky. For almost 20 years, he had been working his way toward that top dugout step. He was ready to implement a positive, high-energy program in which he was in charge, and through which he would win. He had proved he could contribute as a player, a scout, and a coach, and he was eager to prove that he could do it as a manager. He was ready to lead.

▶ **Charlie Manuel:** *When he started managing, he wanted to be the manager. Not only that, he had enough cockiness that made him want to prove to you that he was the best manager. He was a very positive, very strong guy. He was so secure on the field. You know, when I looked at Billy, my first year in the big leagues, I thought when he came in there in Minnesota, he generated a lot of energy.*

▶ **Rod Carew:** *He wasn't going to allow us to just stand still. He gave anyone the steal sign on that ballclub that year. [Harmon] Killebrew stole a few bases. [Bob] Allison, everybody—guys that weren't base-stealing threats . . . He would try and do anything that he possibly could to win a game. He was so far ahead in his thinking than most managers. He just created excitement with the ballclub. He just pushed us to do things that we hadn't done the year before.*

▶ **George Mitterwald:** *We had a different team in '69. We had a tremendous team. We had Killebrew and [Tony] Oliva and Carew and [Cesar]
Tovar. Ted Uhlaender. I mean, we had some great players and a great
pitching staff. We could go in and do different things. We had nine rookies on that team that year, I think. That first [AL Playoff] Series in 1969
[between Minnesota and Baltimore] could have gone either way. We lost
two games in extra innings, and they ended up going to the World Series
that year. They had a tremendous team. Their starting staff was fantastic,
but we were right there with 'em. Our team was just as good, and our
pitching staff was right there with 'em.*

▶ **Charlie Silvera:** *He had the people there in Minnesota. He had Carew
and he had Tovar. And these guys, they'd go to hell for him. I mean, he
protected them. Tovar'd run through a brick wall. If Billy said, "Tell Tovar
to go knock down that brick wall," he'd be out there trying. He might not
do it, but he'd be tryin'.*

That sort of impact on his players is reminiscent of stories sur-
rounding General George S. Patton, a man with whom Billy identified
and had much in common. Interestingly, both men were known for a
seat-of-the-pants decisiveness that often was confused with a lack of
preparedness, and both captured America's imagination as aggressive
"geniuses" full of bravado.

Yet for both men, it was tireless preparation grounded in dedication and a deep-rooted love for their profession that enabled them to
respond in a *seemingly* seat-of-the-pants manner and to trust their gut
hunches. For both men, greatness grew out of intense, lifelong preparation—not wild-eyed bravado.

▶ **Buck Showalter:** *I think people have this perception of Billy just being a
guy that showed up, game time, did a bunch of emotional, wild things,
and somehow got lucky and it worked out. One thing I learned from him
was that basically you use statistics to verify gut feelings, and the gut
feeling comes first. And that's certainly what the case was with Billy.
Billy wasn't afraid. I'm sure some people view him as some swashbuckling, off-the-seat-of-his-pants, "the heck with reason" guy, but Billy*

thought things out very deeply. You don't get lucky over 162 games. That's the great thing about our game. I mean, you play too many games not to have strengths and weaknesses show up over the course of the season. Billy wanted to be prepared. He wanted to know. *He wanted to know about the opposition. He wanted to know umpires' tendencies. He wanted to be prepared to take advantage of anything, and not be caught by surprise.*

In September 1944, just before General Patton's great dash across Europe put the nail in Germany's coffin, Patton reportedly told his nephew Frederick Ayer, Jr., "I have studied the German all my life. I have read the memoirs of his generals and political leaders. I have even read his philosophers and listened to his music. I have studied in detail the accounts of every damned one of his battles. I know exactly how he will react under any given set of circumstances. He hasn't the slightest idea what I'm going to do. Therefore, when the day comes, I'm going to whip hell out of him."[14]

Billy's education in the game of baseball was very similar to that of Patton's education in war. Consider two "quiet" periods in Billy's baseball career—the 1950 and 1951 seasons, when he was riding the bench for the Yankees as a utility infielder, and 1965 through 1967, when he was coaching third base for Sam Mele's Minnesota Twins. In neither case was Billy treading water, waiting for something new to happen. In both cases, he was learning and improving at his trade. As a Yankee bench warmer, he didn't sulk. Instead, he paid attention and learned from Stengel.

▶ **Gil McDougald:** *I think Casey, in his own way, was teaching Billy when Billy was on the ballclub. Billy was on the bench a lot. Billy watched every move that Casey made and questioned every move in his own mind. In other words, Billy was managing, and Casey was managing. If you sit on the bench, you can go crazy, but Billy made himself involved in every minute of the ballgame. And that is extremely unusual. But this was Billy.*

Billy learned from Joe DiMaggio, too.

▶ **Charlie Silvera:** *We'd hang around with DiMaggio after the day games for hours sometimes. Just Hank [Bauer], and I, and Billy, and Joe. Just sit there and talk. You know, we'd have a few beers—two, three, maybe. We'd pick his brain. We'd just talk a little bit about everything. I always said to myself, even when Billy got to managing, "I didn't think that you were paying that much attention." But he was. He was picking things up. Years later, I said, "I give you credit. You made a study of this game."*

And when he was coaching for Sam Mele, the game was never over for Billy.

▶ **Sam Mele:** *He'd come into my office when everybody was gone and we'd just sit there, having a beer, and we'd just talk and talk and talk. And then damn it, he'd call me, I'd go over his house later at night, and get some Kentucky Fried Chicken or something, have another beer, and just talk baseball, baseball, baseball.*

From the days on the sandlots with Augie Galan to the nights eating fried chicken with Sam Mele, Billy was getting ready. He was developing his instincts and intuition for the game. Thus, years later he could say, "A manager has to have good instincts . . . You're not just guessing at it, you actually have an instinct or an intuition about what the other guy is going to do . . . So many times the other manager would go to the mound to talk to his pitcher . . . and I'd say to my players, 'He's telling him, *Billy's going to send the runner, so we're going to pitch out.*' . . . And they'd pitch out and I wouldn't be sending the runner because I knew he was going to pitch out . . . and the players would say, 'How did you know that?' . . . I don't know how I knew it. It's just instinct, or intuition."[15]

Whatever it was, it was largely acquired. Throughout Billy's boyhood years and his 20 years in professional baseball, he built a store of knowledge that, along with an intelligent mind and an energetic spirit, enabled him to become one of the greatest field managers in the history of the game.

▶ **Mickey Morabito:** *I think Billy's feeling for the game came from the amount of time that he spent on the field as a player, coach, and man-*

ager. I think that's what probably sets him apart from a lot of other managers. In talking to baseball people that you respect a lot over the years, they've all told me that there's no one better than Billy. Managers that I respect to this day like Tony LaRussa will tell you that he's probably the best he's ever managed against.

▶ **Tony LaRussa:** *Don't put me in his class—he was one of an elite few ever in this game. I think when you've been in the game for a long time, you make a decision on your gut feel, and then after the game, you go back and you can trace that decision to a game when a similar scenario unfolded. That's the instinct. With Billy, going back to his playing career—and I've read about his relationship with Casey Stengel—I think he just took in everything.*

▶ **Ray Negron:** *Anybody that can tell you exactly how Billy did this or did that is lying. He was a very instinctive type of guy who just had an inner vision of dealing with situations. Everybody always marveled. You couldn't help but to marvel at how he ran a ballgame. You always heard throughout the years, "In the first inning, he already knew what he was going to be doing in the sixth inning." That's something that you can't go to school and learn. That's from years of playing the game, being around people, and it's just in you, a special sixth sense of the game.*

Having seen how Billy got ready, let's look in the next chapters at what he did with his opportunities to lead.

Notes

1. David Falkner, *The Last Yankee* (New York: Simon & Schuster, 1992), pp. 212–213.

2. Ibid., p. 41.

3. Maury Allen, *Damn Yankee: The Billy Martin Story* (New York: Times Books, 1980), p. 29.

4. Maury Allen, "Martin's Problems," *New York Post,* May 9, 1978.

5. Norman Vincent Peale, *The Power of Positive Thinking* (New York: Fawcett Crest, 1992), p. 97.

6. Falkner, p. 34.

7. Ibid., p. 34.

8. Billy Martin and Phil Pepe, *Billyball* (Garden City, N.Y.: Doubleday & Company, 1987), p. 55.

9. Allen, *Damn Yankee*, p. 38.

10. Norman Lewis Smith, *The Return of Billy the Kid* (New York: Coward, McCann & Geoghegan, 1977), pp. 47–48.

11. Billy Martin and Peter Golenbock, *Number 1* (New York: Delacorte Press, 1980), p. 109.

12. Martin and Pepe, p. 96.

13. Ira Berkow, "Emotion Rules the Way Martin Lives and Works," *New York Times,* July 3, 1983.

14. Roger Nye, *The Patton Mind* (Garden City Park, N.Y.: Avery Publishing Group, 1993), p. 92.

15. Martin and Pepe, p. 116.

Building Competitors

ike many of his peers, Billy Martin had a firm grasp of the fundamentals of baseball and the ability to teach his players what he knew. But one of Billy's greatest skills was his ability to look into the hearts of his players, find who really wanted to win, and bring out the greatness in them. Billy's teaching was thus more mental than physical. Billy could get players to *think* like winners. To Billy, winning was a habit that could be taught.

Mastering the Mental Game

Consider the following passage from H. A. Dorfman and Karl Kuehl in their book *The Mental Game of Baseball*: "What percentage of time does a coach or instructor spend teaching mental skills and strategies and working on winning the mental game? Studies by sports psychologists indicate the most common figure to be somewhere near 10 percent . . . Though they're often heard shouting such directions as 'Hang tough!' or 'Be ready!' or 'Keep your eye on the ball!' they have seldom been able to tell their players how to be tough, or what's required in order to be ready and see the ball well."[1]

But many baseball players disagree with Dorfman and Kuehl. These players maintain that pride, desire, and the mental game can indeed be taught—and Billy did just that.

▶ **Toby Harrah:** *You hear that crap all the time. I played for managers, you listen to 'em, and you know they're not speaking from the heart. You know that they've said that same speech over and over. It's almost like a recording. But Billy made winning a personal thing. He pushed you. He tested your pride and your makeup as a man, and he wanted you to go out there and play like an extension of yourself and the way you do everything else.*

Clearly, Billy was different from Dorfman and Kuehl's typical coach. More than any ability to teach physical elements of the game, Billy's talent was in the mental game, and that is what made him special. Billy turned ragtag squads like his 1974 Rangers and 1980 A's into fighting machines in a single season because he got players to think like winners and to execute like winners. Sure, he taught them how to play the game better, but more importantly, he taught them to believe in themselves and to test themselves—something every leader should aspire to do.

▶ **Matt Keough:** *What makes a good leader is he makes people around him better. You show me a baseball team that Billy Martin had for one or two years initially that didn't get better. The bottom line is, if you could be good, Billy showed you how to be good. He taught a lot of guys who didn't know how to play, how to play. And every place he went, he did that. Baseball is a very complex game. Size doesn't matter. Speed doesn't matter. Height doesn't matter. It's a very, very grinding mental game, and Billy, basically, that was him. That epitomized what he was. There's only 600 of us animals in the world. So the difference between one and 600 isn't that big, unless you're talking [Mark] McGwire and [Sammy] Sosa—those guys are at a special level. There's a lot of us that play the game that aren't the best athletes. We grind. It's 162 games, and we learn how to play.*

The "Billyball" style of play Martin implemented during the Oakland years of 1980–1982 was reminiscent of turn-of-the-century baseball with hit-and-runs, sacrifices, squeeze plays, hitting behind the runner, and an all-around fighting style. It was all about attitude—Billy's swaggering, in-your-face attitude.

Being a Leader with Attitude

But how could a team of young ballplayers coming off a 108-loss season, which was Oakland's fate in 1979, suddenly be so in-your-face? By having a leader. By having a plan. By being prepared. In one short spring training, Billy gave a young group of players direction and confidence, and he got them playing a wild brand of exciting, aggressive ball.

Still, it's shocking to think that a team that lost 108 games the previous season is suddenly going to take on a more fundamentally complex style of play and win with it. It required not only a lot of practice but a lot of confidence, and a willingness to take the leader at his word that they weren't "losers" and that they could turn the ship around. Billy was able to do these things.

▶ **Mike Heath:** *We had a pretty good nucleus of a ballclub there, but we needed somebody to lead it. What I mean by that is we needed a manager to implement a system he believed in that we could play by. Billy brought in that sense of winning. "We're going to win, guys. If you listen to me, this is how it's going to get done." And that's exactly the mode that we went after. We needed that after coming from the '79 season like trash. But Billy brought that attitude in, and then he brings in these coaches that got names behind 'em, that was going to teach you how to play the game. It was great.*

Oakland pitcher Matt Keough learned new ways of looking at the game from Billy and his two well-known coaches, Art Fowler and Clete Boyer, that honed his mental toughness. Billy and his coaches were able to do this even in a kid like Keough who had been around baseball all his life as the son of major league outfielder Marty Keough.

▶ **Matt Keough:** *Billy taught us how to win. Art Fowler taught us how to win. Clete Boyer taught us how to win. These guys, they taught us how to do things we'd never been told about. You know, like after your team scores, "Go out and put a zero up on the board the next half inning, you'll win." I never heard that in my whole life, and I was born between Frank Robinson and Vada Pinson. I said, "What do you mean go out and* *put a zero up?" And he says, "If you put a zero up in the third inning after we score, you'll win." I never heard that. Suddenly now, it made an impression on me.*

It was a "one step at a time" type of message, and certainly not nuclear physics. But sometimes helping a person look at his or her job in a simple way, or helping him or her to break it down into smaller parts, can help to clarify the person's job or task. Keough had the talent to pitch in the majors, but still he learned something about winning from Billy in learning to take things one step at a time. Don't worry about the ninth inning here in the third. Just do the job in the third inning.

Mike Norris, a player, and George Mitterwald, a coach, both reflect back on Billy's arrival in Oakland and recall his teaching of both the physical and the mental aspects of the game.

▶ **Mike Norris:** *I think what Billy did was actually strip it down to a little league form of fundamentals. When he came to spring training, he taught guys how to play baseball. Just the little things on what makes you win. I think he embedded in you what he wanted you to do. And it was up to you. Your manhood was tested. Your ballplaying skills were tested at the same time. And it just made you step up your level of play. And you knew that if you were out there making mental mistakes, you were going to have to hear his wrath. So that made you concentrate a lot more. So you got basically 100 percent of your physical abilities out of you all the time. And if you produce 100 percent of the time mentally, you're going to be a winner. The guys that were underachievers were able to fit in and be overachievers. The Mickey Kluttses and guys like that, having better career years than they had ever had. Chicken Stanley, guys like that.*

▶ **George Mitterwald:** *In 1979 we lost 108 games. We won 54 games. It was a miserable season. We had a young team, a very young team. And the players, some of them were good, some of them weren't so good. But Billy came in there the next year and he turned it around. We went from 54 and 108 to winning 83 ballgames with the same identical team. He went through spring training, and we worked on every fundamental you can work on. We did all the basic things. I say the basic things, but other man-*

agers don't do the basic things. Basic things are bunting, stealing, trying to steal home, and first and third situations. A good hitter, like a Dwayne Murphy, who hit with power—Billy had him drag bunting to first with runners on first and third instead of trying to hit a home run, where he may strike out and not get any runs in. He'd bunt the ball. He might get a base hit, drive in a run, and move the runner to second. That was just the way he thought. And he believed in repeating, repeating, repeating. He said, "When you get tired of repeating, repeat it a few times more, because the more you can drum it into these guys' heads, the better they're going to be, and the better we're going to be as a team." He kept drumming and drumming and drumming and drumming. Sometimes, certain guys might get mad at a manager for doing something like that, but you knew what Billy was trying to do. He was trying to make everybody better.

Billy returned a sense of order, teamwork, and winning professionalism to the A's by practicing the fundamentals and demanding execution. It was personal, and each player knew that he had to deliver the basics to Billy if he wanted to be part of the team.

▶ **Mike Heath:** *He really helped me out. Seeing him go about his business reconfirmed me. And what I mean by "his business" is about how he wanted to win the ballgame. It reconfirmed in me that I was doing the right thing. Because I wanted to win. That was the bottom line.*

Raising the Energy and Confidence Level

The reconfirmed A's enjoyed a 29-win improvement in 1980, and a then-record 11-game winning streak to kick off a 1981 season that ended with a trip to the AL Championship Series versus the Yankees. The A's became winners, and for a while, the Billyball show was something to behold. Billyball was fun and kept the players energized.

▶ **Jackie Moore:** *All at once, a club shows up that's a last-place club, and—boom—you're in there, you're competing. I mean, that's a heck of an accomplishment. It's that unexpected showing, and it all starts with your manager. It was Billy's type of ballclub. He could manufacture runs with them. He could do things with them. Billyball! Whoever came up* *with the name, I don't remember, but it was perfect, because he could get 'em to do a lot of things—little things—and it was exciting. That's why the fans came back. They loved it. They loved that style of play.*

▶ **Mike Norris:** *That's what they called Billyball. I had played on the championship team previously with the [Sal] Bandos and the [Reggie] Jacksons and stuff, so I had experienced the success. But what I hadn't experienced was the city being behind it. I mean, coming out to that baseball game was like a rock concert. The fans actually had fun. It was entertainment. And the ballclub was exciting and entertaining. It really brought the city together, that's what I noticed most about it.*

▶ **Matt Keough:** *The energy level was immense, because when you're getting your brains kicked out every day, and all of a sudden you're kicking everybody else's brains in, it was exciting.*

▶ **George Mitterwald:** *They played the "Celebration" song every time we won, and it was just like we knew we were going to win. It was amazing! And I think our pitchers, they had a tremendous confidence in themselves. They gained a lot in '80, but then the next year, they had that much more. They just felt that we weren't going to lose. We had a good ballclub, and we weren't going to give games away. And it's just a confidence thing. The more you win, you just feel like you're going to win.*

Billy infused his club with belief. His ingredients for winning were pride, desire, self-sacrifice, and the will to win. He once said, "These are a lot of little things. Put 'em together, it spells a winner."[2] These are the qualities he brought out in his A's. Billy's turnaround defied all reason, but there it is in the record books. Of course, General George S. Patton once said, "It is not by reason, but most often in spite of it, that are created those sentiments that are the mainsprings of all civilization—sentiments such as honor, self-sacrifice, religious faith, patriotism, and the love of glory."[3] That's a philosophy right in line with Billy's. Billy had such a belief in the team concept and the honor that came from winning that he sparked those urges in his players.

▶ **Mike Heath:** *I'm a guy that really respected him. I really enjoyed playing for him. I just think of a guy that at any price, he wanted to win the ball-game. And that's what thrived him—winning. I was very happy to see something like that, so I was just reaffirming my commitment to the game through Billy, because that's the way I went about my business. I wanted to win no matter what. Hey, if I had a bad game, it didn't matter if we still won the ballgame. I think that's the way Billy was. Winning was the bottom line.*

Billy's greatest leadership skill was his ability to identify and culti-vate the mental strength of his baseball players. He once wrote, "What I look for . . . is what's in [the player's] heart and . . . head."[4] And once he found and encouraged that mental strength in his players, he was ready to let them go and perform. Turning a ballplayer or a ballclub loose was fun for Billy, and because it was fun, he radiated an energy that added to the believability and the motivational impact of his lead-ership. Lenny Randle, who played for Billy's turnaround 1974 Texas Rangers, recalls how Billy got players coming off a 105-loss season to believe that they could challenge the World Champion A's for the pen-nant. They did. They finished just five games behind the A's as com-pared to 37 games behind in 1973.

▶ **Lenny Randle:** *Here's a guy telling you in front of everybody, "You guys play your ass off for me, you're gonna all get raises. Just give me 110 percent and I'll give you 100 percent at the table. And then we're gonna win, and you'll just see all this trickle down, just like it did for the Yan-kees. We have a history of it, and it's going to happen right here in this organization. You gotta believe you can kick Oakland's ass! You gotta start believing that today! My attention is to get you guys fundamentally ready so that you can execute. And you're going to have fun doing it. And if you have fun doing it, you're going to win. I believe in fun. We're going to do some crazy stuff. We're going frog hunting. We're going . . ." You know, he started naming all those little things that he was going to do, because he was still basically a kid. He was still a player's manager. That fired me up!*

▶ **Charlie Manuel:** *I think about how much life he had, and how he walks on the field and he wants to show his burning enthusiasm. He wants to create a high energy level around him. I think his motivation part was actually a factor. He wanted to generate a lot of energy around you, and he could really show people how much he loved the game, and how hard that he wants you to play. Those are the things that to me, I learned from Billy. His spark, his life.*

Achievement in life—reaching our goals—is based as much upon our dedication as it is our intentions, as much upon our efforts as our skills. Billy learned that as a kid from Augie Galan, Cookie Lavagetto, and Casey Stengel. They encouraged him to let it rip, and it helped him to battle his way up to the bright lights of New York as second baseman for the greatest sports dynasty of all time. As a manager, he brought that energy out of his ballplayers, especially the ones who were like he had been.

Building a Team of Talented and Dedicated Players

As a manager (and indeed, as a player), Billy's foundation was desire. He once said, "There's some guys that don't have the ability, speed, strength. But they have more guts and a lot of heart. For where they lack in ability, they want to win so bad that you lean a little bit backwards for a guy like that. There's been so many players that were just borderline but could play for me more than a superstar could, because those guys really wanted to give and put out all the time."[5] As a manager, Billy was able to build competitors out of a wide range of ballplayers—from journeymen like Bobby Meacham, to star hitters like Willie Horton and Rod Carew. The common denominator was desire.

Getting the Players You Want on the Field

One ballplayer Billy loved was Bobby Meacham, a Yankee shortstop in the mid-1980s. Meacham thrived under Billy in 1985, playing in a career-high 156 games despite a nagging wrist injury that took his batting average down to .218. To Billy, injury or no injury, Meacham was the type of player he wanted on the field.

▶ **Bobby Meacham:** *Billy one time came up to me and said, "You know I'll never pinch hit for you with this—I won't mention his name—one player . . . I'll never pinch hit that player for you again because you bust your butt for me every day. You're ready to play. You play as hard as anybody we've got, and you're a good player. You're gonna be a great player. And this guy just sits at the end of the bench, never gets ready to play, and doesn't care if we win or not." He said, "He will never, ever pinch hit for you again." And he never did. And even times when he was the only guy on the bench and it would obviously call for him to pinch hit for me, he never went back on his word. He'd rather put me out there, somebody he knew wanted to win.*

▶ **Buck Showalter:** *I think there's a lot of identification with Billy with players somewhat like him, that had to scrap for everything that they could get. Billy wanted people he could count on, someone that's gonna be loyal. I think along those lines, you're asking, "Can you win with him? Is this a winning player?" I think all managers look for that. At every organization in America, there's some player that a manager's fighting for every off-season or during the year to keep because that's a job playing so many games. And our sport's unlike any other one. We play over 200 times a year counting spring training. And the ability to bring it every day actually shows up on our scoreboard and in our standings. There's a certain amount of ability that it takes to play at this level, but there's so many guys like Billy who are successful who don't necessarily possess the greatest skills in the world.*

Demanding 100 Percent

Most people do want to be the best that they possibly can regardless of their trade, but few are truly willing to do what it takes to get there. Very few, regardless of so-called talent, give 100 percent effort all the time. As a player, Billy had been that way. As a manager, he liked that same type of ballplayer. He was able to infuse these types of players with his attitude and swagger so that they played "above" themselves.

Twins skipper Sam Mele saw firsthand how Billy could turn a player around who wasn't giving it his all. During the Twins' 1965 season, Billy, then a coach, helped defuse a spring training situation with Mele and his shortstop, the late Zoilo Versalles.

▶ **Sam Mele:** *We had a spring training game in St. Petersburg, and a ball went by Zoilo Versalles by maybe four or five feet to his right. He made a very half-assed try to get it. So I pulled him right out of the game right there and brought my second-string shortstop in. Zoilo came in to the bench and oh, he started giving me a lot of b.s. So I fined him. And he kept it up, so I fined him a little more and a little more. Billy finally stopped him and grabbed Zoilo and said, "Get out of here. Come with me." And he had a helluva talk with him. And from that day on, Billy used to take him out. They'd go eat together and talk baseball. He did this continuously. The kid ended up being the Most Valuable Player in that league in 1965! Zoilo and I got along, but it was Billy that did something to help us win the pennant and had the kid play great ball.*

Baseball was serious business to Billy, just as it had been during his playing days with the Yankees. When Billy would join a new organization, he would quickly assess his players' talents, identify the players with the desire and dedication he wanted, and send the remainder to the bench or to other teams. Billy once said, "When I'm managing, you'd better take your job seriously, or you won't be around long. If you play for me, you play the game like you play life. You play it to be successful, you play it with dignity, you play it with pride, and you play it aggressively."[6]

▶ **Mike Heath:** *I think his greatest strength was getting guys to really play aggressive baseball. Either you did it or you didn't. That was the bottom line with him. Billy was a bottom line kind of guy. "Either you go and play hard, or I'm going to get you out of here." And he got a lot of guys to play hard for him.*

▶ **Fred Stanley:** *I think he was a tremendous motivator. I think there were some guys that could not play for him, because they couldn't take the criticism. Billy could be sarcastic. Guys like Graig Nettles, Chris Chambliss, Willie Randolph. Guys that knew where Billy was going, they knew what he was doing, and they were good players, and they were mentally tough. If you were mentally tough, you could play for Billy Martin. If you weren't, you had problems. If you weren't mentally tough, you couldn't be a good player, certainly not with the Yankees.*

▶ **Toby Harrah:** *As a player, if you had some coward in you, you could probably bluff and get by with a lot of managers. Billy found out. Billy could find your weaknesses. And you couldn't hide stuff from this guy. He confronted you. He tested your manhood, man. There wasn't any three ways about it. If you're a chicken shit, if you stayed with him, you didn't stay that way. He made you a tougher competitor. He made you mentally more aggressive. And he made you believe in yourself. And you know as well as I, that if you don't believe in yourself when you're competing, your ass is in a bind. For me, one time, we're playing the White Sox, and Jim Spencer's the hitter in front of me, and he hits a home run. And Stan Bahnsen is pissed. I know I'm going to get drilled, and then 0–2, he threw a fastball that hit me on the elbow, and I thought he'd broke my elbow. And I'm laying at home plate, and I'm thinking Billy's going to come up and say, "Hey Tobe, how ya doin'? What's wrong with ya?" And instead he says, "Listen Toby, when you get on first, I want you to steal on the first pitch." So later I'm over on the bench, my elbow is just puffed up like a son of a bitch. And here comes Billy, and I'm thinking, "Billy's going to say something like, 'Aw, you're OK.'" He just walks right by me, gets a drink of water, turns right around, and goes back the other way. Doesn't say a damn word to me. Never asked me how I'm feeling.*

Billy wanted Harrah to play tough and to play aggressively—not to be looking for any sympathy. Mental toughness is thinking about how to capitalize on being hit by a pitch, not how to get sympathy from the manager. Harrah, already tough, got even tougher playing for Billy, but not everyone made the adjustment.

▶ **Willie Horton:** *Billy Martin's the type of man with fire in him. He challenged me so many times. You find somebody that didn't come from a background that liked to prove themselves, it'll mess them up until they understand it. For me, when Billy got on my butt, I liked that. That just got me going. Some guys couldn't understand that, and I think it all comes back to how you come up as a kid.*

Corporate coach Paul Stoltz, whom we have already referred to in these pages, sees "a deeper compassion" in someone like Billy. These words should ring loud and clear to anyone who has ever been pushed out of a comfort zone to a new level by a teacher, coach, parent, or boss. Being pushed hurts, but in the end, when you reach that new level, you realize the compassion that really was there all along. Stoltz states:

> "This is one of the most refreshing and enervating characteristics of high Adversity Quotient (AQ) individuals. They cannot palate excuses, wimpyness, or helplessness. This can be perceived as cold, hard, and completely void of compassion. But it has a deeper compassion—a belief that every person has the capacity to overcome, improve, and contribute. This is why leaders like Billy Martin still bring tears to their players' eyes. He didn't coddle—he angered, confronted, and inspired their best, time and time again. Like most Climbers, Billy was controversial. He ticked off a lot of people. But the results speak for themselves. Either you're on the rope, or you're not. No in-betweens."

▶ **Rod Carew:** *There were some guys that loved him, and some guys that hated him. The ones that hated him are the ones that didn't want to play the game the way he wanted it to be played. He'd tell you, "The only thing that I ask of you, I don't care what you do after the game, but once you're on the field, I want you to get yourself prepared for the ballgame." And he'd push you to achievement in baseball. Any amount of talent you had, he was going to get it out of you. Even if you were just a player that didn't have a great deal of talent, he was going to get what he could out of the talent that you had.*

Bucky Dent was a player who had a tough time adjusting to Billy when the former came to the Yankees. He was a hard-nosed shortstop who had starred for the White Sox for several seasons before coming to the Bronx, where the pressure was much greater and the bench a lot deeper. Billy was tough on Bucky, and he would pinch hit for him sometimes as early as the sixth inning if he thought it would help the team win. It was no different from what Stengel had done with Billy and his teammates throughout the 1950s. The talent was there—the goal was to win. Still, for Dent it was an adjustment, having come from an organization that didn't pinch hit for him (and also didn't win). Of course, Bucky made the adjustment, was a solid player on the 1977 World Championship team, and emerged as the star of the 1978 post-season, from his big homer in Boston (in a one-game playoff that broke a regular-season tie between the Yankees and the Red Sox to send the Yanks on to the AL Championship Series) to his World Series MVP performance.

▶ **Mickey Rivers:** *Bucky didn't understand him, because he'd always yell at him. But I tell you what, he got the best out of him, and he did his best there. He didn't do his best no other place. He did his best there. He hustle every day. I called him Homey, because Bucky [played college ball] down here in Florida with me. I said, "Homey, what you need to do is stop looking back and go out and do the job you been doing." Because Billy don't like no pussy-puss guy. He liked the guy that go out there and take charge and be loud.*

Players who were willing to play hard, to play aggressively, and to learn from Billy could feel the inordinate amount of faith Billy would put in them.

▶ **Bobby Meacham:** *He treated me like a kid that he saw something in that he could mold and make into a really good player. If he was in New York for the whole time that I was there, there's no doubt in my mind that I would have played ten years for the Yankees, and it would have been a whole different story as far as my career goes. Because it means something when a manager believes in you. And I think he just solely believed* *in me because he saw the way I played. He saw that I played hard, and that was his style. He saw that I didn't back down, and that was his style. And he saw that I was smart enough to learn quickly the things that he was teaching me.*

▶ **Jackie Moore:** *The players knew that he believed in them. If you didn't give up on yourself, he wouldn't give up on you. They knew that "As long as I'm competing, as long as I'm trying, or giving my best, Billy will go along with me." He would give you the opportunity, and he would extend that opportunity probably more so than a lot of managers. Whatever opportunity you needed to become a better player, he presented it to you.*

Once Billy found players with his sort of desire, he would work closely with them, and over the years many stars emerged under Billy Martin's tutelage. Rod Carew, Graig Nettles, Mike Hargrove, Jim Sundberg, Willie Randolph, Ron Guidry, Rickey Henderson, Don Mattingly, Jay Buhner, and many others either first came up or truly emerged as major league regulars under Billy.

Yet when Billy would recall each of these players, it was rarely their pitching velocity, power, running speed, swing, or other ability he discussed. Instead, it was their heart. He wanted players with drive and desire who were dedicated to their trade.

Oftentimes, neither manager nor follower knows exactly the limits of that follower's potential. Billy worked to find that limit so that he could maximize that player's performance.

▶ **Lenny Randle:** *Billy would take 'em to their limit, and then they'd have to find out what their limit was. And he'd help them get to that limit, and not push it beyond that. His thing was timing. His timing was unbelievable on giving guys rest or on giving a guy a day off. Making a guy feel important if he went four innings and pulled him out if we had a 13–3 score and we were ahead. He made guys that weren't totally established feel as good as the guy that was supposed to have been the superstar. And then some can see that this potentially can happen. He was amazing at getting guys to do that. Guys would step up to the plate. Those that didn't, they didn't.*

▶ **Toby Harrah:** *Billy was as good as anyone I've ever seen at taking a ball-club that was a good team and making it better. And I think a lot of it boils back down to his complete knowledge of the game of baseball, and his knowledge of people and what to do to get the most out of each and every one of us. I think half of being a really good manager is putting your players in situations where they can succeed a little bit easier. And Billy was good at that. Billy could get the right matchups, he had the right players that he wanted, and he put 'em in situations where they had a chance to succeed. And a lot of 'em did. He gave Mike Hargrove an opportunity. Here's a guy that was like a 30th or 40th or, I forget, 100th pick, and he made the ballclub out of A ball. Here's a kid nobody ever heard of. Jim Spencer's already the first baseman. And he [Hargrove] makes the team. How does that happen? For any other manager, Mike probably isn't even invited to spring training.*

▶ **George Mitterwald:** *He just instilled confidence in you. Talking person-ally, we [the Minnesota Twins] got in the playoffs in '69, and here I am a rookie, and he puts me in the starting lineup the first two games. I was kind of dumbfounded. But he had confidence in me, and it made me feel great as a player. And it just gave me a tremendous amount of confi-dence, that he would have enough confidence to stick me in a game like that. I only got one hit in that series, but I played tremendous defense. I threw out four guys who tried to steal. I made two diving catches on pop-ups. Defensively, I did everything anybody could do as a catcher. It always stuck with me that Billy was the type of guy that wanted people not to be afraid to do anything. He let people do things that sometimes they didn't even think they could do themselves, but he gave them con-fidence in themselves, just by showing them, "Hey, here's the respect. I want you to do this for me. Go ahead and do it."*

▶ **Buck Showalter:** *I know, managing in AA, and Billy calling and saying, "Listen, I'm supposed to do a report on your club. Why don't you just fill it out and send it to me, and that's good enough for me." Do you know what that meant to a 30-something-year-old manager to have Billy Martin say your opinion's good enough for him? I mean, I was up all night for two nights, making sure those reports were perfect. To* *have your opinion matter to somebody like that, you didn't want to let him down.*

Seeing What Others Did Not See

Because heart was Billy's key evaluation criterion, what was apparent to Billy was not always apparent to everyone else in an organization. The cases of three players in particular stand out: Rod Carew, Ron Guidry, and Rickey Henderson. For example, in Carew, where others saw a moody troublemaker, Billy saw "burning desire and drive to be the best."[7] Billy put in time with Carew, helping him to improve both his physical and mental tools during some difficult years of maturation for the future all-time great.

▶ **Sam Mele:** *He worked a lot with Rod Carew, who used to have hands that weren't as soft as Billy liked them. Billy used to throw a ball against the wall and let the ball come right back to Rod and draw the ball in toward his body. And then he would throw the ball at an angle where Rod would have to go to his right. Then throw it back at an angle and make him go to his left, and back and forth, every day. It all paid off because Rod turned out to be a helluva second baseman besides being a good hitter. One time, our second baseman got taken out of a double play and he hurt his knee bad. Carew was in the minors, and I said to Billy, "Well, what do we do now?" He said, "Send for Carew." And I said, "Billy, is he ready?" He said, "Send for Carew!" And damn it, the kid never went back to the minors. And this again was Billy. He got along with Carew real good. As tough as he was, he could relate to a guy, and if he had to raise his voice a little he did, but it was never in a malicious way.*

▶ **Rod Carew:** *I became his project for the spring. He just pushed me to work hard, I mean, just taught me just about everything that he knew about playing second base, and really not only second base, but playing the game itself. I wasn't the greatest second baseman. I needed to work on turning double plays, staying down on ground balls, and things like that. Every day he would take me out and just work with me on those things. And he could see if a guy was willing to go to war with him. That's just the way Billy was. And I learned from that, I learned that that's*

the way that I wanted to be as a coach. I wanted to be able to have the
patience with young players and teach them until they learned the right
way to play the game. And to this day, that's what I try to do.

Ron Guidry emerged as one of the dominant pitchers of his era, but he didn't make it to the majors to stay until he was 26 years old. Despite a 5'11", 161-pound frame, "Gator" was a power pitcher, and baseball scouts and executives were skeptical that he could last as a big league starter without getting hurt. He also was a slow starter in spring training. During a trying 1977 spring training with the Yankees in which a still unproven Guidry performed absolutely horribly, a frustrated Billy said to him, "Tell me someone you can get out in this league, and I'll let you pitch to him." But for the most part, Billy admired the kid and kept him on the big league squad over some other pitchers who had had better springs. And he never saw Gator's size as an impediment, because again, Billy was looking for heart. Billy recalled, "You're dealing with a human being, not a machine, and . . . calculators and computers can't measure a guy's heart and his toughness, and if Guidry has anything it's heart and toughness."[8]

Billy liked Guidry, and Guidry liked his manager, too.

▶ **Dave Righetti:** *You know, he loved Billy. He trusted him, and Billy was hard on him. Billy had sent him down and treated him hard when he first came up. But Gator's self-motivated and very strong. But I can see where a quiet guy from Louisiana who threw hard but was small might not stand out with all these big star pitchers around. I can see where George [Steinbrenner] wanted him out of there, or Billy felt like he didn't have something because he was quiet. Maybe they didn't understand him. But then when they finally came to an understanding, he loved him and he pitched him. After that, forget it, it's like a bond that never goes away.*

▶ **Ray Negron:** *In his mind, he knew that Ron Guidry was going to be a quality starting pitcher at that time when Guidry had no confidence in himself. Billy wasn't going to take no for an answer from him. In spring training of '77, we had a pitcher by the name of Ed Ricks who totally outpitched Guidry. Totally. And in my mind, that was the first time I ever*

questioned Billy Martin, because I said, "What the hell? Why isn't he giv-
ing Ricks this shot?" Because I liked Ricks. He was a really cool dude.
And you know what? As the season progressed, you found out why Ron
Guidry made that club, and that spoke for itself, because he was one of
the great pitchers in Yankee history. And so there again is a tribute to
Billy Martin, because he had that inner vision.

From the middle of 1977 throughout the entire 1978 season, Guidry was the best and most overpowering pitcher in baseball. Over the years, however, as Guidry matured into a veteran winner, his confidence and poise earned him as many wins as his stuff. Players from the 1985 season—a season in which Gator won 22 games—recall a pitcher who won on confidence, guts, and one dominant pitch, his slider.

▶ **Bobby Meacham:** *In '85—Guidry—I remember playing behind him. I'd*
come home and tell my wife, "You know what, he really doesn't have
that much. I mean, I don't know how he's getting these guys out." And
I think Billy rubbed off on everybody. I think of Guidry, and I think of
Billy. They kind of had that same air about them. They were confident,
and whether they were better or not, they just thought that they were
better than everybody else.

▶ **Ron Hassey:** *In '85, I thought, Ronnie didn't have that fastball that he*
used to, but he had a great slider. It was almost like a curveball, but it
had a slant to it and it went just straight down. And I remember playing
in Detroit, and he called me out. He said, "What'd you forget the fast-
ball?" I said, "No, let's just keep throwing the slider till they hit it." "But
how 'bout my arm?" And that's when I said, "We'll worry about that next
year, but right now this is how you're getting the guy out, so let's stay
with it." I think Ron Guidry and Billy Martin had a great relationship. I
think it was very close, and I think it was very personal. I think they both
respected each other very much.

Then there was Rickey Henderson. When Billy saw Rickey Henderson, he knew he had a once-in-a-lifetime ballplayer to build his new
Oakland team around. Rickey had the talent, and in the early years of

his career, he had Billy, who helped to put him in situations where he would succeed, and who gave him the confidence that he could be one of the greats.

▶ **Dave Righetti:** *Aw, shit, there's nobody like him. Nah, nobody ever. I bet there won't be another one like him for another couple lifetimes in terms of on the field. But again, he's a product of Billy. Not an aggressive person at all off the field, but totally aggressive on the field.*

▶ **Jackie Moore:** *Rickey had so many pluses. And what I mean by pluses, I mean the things that he could do to win a ballgame. What a tool he had as far as making things happen, putting pressure on the opposing club. He fit right in the mold of Billy Martin's type of play. Base on balls, leadoff hitter—boom—steal second base. And I was there the year that he broke the [single-season stolen base] record, and Billy was a big influence there, because he controlled the situations when Rickey ran. In other words, he would give him the steal sign in a breaking ball situation, where the pitcher would be throwing the curveball or off-speed pitch. So he was a big influence there.*

When you are managing young people, one of your jobs is to find ways for that talent to succeed. That means making sure young people aren't overwhelmed and don't get in over their heads. Henderson perhaps has as much talent as anyone who ever set foot on the diamond, but as a man in his early 20s, he was still learning the game and learning about himself. He needed Billy for the guidance he provided at that time. Henderson may have been aggressive on the playing field, but off the field, he needed attention and a little coddling. Billy was willing to coddle Rickey, because he knew he was young, he wanted him on the diamond, and most of all, because he liked him as a person. There was a mutual friendship between the two, much like the friendship between Billy and Casey years earlier.

▶ **Jackie Moore:** *He spent a lot of time with him, and there was a real respect there on both ends. Billy really liked him—it was not just professional association. He spent a lot of time with his players in general,* *but he knew Rickey needed a lot of attention, and he gave Rickey a lot of attention.*

▶ **Mickey Morabito:** *Billy was the best manager for Rickey, because Billy knew how to get Rickey to play. And Rickey loved Billy. He legitimately loved and cared about Billy. I'll never forget when Tony [LaRussa] came here, because Tony had some problems with Rickey. He asked me, "What the hell? How did Billy get Rickey to play?" I said, "You know what he did, Tony? He knew how to kiss his ass." Rickey was one of those guys, especially when he was a younger player, who needed to get a pat on the back. And again, that's what was great about Billy as a manager. I mean it's an old cliché: You've got 25 players, you have to treat 'em equal but individually. And he knew that with Rickey, that he had to kiss his ass a little. He had to tell him how good he was and maybe figure out when Rickey was moping and just give him some time. But he just handled him in a great way to get the most out of him, because he's baffled some other managers.*

▶ **Billy Martin, Jr.:** *One time I was with my dad and we went into the trainer's room, and Rickey was getting worked on. My dad said, "Well, partner, we're gonna have to rest you today. We can't take any chances on this injury getting worse." And Rickey said, "Aw, no, skip, I can play. I can play." And dad says, "It's just not worth it, Rickey. I need you for the rest of the season." Again, Rickey says, "Skip, I'm all right to play. You gotta let me play." Dad said, "You sure, Rickey?" I mean, he had him ready to run through a wall for him. He had a great way with Rickey.*

The mutual love and respect Billy and Rickey shared lasted through the end of Billy's managerial career, and even as Henderson's career has continued on into the new century, he continually refers back to the years he spent with Martin.

Looking at the Intangibles

For all the stars Billy helped get to the top, there were many other so-called journeymen whose entire major league careers were largely the result of Billy Martin believing in the intangibles they could bring to his club. Billy put in a lot of time with these types of players, and he got more out of them than most managers.

▶ **Jackie Moore:** *He was the type of guy that if he saw you in the lobby or wherever, he might say, "C'mon, let's go to lunch," or go fishing with him. You were his friend. You played for him, but you were his friend, and it was always a two-way street. He understood not only the superstar, but he also understood the guy that was going to hit .200, .250, or whatever. If a guy was having a bad night he understood, and I think he would make a point to spend more time with these guys. He knew that they needed him at this particular time more so than the guy that had the good night.*

Fred Stanley was one such player. "Chicken," who played for Martin in both New York and Oakland, was the type of player who learned how to be mentally tough, how to do little things to help the club, and as a utility player, how to stay ready all the time. Suddenly, with Billy in 1976, Stanley's steadiness landed him an everyday job with a Yankee club bound for the World Series.

▶ **Fred Stanley:** *When I got to the big leagues, I was always a utility player. And to be a good utility player, when you come in the game, you have to expect the ball to be hit to you. You have to get yourself mentally focused so that you can take five throws in a warm-up and you're ready to go. One of my whole things was, I did not want to make a mistake— a mental mistake or a physical mistake—that would cost us the ballgame. That was my whole approach. And so when Billy would call on me, sure enough, a ground ball would be hit to me, and I'd make a play. Well, it's easy to like someone if, in the role you put them in, they're doing what you ask 'em to do. And that's what I did. I started playing more, and then we really started playing well. It wasn't just me, but the club really kind of clicked, and we were playing good. All of a sudden when you have a combination that's working—everybody's a little superstitious—I think Billy just felt comfortable with me, being in there, that I wouldn't make a mistake. Even though I was hitting .240 at the time, I wasn't going to make a mistake that would cost him a game. And*

*I think I played in like 110 games, and I was very close to leading the
league in fielding percentage. He gave me that opportunity to play, and
I'll always be grateful for that.*

A few years later, when Billy moved on to Oakland and needed veteran help to tighten up the middle of the infield, he turned to Stanley
again for his steady professionalism. Again, the result was a trip to the
postseason. Billy understood the journeymen players giving everything
they had to stay in the game. He had been in their shoes. And he bent
over backward to show that he believed in them and was glad to have
them on the team.

Mickey Klutts, who also played for Billy in both New York and Oakland, was another Billy Martin overachiever. Klutts was a solid minor
league prospect, having earned co-MVP honors at AAA Syracuse in
1976. He made his Yankee debut during that 1976 season and was
considered by some to be the Yankee shortstop or third baseman of the
future. For Klutts, who had considered retiring from baseball after the
1975 season, Billy Martin would play an important role in his young
career and young life.

▶ **Mickey Klutts:** *I lost my dad in February of 1976, and Billy was a lot
like my dad in ways of discipline and taking your chewing out like a
man, things like that. So father figure? Maybe. I didn't have one at the
time. I think he filled a void in my life at a very, very kind of a down
time, and he picked me back up. Whether we were destined to do that,
I don't know, but it was sure funny because all of a sudden I've got a
man now who stepped into my life and who I had a lot of respect for.
And you know, every day, I just gave him everything I had. He was just
super. He gave me an opportunity. I think he was a wonderful guy, I
really do.*

Before his career could even get started, injuries ate away at Klutts's
body. The first major injury, at the tail end of 1977 spring training, was
perhaps the cruelest. Just days before camp broke, Mickey suffered a
compound fracture in his hand while attempting to tag out a stealing
base runner.

▶ **Mickey Klutts:** *I figured I was finished as a Yankee. Billy was just sick, but he patted me on the back. He said, "Get well. Don't worry." He talked to me after I went to the hospital. I was back in my hotel room. He brought me over a beer and just told me, "Hang in there," because I was really emotionally bad, but he was good to me about it. And then what, four or five days later, they get Bucky Dent, and I'm done. He was disappointed, but I wouldn't have my World Series ring if it wasn't for him sticking with me and putting me on the roster in 1977.*

While Klutts's chances of becoming a Yankee regular essentially did end with that play, he did manage to get a few at-bats wearing Yankee pinstripes, and Billy included him on the postseason roster as the Yankees won their first World Series since 1962. And because Klutts didn't give up despite the injuries, Billy didn't give up on him. Klutts later enjoyed the best years of his injury-plagued career as a platooning third baseman on the Billyball A's.

▶ **Mickey Klutts:** *I think he saw I was a real hard worker. I don't want to say anything about me, but I had a lot of knee surgeries. I have an artificial knee right now because of baseball. I had to fight through a lot of injuries with Billy, but I tried to pattern myself after him. I mean he was cocky, he was hard, he played the game that way. He was very, very aggressive in the way he played. Remember, this guy was small, so he was constantly down at second getting the crap beat out of him. He was a street kid and he was just tough as nails. So I saw that even though I was a very good player, in order for me to stay there and for him to like me, I had to hustle. It was every day, too.*

▶ **Jackie Moore:** *I think in his playing days, everything that Billy accomplished, he had to work extra for, so he could relate to the guy that didn't have all the God-given ability. And I think that's why he was so focused on the mental aspect of it. He'd say, "OK, you might be a little short with your ability, you can't run as fast as certain players, or hit the ball as far as a certain player, but mentally you can be better. You can eliminate these little unnecessary mistakes or things that cost you ballgames, because we can all think and learn the same things mentally."*

Billy wanted the game played correctly, and if you could do that, you could play for him and he would pump you up so that you believed you could compete against the Carews, the Nolan Ryans, and the George Bretts.

▶ **Dave Righetti:** *Mickey Klutts at third base, using him and making the best out of him. [Rick] Langford, the pitcher for Oakland. [Steve] McCatty and Keough. Those guys flourished under him. He believed in them. He believed he could make guys better. A lot of managers don't believe that. They think they can manage the team, to help the team win. Billy felt like he made players better.*

Heart in the Heat of Battle

Again, in considering Billy's notions of what made a ballplayer win, quotes from George S. Patton come to mind. Patton once wrote, "Science changes many things in war but the HEART of man remains unchanged. Greater than discipline or tactics is the HEART OF MAN AS IT WORKS IN THE HEAT OF BATTLE"[9] On another occasion, Patton announced, "The secret of victory lies not wholly in knowledge. It lurks invisible in that vitalizing spark, intangible, yet evident as lightning—the warrior soul."[10] Billy wanted to know who would have heart in the heat of battle. Billy wanted warriors.

▶ **Toby Harrah:** *He was the type of guy, if you played your butt off, if you just gave everything you had, this guy was great to play for. But if you played with any type of fear—if you were scared—then Billy would confront that, and he would make you aware of it. And one way or the other, you either became unscared and played with more desire, or he would just get rid of ya. If you were on the same page as Billy, man, baseball was fun. If you were not on the same page as Billy Martin, you might as well get your ass out of Dodge, because you're going to be miserable.*

Billy's favorite guys might not necessarily stack up the highest in the Sunday morning sports pages. They didn't necessarily hit .300 or drive in 100 runs. But they were the guys who had that "vitalizing spark," who were going to get the job done when the game was on the line.

▶ **Fred Stanley:** *I think he always tried to surround himself with people that he trusted and he knew that he could count on when it got down to grinding time. Those were the guys he could rely on. And I think he had a real good sense of when to put guys into those situations. He loved Lou Piniella. He loved Lou, and he would put Lou in any situation he could put him in, because Lou would deliver. Lou was a good player.*

One Yankee from the late 1970s who delivered for Billy was Paul Blair. Blair was neither the young superstar like Henderson nor the journeyman like Klutts. Instead, Blair was an aging star who came to the Yankees in the spring of 1977, his career on the downswing. He had been the Orioles center fielder since 1965, playing in four World Series and winning eight Gold Gloves. But after a 1974 season in which he hit .261 with 17 homers and 62 RBIs, Blair slipped to .218 with only 5 HRs and 31 RBIs in 1975, and .197 with 3 HRs and 16 RBIs in 1976.

In New York, with Lou Piniella, Roy White, Mickey Rivers, and Reggie Jackson already in the Yankee outfield, there didn't seem to be much role for Blair except as a late-inning defensive replacement. Yet together, Paul Blair and Billy Martin managed to put an interesting cap onto Blair's already great career.

▶ **Ray Negron:** *You know, even veteran guys need that boost. He gave Paul Blair a second boost. He said to Paul, "You're still the greatest center fielder that ever played the game." Defensively. Defensively. Not taking anything away from Joe DiMaggio, . . . but from the standpoint of just going to catch the baseball, you're talking about a guy who won eight Gold Gloves. He was that great. And when he went to the Yankees, he was supposed to be going downhill, but he caught new life. That's what Billy gave him, new life. Billy said all the right things to him, like in essence, he was going to be an integral part of that ballclub.*

Blair became more than an integral part of the club. Not only did he do the job for the Yankees defensively, but he also did it with the bat in the clutch. In 164 at-bats, Blair hit .262 with 4 home runs and 25 RBIs. More importantly, Blair had six game-winning hits, with three coming against right-handed pitchers. Probably no other manager in baseball would have allowed Blair to hit against those righties, but Billy Martin did.

▶ **Paul Blair:** *The thing I remember about that whole year with Billy was the fact that he had complete confidence in my ability. He put me in all kinds of situations, where all it did was enhance my feelings about myself as a player. At that time, being a part-timer, you usually don't have a manager show that kind of confidence in you to put you in all those different situations where he just let me go ahead and do my thing.*

In the postseason, Billy's faith in Blair took to the national stage. First, he started Blair in place of Reggie Jackson in the final game of the AL playoffs against the Royals. Then, in the ninth inning, instead of sending in a pinch hitter, Billy let Blair lead off against right-handed ace Dennis Leonard, a season's worth of confidence-building put to the ultimate test.

▶ **Paul Blair:** *The key spot was when he let me hit in the ninth inning against Dennis Leonard in the playoff. I replaced Reggie because [Paul] Splittorff was pitching the game, and I was 0 for 3 at the time, even though I had hit the ball good. I'm starting the ninth inning, and they're bringing in Dennis Leonard, and I just took it for granted that they're definitely going to pinch hit for me in this situation. But when I got to the top of the dugout, Billy said, "Come on! Get the bat, and let's get the rally started!" And luckily I got the base hit to start the rally.*

A few days later, Blair again found himself in a clutch situation, this time in the bottom of the 12th inning of the first game of the 1977 World Series against the Dodgers. The Yankees had been swept by the Reds in the 1976 Fall Classic, and it was imperative that they get the World Series monkey off their back with a win. With men on first and second and no outs, Blair stepped to the plate, a great bunter in an obvious bunt situation.

▶ **Paul Blair:** *1977, in the 12th inning. The thing about that, it was first and second, no out. I'm supposed to be a good bunter, that's my whole* *career. And then I get in this situation, and I miss two bunts! I foul off two pitches. Now it's 0–2, and [Rick] Rhoden is the pitcher. He throws me a fastball, I get a base hit in the hole, and we win the ballgame. But again, it's the situation where you don't want to let Billy down because he leaves you in a key situation. And fortunate for me, everything came out all right. I went from the outhouse to the penthouse!*

Billy had a different impact on another veteran, Detroit slugger Willie Horton. Horton's confidence hadn't slipped like Paul Blair's had, but as a man who had accumulated all sorts of credentials in the game throughout the 1960s, including a World Series championship, Horton had lost a little bit of the determination that had gotten him to the top. He credits the arrival of Billy in Detroit in 1971 with restoring the fire that enabled him to play through 1980, cracking 29 homers and 106 RBIs as late as 1979.

▶ **Willie Horton:** *I tell ya, he'd give you incentive. Billy's the type of guy that'd say some things you might not like to hear, but if you sit down and think about what he'd say, you knew he was right. At that time, guys didn't understand it, but they look back in life, they appreciate it. That's all I ever said when I left. I respect every manager I ever played for, but Billy had a little extra ingredient for me. He came along when I could have gone home, and he gave me some incentive that I could still play this game. When I retired, I was enjoying the game the same as when I was 18. I had some years after Billy that I think he prepared me to have. A lot of people say, "Ah, he didn't do that." I say, "I think so." Because it goes back to how you can go out there and go through the motions, but I played and I enjoyed it. He taught me how to enjoy the game.*

In any given game situation, Billy played the guy he felt was going to get him the win, regardless of this or that statistic against this or that guy. If somebody was hot, he might use him as a pinch hitter, regardless of whom "the book" said he should play.

▶ **Tom Grieve:** *When a relief pitcher would come in, he'd ask the guys themselves, "How do you feel about hitting against this guy?" He didn't* *really care what you'd done in the past. He kind of looked at your eyes. If you said, "Yeah, I can hit this guy," he'd say, "Fine, go up there and get a hit off of him." It's almost like he said, "Hey, he feels like he can do it right now. I'm going to send him up there and give him a chance to do it."*

And he didn't care if the second-guessers in the stands or with the pens didn't understand his motives. For instance, late in the 1985 season, Billy's shortstop, Bobby Meacham, injured his wrist badly. Billy didn't care: He wanted Bobby in the lineup.

▶ **Bobby Meacham:** *Billy really wanted me to play, and so that's why I wanted to play. My average started going down so low that it got really bad. And that was tough, but it was one of those things where Billy really wanted me to play. During the time when he knew I was in a lot of pain, he came up to me and said, "I know you're hurting, but we need you out there." He said, "I don't care if you bunt every time up, we need you out there." How could you not play? Even though you know your batting average is going down and all of your buddies are saying, "You're crazy. They're not going to pay you the following year. You're gonna get screwed in the end." I loved the guy. I loved playing for him. Anything to do with baseball, I'd of done for him. I played the rest of the season. And the day after the season was over, I had surgery.*

That type of toughness and desire was what Billy admired. He didn't care about batting averages. He cared about winning—the ultimate bottom line. While some fans perhaps wondered how Billy could stick with a shortstop whose batting average was plunging, Billy knew what he needed to keep his team going in the right direction, and in the 1985 pennant race, he needed Bobby Meacham on the field.

Substance over Style

If a player was effective with a particular manner of hitting or fielding, that was all Billy cared about. Billy would rather have an unorthodox but effective player than an orthodox mess. That, in and of itself, was a confidence booster for many players.

▶ **Bobby Meacham:** *When I got to Yankee camp my first spring, it was kind of funny. I look like a Latin player, so the first few days, most of the coaches thought I was from Puerto Rico or something. And I used to field with one hand, and throw sidearm or three-quarters like a lot of Latin players do. I'd take infield, and I could tell the coaches were thinking, "Wow, he's pretty good." But once they found out I was American, they decided to teach me to field with two hands and to throw the ball over the top. Finally, I remember Billy about the fourth day coming up and saying, "Hey kid, I've talked to every coach and nobody's to mess with you. If you need to know something, you're going to talk with me, and I'm going to teach you everything I know. Anybody else messes with you, you tell me, and I'll make sure they don't bother you." And I was like "Great!" I did do a lot of unorthodox things, and so it was good to know, at least for me, that there was a baseball man that saw that I knew how to play, and I was doing fine the way I was doing it and didn't need to be changed.*

▶ **Mickey Morabito:** *He really wasn't a big mechanical guy in a lot of areas, and I think he just figured guys got to where they were by having some natural ability and playing the way they do. A lot of time it was just let them play the way they play, the way they're comfortable, and then through confidence, they'll get better as they get more confidence in their abilities. As much as he was intense about managing the game and controlling it, as far as development of players, he just thought guys would develop by doing what they did and just by getting better.*

To Billy, the only way the game had to be played was with an eye on winning. That meant that certain things had to be done. Cut-off men had to be hit, double plays had to be turned, and so on. If you had a way to get those tasks done effectively, you could do it however you wanted. He wasn't going to make you do it one specific way just because that's how all the old baseball men have been saying to do it since 1900. Billy just wanted results, something all true leaders want to achieve.

▶ **Jackie Moore:** *He wanted results, and how you got there, that was your style. If you were doing something wrong and didn't get results out of it,* *well then either you were going to change it or not going to play. But if you could do something, and do it consistently, and get good results out of it, "Well then, OK, hey, that doesn't make any difference to me." It's not how good you look doing it or how bad you look doing it, it's just the bottom line is let's get results with it.*

▶ **Bobby Meacham:** *Billy told me many times, "You do it the way I want you to do it. You listen to me and I'll teach you all I know." He said, "I'll teach you how to play the game." What he meant by that was that you don't have to go out and read a book or listen to steps one through three that these coaches are teaching you. You just go out and play, and I'll let you know if you're doing it the right way or not. He could really see a player, and one of his strengths was being able to see what kind of player he had just by watching that guy go about his business for a few days. Then he knew what he was working with.*

Developing the Talents of Individuals

Getting a young person over the top is not always easy whether in baseball, accounting, or dry cleaning. Regardless of talent, it can take time for a young person to mature, to let go of fears and tensions, and to let ability flow. It can take time to learn to focus. Billy analyzed the developmental needs of his players and came up with different solutions for different problems. What he basically did was build confidence and self-esteem differently with each player.

Martin had a way of making the player really want to do the job for him and for the team. Billy made his points very clearly, and he was tough, but he cared for his players, and he wanted to see them become real competitors. If you played aggressively, you didn't have to worry if you made a mistake. But while he was concerned about building his players' confidence and self-esteem, if they played the game wrong, he would really rip into them. Yet in coming down hard on his players, he was teaching them lessons about playing the game.

▶ **Toby Harrah:** *There would be ballgames where you went out there and you didn't play up to your capabilities, whether you even won or lost,* *and he would just come in there and embarrass you. I've seen him go into locker rooms. I've seen him go into showers. In his uniform in the shower! And scream! Scream at players in the shower who are already undressed. Him in his full uniform screaming at them, and really confronting their manhood.*

Most of Billy's players vividly recall occasions in which Billy exploded in anger at them, but in each case, they learned something about the game and themselves. In the following two anecdotes, Bobby Meacham and Mickey Klutts each recall Billy jumping on them for allowing another player to dictate their response to a situation.

▶ **Bobby Meacham:** *He chewed me out one time ever, and that was when on a double play ball, the runner didn't slide, he tried to veer off to the side. And I always throw sidearm on a double play ball, and I thought I was gonna hit the runner, so I threw over the top, and I threw it away. We were winning by a lot of runs, and it didn't matter, but when I got to the dugout, he met me there, and he said, "What are you doing?" I said, "Well, I don't know, I just threw that one away." And he just said, "You tried to throw around him, didn't you?" And I said, "Yeah." And he just went off. He just went crazy! I can't even repeat what he said, and he said, "Don't you ever do that again! You throw it right through him! Don't you change because he's not playing the game right! You play the game right! Don't ever do that again!"*

▶ **Mickey Klutts:** *He didn't say things to make you look stupid, unless you really did a stupid thing. But there was a firmness about his discipline. In his line of disciplining, he was constantly tearing you down, but his breath would not stop until he would start building you back up. "You're too f—ing good for this! You're too f—ing good to be playing like this!" In other words, there was a criticism, but a positive—something in the end of that sentence that leaves you thinking, "You're a good ballplayer, man. Why are you playing like this? You're better than that! You're better than that!" He yelled at me so bad one night, I'll never forget this game. Mike Norris has got a 4–3 lead in the ninth, they got a guy on first. I get a routine two-hopper at third and I throw it into right* *field. Of course, I had Davey Lopes at second who's pretty short, and I had to take the error, but that's still debatable. Anyway, I hear this voice from the dugout, and it was Billy yelling at Clete [Boyer], because Clete was our infield coach. And he's saying, "Clete, the f—ing gamblers have gotten to him! The f—ing gamblers have gotten to him!" And now he's yelling at me, "Have the f—ing gamblers gotten to you?" He was just screaming at me. What was bad was we went 16 innings because of me. That night on the plane I'm sitting there with my headphones on, kind of half sleeping, and somebody sits down next to me. It was Billy. I didn't know what to say, because I kind of threw the ball short-armed. He said, "You know what?" He said, "I want you to take the ball the next time and throw it through that little f—er's chest." He knew it wasn't all my fault, he was just mad at me. I said, "Well, I screwed it up, and I'll make it up to you." He'd had a couple of cold ones, and he was in pretty good shape, but he made it a point to come back and talk. He always would make it a point.*

In each case, Billy was mad because the player held something back. It wasn't the error so much as the holding back that set him off. He wanted his players to let it rip all the time.

Billy freely gave criticism, but he could take it as well. As much as Billy demanded the respect that his leadership role required, he didn't mind a competitor jumping on him in the heat of the moment. In fact, depending on his analysis of what made that player tick, he might actually instigate confrontation. Or, if on a rare occasion a player stood up to him and disagreed with him, he might actually admire that player for standing up to Billy Martin. After all, in most cases, that would be the kind of guy he'd want on the field playing for him. That's what he would have done. And taking criticism from a player was in essence another way to build that player up.

▶ **Mike Pagliarulo:** *One of the things that I really liked about Billy was he told you what he thought—if he liked you. And it wouldn't be in a nice way at all. But probably the best situation that I can think of was a real close ballgame in Anaheim. They bunted the ball, and it was a one hop to me. I threw the ball to second base and the guy was safe. My throw* *really pulled the guy off the base. The run ended up scoring, and when the inning ended, Billy was at the top step screaming his lungs out, and he was all over me. What I did was, I yelled back at him. I said, "Billy, that was the right play!" He goes, "That wasn't the right play! It wasn't the right play at all! You gotta go to first base!" I said, "No, it was the right play! It was a bad throw, but it was the right play!" And he was screaming at me, and I was screaming at him. He says, "Just go sit on the end of the bench." So I went down there, and later on he came up to me, after the game, and said, "Maybe that was the right play." And I remember feeling that he liked when you yelled back at him. He liked putting guys out on the field that would stand up for themselves. Billy was harmless really, but he had this loud roar about him. He had a big bark. And the guys that would kind of cower and be real quiet, I don't think he liked those guys.*

▶ **Mike Heath:** *He would get on me quite a bit. He got on a lot of his catchers. But you know what? I kind of let it roll off my back to a certain degree, and he and I would argue a little bit. If it was something he told me in the past, I would bring it up to him again in our conversation. And I think that really helped out a lot, and I remember he talked to me when he was leaving Oakland. He said I was a little stubborn, but that was a good quality in me because I stand up for what I believe, and he really liked that about me.*

Billy wanted intensity from his players all the time—every play, every pitch.

▶ **Dave Righetti:** *I wanted to win so damn bad, 'cause I couldn't get a cheap win. And the one time I did, he mf's me . . . I could hear him from the dugout. He disrespected a lot of guys, and there's a few guys he never did, and I was one of the guys. But he did this time, and I heard him. I hung a curveball on 0–2 to Larry Parrish, and I don't know where in the hell he hit it, in the monuments probably. It was a horrible pitch. It was something that I was hoping he'd go after, but I left it in the zone, and he hit it out. And Billy screams, "Mother f—ing pitcher my ass!" And this is right after I threw the no-hitter! He was mad at me for doing* *that, but that was my only game of the year where I did relax and didn't bear down like I should have. So in a way it helped.*

The fact that Billy wouldn't let you get away with letting up was part of how he motivated and taught what the game was all about. You learned that you had to be on all the time—even if you threw a no-hitter, and even if the team was well ahead in the game.

▶ **Jackie Brown:** *Billy was loud, and I don't mean that in a bad way. When he said something, it kind of rang. There was something about him. But if you couldn't handle being screamed at or being hollered at, it could really be tough to play for the man. I know that because I always felt that when he hollered at me, he was hollering for me. In other words, he knew I could have done better, and I didn't . . . He challenged you to do the best you can do.*

▶ **Mickey Klutts:** *I watched how Billy criticized, or how he was pretty hard on the young guys like me. But in the same sentence when he's telling me what I did wrong, at the turn of that sentence, he's pumping you back up so you never have a chance to get down or get where you sulk or pout. He always made it a point to tell you what you did wrong, and tell you, "You are better than that. You're a much better player than what you're showing." And so in that kind of a sentence, you're thinking, "Maybe I am better. Maybe I'm not getting to that next level."*

While Billy could be tough on his players, he didn't hold grudges, which was critical. For Billy, when it was over, it was over. He was going to call you on your mistake and make you realize in no uncertain terms that you had let him down. But then it was over. Billy didn't beat somebody up endlessly for a mistake. He made his point—maybe even pretty loudly—but then he moved on.

▶ **Tom Grieve:** *You know, he was tough. He would yell, and he would scream, and he would fight. But the good thing about it was, when the game was over, he forgot about it. He didn't carry grudges. In a lot of situations, someone gets that mad at you, it carries over, and then you're* *not talking, and then he wants to get rid of you. In Billy's case, if you were a guy that could help the team, and he screamed and yelled at something you did, he had a way of making you feel good. He might buy you a beer at the bar that night, and the next day, come up and pat you on the back and smile. You say, "Jeez, he must not even remember last night." There were no grudges held. He had a fiery determination, and the way he yelled and the way he ranted and raved—it wasn't even a lot—but when he did it, it was effective, and no one held it against him, because they knew he wasn't going to hold a grudge.*

▶**Jackie Moore:** *You hear stories about how tough Billy was, but there was such a loyalty there, whether you were a coach of his or a player of his. He might chew your butt out one day, and it might be a situation where you screw up, where you're a coach or you're a player. He's not going to turn his head or let you get away without a discussion or telling you how you should do this. But once that was over with, it was forgotten. It wasn't like you come back the next day and start over the same conversation or hold grudges. You screwed up yesterday, you cost us the ballgame, or you made a wrong decision or whatever. Once he finished with it, that was it, you were on the same page again.*

Being a Teacher

Billy believed that "The whole thing to managing is building up the ego, making a player feel he can do it. Showing him how to do it. Get him over the humps. And once you get him over the humps on the baseball field, that player will make it in any walk of life, because he'll have learned to be a competitor. But you have to have patience, especially with a young kid. I have patience, and when I get angry, I get angry, but I always try not to allow my anger to affect my thinking."[11]

It is important to note Billy's use of the word "feel." Confidence is all about feeling that you can succeed, feeling that you can take a risk, feeling that you are in command. With that feeling, energy flows instead of being choked by fear. Even a veteran like Paul Blair, who had succeeded in the game for years, could benefit from feeling better about himself.

▶ **Paul Blair:** *The thing that I remember about Billy was that he had total, total confidence that I could do anything in any situation that he put me in. He made me feel that way, and he just had all the confidence in the world in me. He put me in left, center, right, third, second, short. Wherever he needed somebody to go in for any short period of time—if he had to pinch hit for somebody or whatever—he put me in.*

Fear comes from uncertainty, but Billy broke uncertainty down by taking it away and thus built confidence up.

▶ **Bobby Meacham:** *The main thing with Billy was that he wanted us to feel confident and to play aggressively. I mean, my gosh, you couldn't be any more aggressive than him. So you knew. He didn't even have to say it. So you knew that's what he wanted and once you did that, man, he was happy with ya.*

▶ **Jackie Brown:** *Again, confidence is best for pitching. I don't know how many times I have stood on the mound. I was never afraid of a hitter in my life, but I had doubts whether I could get a hitter out consistently. Any time I started in my windup, and I said, "Ohhh"—have doubt in myself—the hitter would hit me. And if I stood out there and knew I could get this guy out, I had success. Confidence is a big important factor. And that's one thing that Billy Martin seemed to give me, in the way that he handled me. Billy's swagger is part of it, that goes along with all of it. The way he goes about approaching you. The confidence that he has in his voice, telling you who you are, and what you are, and what you can do. That all goes together.*

▶ **Bobby Meacham:** *Billy made me feel at ease when I was playing. I knew he wanted me out there. I went out there thinking, "This is how Billy wants me to play, and he's happy with the way I'm playing, and he's glad I'm out there." And so it was easy to play for Billy. For me, every time I think about helping players, I think about putting myself in their place. I think that's what Billy did. And I tell them, "OK, the most important thing I ever learned was when you step on that field, you need to know what your manager wants you to do in certain situations." I tell them, you* *need to have some kind of a way to communicate with your manager without having to talk to him a lot. I got that from Billy. Simplify it all. It's not brain surgery. It's baseball. I tell my players, "Think about what you're doing out there. If it makes sense, go ahead and do it, and then we'll talk about it later. If it doesn't jive with what's going on, then we'll straighten it out. But if it makes sense, do it."*

In other words, don't play in fear of your manager—just play. The reason Billy loved Meacham or Ron Hassey, who also blossomed under Billy, was not lost on other players.

▶ **Mike Pagliarulo:** *I can tell you what those players had in common. Those players weren't afraid. Bobby Meacham came up at a hard time, but he ran every ball out, he played hard. He tried hard, he switch hit. He wasn't afraid. Meach, you could throw him out there. Bobby Meacham and Ron Hassey, those guys, they had been through a lot of stuff, and they weren't afraid. They weren't afraid no matter who we played or who we faced. And I think that good managers can sense when other guys get intimidated. And those guys didn't get intimidated.*

▶ **Marty Appel:** *He was a good manager because of his intensity and his knowledge and his fearless approach to not being afraid to try anything. And that made the ballplayers take the field in a fearless manner and not play with any reserve or hesitation. I think that's what he brought most to the job.*

Billy believed that the competitors that he selected for his teams would respond to his tactics, learn to play the game his way, dig a little deeper for strength, and become professionals. Consider Toby Harrah. Toby was a tough player, the kind whom Billy Martin had no problem managing. That doesn't mean that Toby couldn't get even tougher under Billy's tutelage. With Toby, Billy took an approach to toughening him that he never explained, but which in retrospect is obvious to Harrah today.

▶ **Toby Harrah:** *I played for two years for Billy, and I don't think I missed a ballgame. I remember one time Billy said to me, "Toby, tell me a* *pitcher that gives you a problem, and I'll rest you that day." And I said, "Sure. Luis Tiant. I can't hit Luis Tiant with a paddle, Billy." So sure enough, I think we faced Tiant three or four times that year. I played every damned ballgame! I said, "Billy, I thought you said you were going to rest me." He said, "Well, I was going to rest your bat. I know you have trouble with him. But I need you out there, because I need you to take charge, I need you to be one of my leaders out there on the field." Now that I look back on it, I know what he was doing. He was strictly doing that to say, "Hey, it doesn't make a damn bit of difference if you have trouble against this guy or not, you still gotta toe the line." And you know what, I started hitting Tiant better after that. He wasn't going to let me slide, he was not going to let me slide. And I should have known!*

Yet as previously stated, Billy had to use different tactics for different personalities, much like his mentor Stengel had done in the 1950s with the Yankees. Martin's approach with Rod Carew had nothing to do with the loud Billy Martin so well known to baseball fans. In a 1983 *Sports Illustrated* feature,[12] both Billy and Carew recalled the days of 1967, which would eventually see Carew emerge as Rookie of the Year. Martin, then the Twins' third base coach, recalled an incident where Carew actually walked off the field in the middle of the game.

According to Billy, "I followed him into the clubhouse and found him there crying. He told me about his mom and dad [who were separating at the time]. I had come from a broken home myself, so we talked." Rather than tell him that his personal problems had nothing to do with the game on the field, Martin talked with him, knowing that Carew's peace of mind was as vital to his batting stroke as his wrists and forearms.

▶ **Rod Carew:** *I had heard so much about how hot-headed Billy was—he was tough to get along with, things like that, and I never saw that. I never saw that person. I saw a person that took a young kid, worked with him, and talked with him every day. He was always talking to me about what I wanted to do, where I was headed. Just things that I think your dad would talk to you about. And we became very, very good friends, very close friends. If I had any problems, anything at all, I could always go and talk to him. He would give me advice. I guess Billy saw* *something in me that he liked. I liked to play the game, but I was a quiet kid. He used to push me to be more aggressive on the field, talking more. He just saw something in me that he liked that he felt that he was going to draw out. He had tremendous patience with me, because he knew that there were a lot of things that I had to learn, and I was still young, and I was still raw.*

With Carew, Billy showed compassion, and he worked to bring the player's emotions under control. Even though Billy wanted players to take their jobs seriously, with Carew, Billy knew a little kidding and relaxation would help him to play better, so he focused on that.

The relationship that developed between Billy and Carew deepened over the years, as Carew became the dominant hitter of the era, and Billy went on to great fame as manager of his beloved Yankees, a testimony to just how important Billy's leadership with Carew was. In July 1978, moments before Billy would be reintroduced as Yankee manager in a stunning Old-Timers' Day announcement, he was hiding in a Yankee Stadium boiler room. Of all the people in the park that day who were special to Billy, it was Rod Carew whom he asked Ray Negron to bring in to see him.

▶ **Rod Carew:** *I was happy for him. I knew the emotions that were going through him that day, and I wanted to go hug him. He became a very special part of my career, what I had done in baseball. He became like a dad to me, and I was happy for him. It was great to see him back, and I wanted to wish him the best. He grabbed onto me and hugged me, and I said, "You're the greatest. Everything that I have been able to achieve playing the game is because of you and how you took me under your wing and counseled me as if I was your son." I was just happy to see him come back. The man knew the game, and it's hard to keep people like that away from the game.*

Carew also made a wonderful gesture of thanks to Billy by having him act as the godfather to his daughter Stephanie. Billy had been there for Carew as a young player and as a young man, and Carew never forgot what Billy had done for him.

▶ **Rod Carew:** *I couldn't have thought of anyone else that I wanted to be the godfather to my daughter, because we had become such good friends. I had learned so much from him. Underneath, I had seen that he could be a very easygoing person, contrary to what everyone else thought. He was like a father to me. He taught me everything that I knew on playing the game. If I needed advice on anything, I could go to him. I felt comfortable going to him, I didn't have to worry about anyone else knowing about what we had spoken about. And he became a father figure to me; he became somebody that I admired as a person. And there wasn't a second thought about asking him to be a godfather to my second daughter.*

▶ **Sam Mele:** *You don't treat 'em all alike. You can't. If this guy needs a little discipline, be a little stern with him. If this guy, like Carew who was an introvert, didn't laugh much, didn't joke around much, get in his mind that, "Hey, let's laugh it up a little bit." Tell him a joke, put him at ease. He had a knack at doing that, and getting pissed at a guy, too, which made the guy get mad to show Billy he can do it. Reverse psychology.*

So whether with Carew, Harrah, Brown, Horton, Meacham, Righetti, Blair, or Klutts, Martin really was not the mean, loud, obnoxious Billy Martin so well advertised to baseball fans. He could be loud, he could be mean, but he could also be quiet and understanding. There was a method to his madness, and he knew what he was doing with his players and where he was going with each of them. He wanted to see them succeed to generate victories, and also to become competitive as ballplayers and people.

Because Billy could communicate, he worked on the head and the heart as much as the bat and the glove. Charlie Manuel, now the manager of the Cleveland Indians, was a rookie on Billy's 1969 Minnesota Twins team, and he remembers how he and his former teammate and now first base coach, Ted Uhlaender, learned from Billy to communicate with each player daily in some shape or form.

▶ **Charlie Manuel:** *We learned a lot from Billy, and we were Billy's type, and we thought a lot like Billy. I believe in communicating with my players. I* *got guys on our team, now that I've become a manager, like Einar Diaz or Alex Ramirez or Manny Ramirez. These are guys I can play with, basically like Billy used to play with us. I can hit them, and they'll laugh and they'll hit me back. But I feel like that's how I communicate with them. That's who they are. And then there's guys that I got to be more diplomatic with, and understanding with, and carry on a more intelligent conversation, and forget about the kidding and joking. One of the best things I do is when I go to the ballpark every day, everybody that walks through the door, I meet 'em, and I talk to 'em in some way. I have eye-to-eye contact with them, and I have some kind of conversation with them, whether it be real serious or just loose and laughing. To me, those are a lot of things that I learned from Billy when he first started managing.*

▶ **Toby Harrah:** *Billy did treat you with respect. He did treat you like a man. And those are things that you like. You weren't just a player to Billy. You were an individual. And you had to like that. I played for a lot of managers, who pretty much about five minutes before the game would come out of their office, say "hi" to a few guys on their way down to the dugout, and go to the end of the bench, and sit on the end of the bench. And then when the game was over, they go back to their office and talk to the sportswriters.*

▶ **Mike Pagliarulo:** *Some guys are more outspoken and some guys more quiet. Some guys can take a little ribbing, and some guys can't. Billy's style was to give a good ribbing every once in a while, and tease you and make fun of you—old school stuff. It just so happens that I liked that stuff. I remember . . . there was a period of time when I wasn't doing so good. There were times when he was able to get on me, and there were times when he said that I needed to relax a little more. One time he said, "C'mon, we'll go out tonight," because he liked to hang out with the boys sometimes. He goes, "We'll go out tonight and relax after the game." And that was great for me. I relaxed, went out and had a few beers with him, and talked baseball and stuff like that. And that was very good. You get your mind off stuff, and you get out there and relax instead of going back to your hotel room. And me, I was the type of guy that would think about it all night with my bat in my room. And he's like,*

"Look, let's take a break tonight." In that way, that was support. And in other times, when I was going good, he made sure I didn't get too high by knocking me down a little bit. "Hey, lookit, you only got two hits, don't get too crazy." So motivating—certain guys don't have to be motivated—you have to just push their buttons every once in a while. And they have to be the right ones.

Billy talked to some players a lot, while to others he did not. Some he riled up, some he calmed down. As Pags says, Billy pushed the right buttons. As a leader, you have to get the job done with the personnel at your disposal. You need to motivate each individual within your organization to get the most out of his or her potential by making each one believe in him or herself and perform at his or her best.

The Case of Mickey Rivers

Billy did just that with Mickey Rivers, a player equally renowned for his great abilities and his tendency to become distracted. A center fielder during his years with the Yankees, "Mick the Quick" encountered family and financial problems that distracted him on the field. Rivers was a lovable man, and lethal on the diamond, and Billy was very patient with him. Throughout 1976, a season in which Rivers hit .312 with 95 runs scored and 67 driven in, the two got to know one another, and they had their fights. But the foundation was being laid for a lifetime relationship.

▶ **Mickey Rivers:** *The reason we got together, why he loved me and take care of me, because understand, we had time to argue. We'd argue and fight that whole first year, because I guess we're too alike. So as the time build up, he got to just say, "All right, now, Quick, come in here. We going to have a talk in the room down here. Anything goes wrong, I got your back, I know what to do. Any time you need something, here's my numbers. Call me." And every day, we got a better understanding. That's what I appreciate. Most of the managers didn't have the time to talk to the guys individually, little things. And he was behind me 100 percent on anything I did. If I had to go somewhere, he'd say, "Let me know in*

plenty of time." Sometimes I'd call, "Skip, I'll be a little late." He didn't
mind nothing like that, 'cause he know.

As 1976 turned into 1977, Rivers continued to mix periods of dis-
traction with periods of explosive baseball. Billy disciplined Rivers to an
extent, but he also continued to protect and to help Mickey, not only
because he cared for him but also because he needed him to perform
if the Yankees were going to win. Unfortunately, Rivers was going
through a divorce, and it was a difficult time for the speedster. In one
well-reported incident, Rivers's wife waited for him in the Yankee Stadium parking lot in her Mercedes. When Rivers pulled into the lot in
his Cadillac, she began playing bumper cars at his expense. Billy did his
best to help take the stress off Mickey's shoulders so he could play ball.

▶ **Mickey Rivers:** *I was going through a divorce. I was going through all*
that. It was giving me a headache. A lot of guys, that's an aggravation,
you can't play with all that. He told me, "Don't worry about all that. I'll
take care of all that." I didn't have to take care of all that. When she came
in there, tore up the cars in the parking lot, that's in the paper, and he
took care of all that. She come in there, . . . we had a big old thing in the
parking lot. Boom, boom, boom, boom. He squashed all that, and I just
had to play ball. He said, "All I want you to do is play ball. I'll handle all
this. Don't worry about it. I handle all of this, you just play ball."

Very few bosses, in baseball or in any other line of work, would go
to such lengths to help a subordinate, no matter how talented and
important to the team. Billy would go that extra mile, and Rivers
responded. Beginning in August 1977, Quick spearheaded the Yankee
turnaround that ended with a championship. He hit .405 for the
month, with 5 homers and 21 RBIs, and the team launched a streak of
40 wins in 50 games.

▶ **Mickey Rivers:** *I just took off! I know where it had to come from. He*
gave me everything I needed. If I needed something, what I do? I say,
"Skip, I need so and so . . ." He'd say, "OK, what I want you to do, just
go out there and play ball. I don't want you worry about nothin'!" And

that's why I did well for Billy. We had arguments, like everybody, when you don't think things are right. But then after when I got a chance to see how he was helping me, then that's my strong point. He had the confidence in me. He knew I had something in me, and this was my blessing. And that was my strong point, because I know what he did for me.

Other people in that 1977 clubhouse saw how Billy worked with Mickey and with the other players. In that 1977 locker room, it was Billy's job to keep all of his players moving forward on the field, even as there were continual distractions off the field.

▶ **Paul Blair:** *Well, what I think I took from Billy is you have to understand your players. You try to understand each and every one and their needs. You gotta treat 'em all differently. Billy knew who he could push the buttons on, who he couldn't push the buttons on. Who he could trust, who he couldn't trust. Who he could rely on, who he can't. This is what I'm trying to do with my guys at Coppin State.*

▶ **Ray Negron:** *If it was just to manage a baseball game every day, that would be one thing, but there was always something going on. Because that was a wild bunch. Wild bunch! Certain players, when something was going on, players loved it. When there was a fight going on, players loved it. That's how it always was, and there was always one fight or another. The Yankees were nasty. They could be a very nasty bunch of guys, and Billy knew that. They were hardcore. The fading of the 1970s represented the end of the old baseball. They were the end of an era.*

The Importance of Being Confident

The aura around Billy bolstered the confidence and self-esteem of his players, even as he worked on their own self-images. Billy's confidence and his skills lent credibility to his message of belief. At the same time, it was infectious.

▶ **Tom Grieve:** *When you went onto the field, when you traveled to another ballpark, when someone came to your ballpark, you had a good* *feeling knowing your manager was Billy Martin. When you took the field, you had a different feeling inside, like we're a different team with Billy Martin. It's like going to war with a general that you know is going to lead you in the right direction. You're just more confident about the war ahead of you. If you go to war with some guy that's not a strong personality, that you don't have confidence in, you just don't approach the job the same way. To me, that was what made Billy Martin.*

▶ **Mike Heath:** *He taught me really to be confident in myself—like he was. He was really confident in his self and what he believed in, and I think that rubbed off on me quite a bit.*

▶ **Mike Norris:** *You can feed off a person. In other words, if it's your teacher or your boss, you can feed off him when he's having a bad day or when he's having a good day. And that's what we did off of him. Billy would always be so strong and so demanding.*

▶ **Bobby Meacham:** *I looked at Billy and I said, "Man, this guy played for the New York Yankees. He's got World Series championships as a player. He played with one of the greatest, Mickey Mantle. He obviously knows what he's doing. Man, he looks like he's confident." And all of a sudden, that's the type of guy you really hone in on and just kinda feed off. It's one of those things where you know the guy did everything really well and was successful in everything he did. You can't help but respect that and want to feed off that. But most of all, it's the confidence factor. The confidence he had—I mean it's stupid, but he'd try to fight Frank Howard. The whole aura of his being able to be confident in every situation because he knew he was good, that's what I try to help my players with when I'm coaching now. Become good, and then you're as confident as anybody else, and therefore you're probably better than anybody else. That's what Billy left me with.*

▶ **Lenny Randle:** *I can name some lives that he's changed from the swagger, from pitchers to infielders or whatever. Or some people that went into their shell as well who couldn't handle it. Toby [Harrah] could handle it. It changed Toby Harrah's whole life. He took him from thinking* singles to thinking like a champion: *"I can win World Series, I can win shortstop Gold Gloves, I can hit 20 to 30 home runs. I can knock a guy down on a double play. You try to knock me down on a double play, it's like dealing with a Green Beret. It's gonna be an invasion on your life. You don't want to knock me down at shortstop."*

▶ **Toby Harrah:** *He pushes you in a way that maybe a best friend would push you, as far as competing goes. He could just get you going. Billy made me believe I was the best shortstop in baseball. And half of really succeeding is believing in oneself. And Billy was that way. Billy made it personal. He made every ballgame almost a personal quest. It was never just a game. It was an extension of one's life and the way one thought about themselves as far as competing goes. And that's what it's all about—it's competing. He just made the game fun, because he made you believe that if you played properly, and you executed the fundamentals, and you played up to your ability—and no more—you could beat anybody. Any team on any day!*

The players wanted to do well not just for themselves, not just for the team, but *for Billy*. When a leader has a strong personality and really stands for something, a responsibility to live up to that leader's ideals gets passed down.

▶ **Mickey Klutts:** *Even when he would go out for the lineup card, people would cheer and boo, you know what I mean? And you as a player, you say, "OK, this is my leader here of this team!" You've got to try to live up to it. He's not going to stand with his neck out. He's representing something; you better follow along. You're gonna represent what he's representing, which is toughness, being aggressive, and never knowing what we're going to do. That's what Billyball was all about.*

▶ **Buck Showalter:** *It's one thing to want to do a lot of aggressive things on the field. It's another thing to get your players to execute 'em. With all great leaders, it seems like they present this feeling onto their teams, that the team doesn't want to let this guy down. With Billy, "Jeez, Billy's going to put the squeeze play on," or "Billy's gonna hit and run with me," or "He's gonna go double steal here." [They feel like], "Man, he's* *got this great confidence in me that I can do this, and I've got to execute it." So it's one thing to want to do all those things, another thing to have the people to execute 'em, and be able to present and capture the atmosphere that allows you to do 'em in.*

▶ **Toby Harrah:** *I know as a player, I was more afraid of letting Billy Martin down, my manager, then I was [afraid of] the other ballclub. He was that type. Because after the game, you have to go in the locker room and have to deal with Billy and look him eye to eye. And Billy would know whether you gave it your all or not. He was the type of manager that you loved to play for because he did take it personal. He was awesome. It was kind of like pleasing your father. To me, he wasn't my dad, but I wanted to make him proud of me. That's what I always wanted Billy to do, to be proud of me as a player, and to like the way I played the game. And I felt like I accomplished that . . . I really respected him on the field. I've seen other managers that were really good managers on the field too, but for me, our relationship went farther than on the field. I liked the way he treated me. I just felt like Billy Martin really cared about me.*

Getting Beat with Your Best

With the swagger of confidence comes the ability to go right into the teeth of the opponent, whatever or whoever that opponent is. Here's my best shot—let's see what happens, and to hell with it. When a player could digest this aspect of Billy's personality, they could "let go" and play the game with flow.

Lenny Randle had been up and down with the Rangers for several seasons, hadn't hit a lick, and was considering giving professional football a shot when Billy took over the team. Though Randle had never met Billy until late 1973, he had learned of Billy while playing for the Rangers' AAA team in Denver, where Art Fowler was the pitching coach. Fowler's tales of Billy had a profound impact on Randle at the time.

▶ **Lenny Randle:** *Art would talk about him. He would say, "Now look, Billy likes speed, and he likes guys who got guts, guys that can play hard. If* *you're gonna be la-dee-da-dee like, there's no way." He started naming a couple of guys. He said, "I can tell you right now, he might be able to pick it, he might be a big bonus baby, but Billy ain't gonna like him. And I can tell you right now." And I went, "Oh, wow!" And he was just totally giving stories about Billy, how he played, what he did, and how he did it. How one time he bunted three times in a game, and knocked the guy down on a double play, got hit by the ball, and won the game. Whatever it took. I was thinking, "This guy is like a samurai." We had heard stories about him and Stengel, and those stories are just passed on. Then when we saw him, he had this aura.*

Rather than shrink from the aura, Randle responded to it. He forgot about football and established himself as a big leaguer.

▶ **Lenny Randle:** *In spring training 1974, man at third, two outs, he calls me in to pinch hit. And I went, "OK? Well, let's see, what am I going to do in this situation?" I bunted! He went nuts! He came running out on the field, hugging me. "This is it! You know how many guys would do that? Not too many guys! That's what I'm talking about, that's the kind of ball we're going to play!" I said, "OK, OK, coach. Cool. I'll do it all the time." I was just shaken that he was so shaken. That was a big deal.*

Billy Martin's philosophy was that if you had a strong weapon, you used it. Randle could bunt, and he had speed, and in that pressure situation, he acted, exploiting those strengths. He challenged the opposition with his best stuff. That's the type of confidence Billy wanted to see. And when he saw it, he got excited about it and made Randle understand that he had done the right thing. From then on, the two had that energy together.

It sounds so easy, but putting your best out there in a really aggressive fashion can be tough. It's like the singer who won't go on stage, the poet who keeps her poems locked in her room, the entrepreneur still working for that giant corporation rather than striking out on her own. Fear holds back the greatness that many people have to offer. Just ask pitcher Jackie Brown.

The Case of Jackie Brown

Jackie Brown had been a lifetime minor league pitcher, but in 1974, Billy Martin put the 30-year-old Brown into his starting rotation in Texas, because he recognized that Brown had one big league product—a curveball. And he expected him to use it.

▶ **Jackie Brown:** *I would go out and throw 135–140 pitches, and 120 of them was curveballs. He didn't expect me to be perfect with it. He knew that throwing as many of them as I did, I was going to throw some down the middle of the plate and some up. I never one time remember him getting on me about getting beat on a curveball. But now, if I got beat on a fastball, he would have something to say, and he would scream at me. They always kidded me that if you throw 150 pitches, at least 120 of them were curves. He believed in my curveball that much. I mean, here's the manager of the ballclub telling me, "Your curveball is that good, you can tell 'em what's coming and they can't hit it." Billy Martin made that statement to me. He said, "Jackie, you can tell 'em it's coming. They can't hit it."*

Throw your curve. Sing your song. Recite your poem. Start your company. Put your best out there for the world to see. It's very hard for many of us to do, just like it was for Jackie Brown. Brown's journey to the major leagues was a long one, partially because it took him a long time to learn to get beat with his best. Luckily, Billy's pitching coach, Art Fowler, finally got through to Brown.

▶ **Jackie Brown:** *Art Fowler . . . was almost like a dad to me. His philosophy was "throw strikes." That's all he harped on. You'd be in the bullpen, and if you were throwing balls in the dirt or throwing balls over the catcher's head, he would just tell you to stop. He'd push you off the mound, say, "Give me the ball," and he'd stand on the mound, and he would just throw strike after strike after strike. He'd say, "Hot damn, Brownie, I can do this, and I'm 52 years old." And you'd step back on the mound, and you'd start throwing strikes. He used to tell me I was a nib-*

bler. I never had confidence in my stuff, I guess the way you should have. I knew I had a good curveball, but I was leery of throwing it down the middle of the plate. I thought everything I threw down the middle of the plate was supposed to get hit. That's what I'd been taught to this point. Well, if you don't throw the ball down the middle of the plate, that means you have to throw it on the corners. Well, that black is not very big, and if you're trying to hit that black all the time, your percentage of throwing strikes is pretty slim. For Catfish Hunter or Fergie Jenkins, that was their living, but the rest of us had to throw the ball over to get ahead. Well, Art taught me that I didn't have to be perfect with every pitch I threw. Throw strikes first, and then go and try to make a perfect pitch.

Art and Billy taught Brown to take risks. Art and Billy taught Brown that his stuff was better than he thought. Brown had not been taught a message of confidence until he met Art and Billy. He had been taught that perfection was the way to success, not aggressiveness and a challenging attitude of laying it out there. But Billy Martin and his career-long sidekick Fowler permanently changed Brown's mindset. Brown remembers the night the message finally registered deep within him.

▶ **Jackie Brown:** *Art had told me and he had told me, "Hot damn, Brownie, Babe Ruth's dead! Throw the ball over the plate!" Finally, I come in off the field one night, and he walked over and sat down and said, "Throw the ball over the plate. Babe Ruth's dead!" And I said, "I'll show you what happens when I throw the ball over the plate." So I walk on the mound, and I had gotten mad at him, and I was going to go out there and show him what happens if I throw the ball over the plate. I threw a shutout! I didn't throw nothin' but strikes the rest of the game. The game is over, I'm walkin' off the field, and here comes Art, his little penguin walk out toward me. He just shook my hand and said, "Good game." Never said another word, and never again mentioned that to me. And from that day on is when I actually started throwing. Every time I raised my leg above the ground, the pitch was intended to get a hitter out. It was going to be a strike. That was the way I played. So Art Fowler was a big part of what success I had in the big leagues.*

Fowler's message was so straightforward that he is often presented as a clown, as a man who was along for Billy's ride through the big time. But he helped to change Jackie Brown's life and pitching career with his message. Too many people go through life being given a message of caution like Brown had been given. Art Fowler, the mellow, joking Southerner, had a message of aggressiveness, confidence, and risk taking. Don't try to be perfect. Make the hitter do something perfect. There is genius in those five simple words: "Throw strikes. Babe Ruth's dead." And Billy shared Art's philosophy.

▶ **Bobby Meacham:** *Billy would bring in a pitcher like Brian Fisher, for instance, who was my roommate on the road. And I would try to tell Brian, "Brian, I know Billy. You throw 94 miles per hour. He wants to see fastballs, OK? If you lose with your fastball, it's no problem. If you lose over and over with your fastball, then your fastball's not that good and you're gone. But don't come in throwing sliders thinking your slider's good today." Because he'd sometimes say back in the hotel, "Man, my slider looked good in the bullpen." I'd say, "I'm telling ya, if you lose with that slider, he's gonna kill you, and you're not gonna throw it anymore. Don't lose with the slider." Billy was one to not second-guess. If he wanted you to throw fastballs, throw fastballs. [Then Billy would say,] "If you lose, so be it. My fault. I brought in the wrong guy."*

Blame and Responsibility

Billy wanted his players to take responsibility for their jobs on the field. If they did so, he shrugged off their mistakes, and gave them the confidence to produce. However, anyone unwilling to assume responsibility for themselves would feel Billy's wrath.

Taking the Blame for Your Players

Meacham recalls that Billy did more than preach his message. If you gave a good effort, played the game right, and messed up, he would be there for you.

▶ **Bobby Meacham:** *He wasn't a front runner. If he strongly believed in something, and it went wrong in a game, he didn't blame you. Billy was pretty good at putting a lot of the onus on himself. He decided this is the way we're going to play the game, and if we don't come out on top, I'll take the heat for it. And also, when we do come out on top, I want all the glory. That's the way I believe the manager best is able to take all of the pressure off of the player. I remember one time we lost a game because I had made an error, and I was sitting in front of my locker just kind of bumming out on how we blew that game. If I make the play, we win. And he walked out, and I looked up, and he was kinda standing around the corner of my locker, three lockers down, and he's smoking his pipe. He kinda looks at me with a little smirk on his face, and he says, "What's wrong with you?" And I said, "Well, you know, I'm sorry. If it wasn't for me, we'd have won that game. I gotta make that play. I just blew it." And he just said, "It's not your fault, kid. It's my fault for putting you out there." He had a little smile on his face and went back into his office. Basically, he was saying, "You're going to make mistakes—that's the way it goes. I play the guys I think are gonna help us win out there. If we lose, it's not your fault—it's my fault, too."*

▶ **Matt Keough:** *Nothing is better than to have a manager come out and tell you, "I want you to pitch this guy this way, and if it goes wrong, I'll take the blame." Because then, all the thought process is out, and all you have to do is produce. Just do it. So when he would leave the mound after that, I felt like, "Great, man, I can breathe again." But if it went wrong, he would tell the press, "I told him to pitch him that way, and we got beat." But 99 out of 100 times, it worked. That's one thing Billy did for all the pitchers that people don't talk about.*

▶ **Mike Pagliarulo:** *There was one time in Toronto in a pennant race. George Bell was on second base and Jesse Barfield hit me a ball. I threw the ball away, and Toronto won the game. I have never felt as bad as I did this day. And Billy just come up, and he put his arm around me, and he said, "Lookit, kid, don't worry about it. There's going to be other games." . . . And I did feel bad, but the next day I felt all right. That* *helped me deal with it. Because it was a big game, big pressure situation. You're playing for the Yankees, playing for first place, and it was amazing. I just felt terrible, but he made me feel a lot better. Sometimes, those kind of things, they can kill young players. A manager or a player can say something to a guy at that moment and it can really destroy some guys. And that helped me an awful lot.*

Martin wanted his players to feel all right after blowing one, because he needed them to go out the next day and play ball the same way. He was tough, but at the same time, he didn't want players to be afraid to make mistakes on the diamond.

▶ **Mike Heath:** *He treated me good. I mean, he would get on me, and then maybe a couple hours later he'd come to me and he'd say, "Hey, I'm just trying to make you better." But I respected the man, I really did. I wasn't afraid to make a mistake around Billy. You went out there and played hard every day. You could not be afraid to make a mistake, because if you did that, you'd start making mistakes. Some people would question the point and say, "Well, he would make you tentative." But me as a player, I didn't worry about that. I played aggressive and I didn't look over there in the corner and think, "Oh, well, if I throw this ball away, Billy's going to get mad at me." Heck no, that's my job, I have to perform.*

Assuming Responsibility for Your Errors

Heath's "that's my job" attitude spells out another Martin credo: that of taking personal responsibility for the job one has to do. Making mistakes can be painful and embarrassing, and to save face, one's defense mechanisms can kick in, even if subconsciously. Since sometimes bad things happen to us that are not our fault, the temptation exists to let our minds maneuver us into excusing away *all* the bad things that happen to us as somebody else's fault. Yet by not being honest with ourselves and taking responsibility for those things that we do incorrectly, we limit our ability to reach our full potential and to build our own self-confidence and self-image.

Billy Martin demanded that his players take responsibility for their performance. This meant three things: (1) eliminating mental errors altogether, (2) always being in the game, whether you were playing or not, and (3) admitting your fault in the physical errors that were an inevitable part of playing aggressively.

▶ **Mike Heath:** *Mental errors in the game are unacceptable. I mean, a physical mistake is going to happen on occasion. But mental mistakes should never happen in the game. You should know at all times what you need to do with the ball out there. Today it seems like you see a lot of mental mistakes—guys throwing to the wrong bag or guys in the cutoff situation coming up throwing, they don't know where to throw the ball. . . . You gotta know the game situation and want the ball before the ball is hit. Expect it's going to be hit to you, and know what you're going to do with it.*

▶ **Mickey Klutts:** *He couldn't tolerate mental errors at all. He had a real problem with it. If you didn't know where to throw the ball, if you overthrew cutoff men, you'd get in the doghouse quick doing that. So he wanted smart people. I think that's why he was a little intolerant of young guys at first. He was real hard on young guys to make the Yankees. He was very intolerant of the mental mistakes by myself and a Brian Doyle and a Mike Heath, and people like that. He was very tough on young guys. Not in a belligerent way, just tough.*

Taking responsibility also meant being in the game and being alert, even if you weren't playing at the time.

▶ **Tom Grieve:** *You were on your toes for nine innings, whether you were sitting on the bench or whether you were in the game. You did not feel comfortable if you weren't giving 100 percent of your attention to that ballgame, because you knew you were going to hear about it if you didn't get the bunt down, if you didn't hit the cutoff man, if you didn't put the ball in play with a man on third and less than two outs. You knew you were going to hear it.*

▶ **Charlie Manuel:** *Once the game started, Billy was probably one of the most serious guys I've ever been around. He required you to sit on the* *bench and watch the whole game. He wanted you there watching the game, he wanted you to see everything about the game, he wanted you to try to pick up things, like signs, or infielders moving, or catchers giving away pitches. Billy was trying to teach you how to study the game, and he kept you in the game. He loved baseball to the extent where he thought everybody around him, when that game started, should be there and be in the game.*

It's human nature to let down. Billy's job as leader was to prevent it. A ballplayer ought to feel uncomfortable if he isn't giving 100 percent of his attention to the game. After all, that's his livelihood. That's what he's doing at that time. But human nature being what it is, ballplayers slip just like the rest of us. The threat of Billy's wrath helped stop that slippage. If a guy was tired and needed a day off, Billy could see that, but if a guy was simply dogging it, Billy was going to let him know it.

Making players take responsibility for themselves and the mistakes that they made was one of his keys to building competitors. He insisted at all times that players be responsible, accepting control over what they've done, caused to be done, and could still do. In 1971, Billy told *Sporting News* columnist Watson Spolestra, "I won't put up with liars, alibi Ikes, or con-artists."[13] And he didn't.

▶ **Rod Carew:** *He always told me, "Don't ever alibi when you make a mistake on the field. Just fess up to it, and that's how you learn, because if you make alibis, the same play might happen again, and instead of knowing what you did the first time, then you'll continue to do it again the second time, and just make matters worse."*

▶ **Jackie Moore:** *I remember coaching first base for him one time, and it was one out, and it was an important run. Billy was getting my attention from the dugout, pointing, "Tell him [the runner on first] watch the line drive." So I was telling him, "Watch the line drive, don't be lined off in the infield." Sure enough, about five pitches later, there was a line drive and—boom—the runner reacts toward second base and they double him off first base. I knew that when I got back to the dugout that Billy was going to have something to say, and he said, "You can't let him get lined* *out in that situation!" I said, "Billy, I told him eight times. You saw me. I walked up to him eight times and told him that." He said, "Well, you gotta tell him nine. You know they're all stupid!" And I never forgot that—that eight times wasn't good enough. He said, "You gotta tell 'em nine times!"*

▶ **Willie Horton:** *I believe in discipline. But now they say, "Something got in my eye." I just don't see it. Billy used to get mad when people started making excuses. I think, what Billy didn't like, a lot of people start hiding mistakes and are scared to admit to mistakes. You do that, you're going to hide instead of try to overcome. If you understand you're going to make mistakes, you'll win all the time, because you're going to benefit.*

Billy drilled a sense of responsibility and honesty into his players. He would tell a pitcher who had lost, for example, that it wasn't his fault because he hadn't pitched in a couple of days—it was his fault because he didn't get the ball over the plate. He would tell the pitcher not to claim that it was the shortstop's fault—it was his own fault because he made the wrong pitch. Billy wanted his players to go out and be aggressive, but not to make alibis and excuses and blame others. Instead, they should admit that they had made a mistake.[14]

▶ **Mike Pagliarulo:** *I certainly got that feeling from Billy right away. I just really got the feeling that he didn't like guys blaming other guys. And from time to time, he would just yell that out, "Say you screwed up! Everybody screws up! Everybody f—s up! So just take the heat, suck it up, and go out there and let's see what you got now. It's going to happen. It's going to happen again."*

To get a player to take responsibility for himself, Billy had a technique of berating a coach over that player's mistake. The goal was to guilt that player into taking responsibility for himself by watching somebody else take the rap for his mistake.

▶ **Jackie Moore:** *He made sure the player was listening. What he was doing, not only he was letting the player know that he was wrong and that's not the way to do it, but someone else was taking the blame for* *what you had just messed up. In other words, not only did you do something wrong, but you got someone else in trouble. Someone else is taking the heat for how you goofed up. And I think it left a double impression. The player, if he has any feeling at all, he's gotta say, "Jeez, not only did I goof up, my coach is having to take the heat for it." Billy had a reason for doing this. It left an impression. It was a lasting impression.*

In the end, it was about taking responsibility for doing your best every day. It was an empowering lesson for those who could do it, yet many players and people struggle to make that leap. Billy's greatest success stories always made that leap.

A Passion for Winning

In addition, Martin made sure his players also took responsibility for the gradual accumulation of a season's results. Martin had a unique turn-around ability because there was no excuse for playing losing ball in his mind. Whatever the case—young, old, fast, or slow—he believed you were capable of winning. You couldn't ride out your rookie year or coast through your final days in the majors with Billy. You were expected to win today.

▶ **Jackie Moore:** *He only thought one way, and that was winning. It was not win two years down the road or three years down the road. If we had a ballgame today, we were supposed to win this ballgame. And that was the only thing that he really accepted. "Hey, we're not satisfied unless we win today, and then we win tomorrow, and if we do that, then we win the following day." Although these guys were young, it's one thing that he told these guys, "Hey, regardless of how you are—first year or what- ever—we need to win." And I think that was good for them, because it was teaching them the right approach to how to play the game.*

▶ **Tom Grieve:** *He hated to lose. No manager likes to lose, but I never played for a manager who hated to lose more than Billy Martin. It was uncomfortable after a game that you lost to be around him—to look at* *him, to bump into him, to talk to him in the clubhouse. That rubbed off on the players, that desire to win.*

▶ **Mickey Klutts:** *He hated to lose, dude. There was never a good loss. You could win 20 in a row, you lose one and it would kill him. He hated it. He just hated it. By the next day, he's ready to go, but he hated— hated—to lose.*

▶ **Matt Keough:** *I never heard that word "rebuilding" used by him. If you gave him the Long Beach Junior College baseball team tomorrow and put him in the big leagues, he's not going to talk about rebuilding. He's going to try to figure out how to beat you.*

It was more than just losing that Billy hated. He hated not playing your best and not improving. In the game of baseball, a .600 winning percentage is usually good for first place, so you know going in that four times in ten, your team is going to lose. Billy's goal was to not give away any of the six you could win.

Building Young Coaches and Managers

Billy also took an interest in young coaches and managers who showed a love for the game, putting in time with those whom he saw potential in. Two examples who are among the top managers in the game today are Buck Showalter and Tony LaRussa. Billy took an interest in Showalter during spring trainings, while Buck was a manager at the lowest rungs of the Yankees' minor league system. Billy took an interest in LaRussa when Tony became the pilot of the White Sox, and later the A's. Martin became the sort of managerial mentor to these men that he himself had had in Sam Mele.

▶ **Buck Showalter:** *Billy was a lot of fun to talk to—I should say listen to more than anything. I had a lot of respect for him, and I think that maybe caught his eye. He knew that I was basically listening and trying to learn. You know what they say, the true test of a man is how he treats those*

who can be of no possible use to him, and that was certainly Billy. I was
a minor league manager, and he didn't have to give me the time of day,
but he did, and he made it a lot easier. That was a real highlight for me.

From Showalter's perspective, Martin had that type of empathy that all great leaders possess—the ability to put himself in the spikes of young managers and to do what he could to give them a little boost. The attention Billy paid to a "nobody" had an impact, and Buck has not forgotten Billy now that he is one of the game's best managers. Nor has LaRussa.

▶ **Buck Showalter:** *I've learned to make up my own mind on people. There are so many things that are publicly perceived that are completely false. I can only go by the way he treated me. There were so many things that he would do that never came to light publicly, but he wasn't in it for that. To keep me in camp, when I was supposed to be going across to Tampa to the minor leagues, that's a big financial thing for a manager making $13,000 a year to stay in big league camp and take big league meal money for an extra two weeks. I'm sure that was part of Billy's thinking. And through it, I got to drive him around some, and sit there and listen to him, and it was special. Billy always felt like, if you weren't sure about his character, just look at his friends and the people around him. He felt like that was enough. If you like it, and want to be a part of it, there was always room.*

▶ **Tony LaRussa:** *Billy was good to me when I first came into the big leagues. He took the time to talk with me and to see how I was doing. I think a mutual friend told him, "Hey, he's another Italian. Take it easy on him." And I did get to spend time with him, mostly during the winter meetings. I had the opportunity to spend a few afternoons and a few evenings with him. Just talking with him, and talking baseball. And you really got a sense for how much he cared about the game of baseball. Sure, Billy wasn't perfect. He had his dark side, and he had a side no one understood. It was just Billy. But if he trusted you, he would do anything for you. He was very good-hearted and fun to be around, so when*

one of those things happened from time to time, you felt bad about it,
because he was a good guy.

In the next chapter, we'll look at how Billy taught losing teams how
to become winners, and the moves he made to engineer turnarounds.

Notes

1. H. A. Dorfman and Karl Kuehl, *The Mental Game of Baseball* (Southbend,
   Ind.: Diamond Communications, 1995), p. x.

2. "Baseball in the 1970s," *This Week in Baseball* video (Major League Baseball Productions, 1991).

3. Roger Nye, *The Patton Mind* (Garden City Park, N.Y.: Avery Publishing
   Group, 1993), p. 36.

4. News clip dated September 29, 1973, found in the National Baseball Hall of
   Fame Library.

5. *Billy Martin: The Man, The Myth, The Manager*, videotape (Cabinfever
   Entertainment, 1990).

6. Billy Martin and Peter Golenbock, *Number 1* (New York: Delacorte Press,
   1980), p. 10.

7. Billy Martin and Phil Pepe, *Billyball* (Garden City, N.Y.: Doubleday & Company, 1987), p. 101.

8. Martin and Golenbock, p. 75.

9. Nye, p. 74.

10. Ibid., p. 78.

11. Martin and Golenbock, p. 98.

12. Ron Fimrite, "Portrait of the Artist as a Hitter," *Sports Illustrated,* June 13,
    1983.

13. Watson Spolestra, "Tigers Column," *Sporting News,* January 30, 1971.

14. *Billy Martin: The Man, The Myth, The Manager.*

Chapter 3

Preparing for the Turnaround

n October 1973—only months before he began to negotiate an amazing 27-win improvement with the 1974 Texas Rangers, taking the team to an 84–76 season after its 1973 season of 57–105—Billy told writer Randy Galloway, "Losing is just like winning. It becomes a habit . . . In spring training we are going to show them how to win. When they see our program, they are going to believe they can win. Winning isn't that difficult if you know how . . . And they are going to learn."[1] In late 1973, Martin had scoured the Rangers organization for his style of players. In the spring of 1974, he would have the chance to mold them.

▶ **Charlie Silvera:** *He took 'em all to spring training. He took every prospect that they had down there. In fact, I had gone down to see the Instructional League team, and they had the best lookin' kids down there of any organization. [Jim] Sundberg, [Ron] Pruitt, [Mike] Hargrove, [Roy] Howell. So he took 'em all, and you know, they made the club.*

When you consider Martin's statements about a team that had managed a .352 winning percentage the previous season, you see a man with confidence in his abilities to build a winning unit, but you also see a man already at work setting a new tone for his players. Billy wanted his players to understand that things were going to be different—that for the turnaround to take place, a revival was about to occur.

▶ **Lenny Randle:** *In '74, he took a nucleus of guys that were winners and didn't know it. They were gamers that didn't know it. They were 10- or 15-game winners—he made them 19- or 20-game winners. He took .220 or .250 hitters and made them .300 hitters by letting them know that he believed that they could hit a pitcher in a certain situation, like a 3–1 count. He got guys to put the ball on the ground and move a guy from first to third. We learned to cause chaos offensively. He'd say, "I can win a game with one run, but I need guys that are going to execute to do that. I'm not saying it's me, I am saying we. We can win a game with just one run." A lot of guys never played like that before. That team gelled.*

It didn't take long or grueling practices for Billy to get a team to gel. It did take perfect practices. Most of us don't practice perfectly, regardless of our trade. We want to work on what is most fun or what we are already good at. Billy Martin made his players work on the things he knew would win ballgames.

Making Efficient Use of Time

Billy's spring training camps were short on "face time" but long on efficiency. Billy didn't care if you worked long hours as long as you worked smart hours. He knew you could get more done in four hours than in 12 if there was a rhyme and reason to the effort. In today's competitive times, long hours are the norm, but it's still productivity that gets the results that drive growth and lead to success. Do things right. Concentrate on the task at hand completely. Work on getting better rather than just working. And when you're done for the day, go home. That was Billy's way.

▶ **Tom Grieve:** *Billy wasn't a workaholic. I mean, I see managers today that get out to the ballpark at one o'clock and plan elaborate prepractice workouts and that kind of thing. Billy wasn't like that at all. As a team, we* *weren't out there in the middle of the afternoon practicing all day long before batting practice. And there's plenty of times where he got to the ballpark after batting practice already started. He just had a great way of demanding that his team perform at a high level. He got you to do it. He was a master motivator really, and psychologist.*

Billy was able to minimize hours by keeping things organized. Recalled Billy:

> "When camp opened, everyone was ready, and I ran it exactly as I said I would. I have my own system for running a spring training camp. We start about ten in the morning and only go until one, but during that time everything is so organized that everyone gets more work than most guys on other teams who work out twice a day. Nobody stands around for a second. Every day the hitters practice their bunting on the machines, with instructors there to make sure they learn correctly. We work on relays, rundowns, pickoff plays, on both fields every day. I have my pitchers practice covering first base on grounders to the first baseman. In other words, I make sure that by the time the season starts, everyone has his fundamentals down."[2]

▶ **Buck Showalter:** *Billy expected you to work when you were there. There were certain things that he wanted to accomplish each day, and once those things were accomplished, we moved on to the next day. It's one of those things where you were working, but you didn't know you were working. It was obviously a labor of love for him. He didn't want a club to peak too early. He knew where the finish line was, and it wasn't in February.*

▶ **Jackie Moore:** *When Billy does something, it's not just to do it because, "Well, OK, it's something to do this day." When there was a drill or fundamental that was worked on, it was the most important thing of that day. And . . . the players came away from it saying, "Well, this is the way* *it's going to be." It gets back to little things taking care of the big things. Billy would not tolerate any other way than doing it right. And if you didn't do it right, you stayed out until it was accomplished. And I think once the players realized this, they said, "Hey, we're going to be here all day, or we're going to do it right."*

Billy's teams worked very hard on the fundamentals, because that's where Billy believed much of the key to winning came from.

▶ **George Mitterwald:** *He told that 1980 A's team, "Look, you lost 43 games by one run. You weren't that far away from being pretty good. The reason you weren't good is because you didn't do the little things. We're going to do the little things." I remember playing San Diego, and he told the manager before the game, "Look, we're going to do things, and I don't want you to be getting mad at us. If it's a 13–2 or 13–3 lead, we're still going to be stealing, we're going to be doing different things, because we got to work on these things and that's part of our spring training to get better."*

▶ **Mickey Klutts:** *The first spring we had with him, we worked. I've never worked on fundamentals like that. And I told the guys on the A's, "We're going to work on fundamentals like you cannot believe." We were green. Half the guys were out of the International League with me, and we worked real hard on fundamentals. We might work three, four, five hours straight handling bunts.*

Billy was a hands-on teacher. He wasn't buried in an office somewhere, having delegated the entire camp to his coaches. He was out there with his men—in essence, not just talking the talk but walking the walk—because he wanted to show them how strongly he felt about the work they were doing and wanted to know that they were learning things correctly.

▶ **Mike Heath:** *He would show us. He would literally physically get out there and show us what he wanted to do. If we did it wrong, he would* *halt the practice and start the play over again. He literally showed us what to do, what to look for, and how to read it.*

▶ **Bobby Meacham:** *The younger guys—myself, [Mike] Pagliarulo, [Don] Mattingly—we worked on a lot of things. Fundamentally sound things like rundowns. What side of the ball do you want to be on? On tags where do you want to be? And Billy was the only manager that I ever had who got out there with the infielders and actually showed you how to turn the double play, how to make a tag, or how to execute a rundown. The rest of 'em, they let somebody else do it. But Billy used to get out there with me and school me on what he wanted done.*

Thus, Billy Martin's spring drills were short in hours but long on substance. Players drilled on the fundamentals of the game so that the response in the actual game would be automatic. And when the work was done, you were expected to get out and have some fun.

▶ **Tom Grieve:** *Billy's spring trainings were pretty remarkable, really. In every other spring training I had been to—and they're a lot different now than they were back then—you did calisthenics and running before the practice started. When Billy took over, the first thing he did was pretty much start the practice. The pitchers got loose, the hitters hit. We didn't have any calisthenics. We just went out and practiced. You got the work in, you concentrated on the baseball part of it, and then very early in the afternoon you were free. And he set things up at different golf courses where you could go and play for free. So his camps were very relaxed camps.*

▶ **Charlie Manuel:** *We worked a lot on bunt plays, cutoffs, and relays. He would sit there in the dugout, and he would supervise, and it was up to you to do it. As far as running a real big conditioning program, Billy was not big on that like some other organizations like the Dodgers. At the same time, if you weren't in shape, he would really jump on your butt. But it was knowledge, knowing how to play the game, those are things we worked on, and we did it every day in spring training. We worked on the right way to play the game every day in spring training.*

The end result was a component of mutual respect that grew out of Billy's camps that created a good starting point from which to begin the season. The manager knew what he wanted done and expected the players to do it. And if a player needed something, Billy made sure he got it. There was a good balance.

▶ **Mike Pagliarulo:** *If you were one of the regular players, whatever you needed to get ready for the season, you got it. Pete Filson, the left-handed pitcher, used to have to go out there and throw me breaking balls, because I'm the third baseman. Or if I needed extra grounders, three coaches will be out there hitting me ground balls. And I'd have a first baseman, and I'd have a second baseman. If I wanted to hit early, I got early hitting. Whatever I needed. So from my standpoint, it was great. Anything I needed to get. But it was hitting, grounders, running, or a day off. "I need a day off, Billy, I gotta work out some kinks in my swing." "All right, we'll do it." Anything for the player, that's how I saw it. So I thought it was great.*

▶ **Tom Grieve:** *You can't just do nice-guy things and get the players behind you—otherwise it'd be a pretty easy job to be a manager. You'd just let your players go golfing and everybody likes you. It doesn't work that way. He was demanding when you were out on the field. He expected the fundamentals to be worked on. He expected you to work hard while you were out there. But when you were done, he didn't have a problem with you golfing.*

Emphasizing the Necessary Skills

Billy's players practiced ways to win games, not ways to enhance their personal statistics. It's common sense that you want to hone your skills to the best of your ability: That's what wins games. But home runs and statistics are what earns the money and garners the recognition on ESPN. Many ballplayers lack the full repertoire of skills that managers like Billy Martin looked for in the 1960s and 1970s, especially in today's power game. But those skills can still be crucial to helping your team win, and Billy loved the guys who wanted to do those things.

▶ **Toby Harrah:** *Billy wasn't really interested in stats, I can tell you that. He came up to me one day and he said, "Toby, don't ever worry about statistics. You play the game one day at a time. Do whatever it takes to help your team win. When the end of the season rolls around, those stats will be there." After you've played for a while, you realize that so many ballgames are really won and lost in late innings. You can get a couple of hits in the first five innings, but the game hasn't been won yet, so Billy wasn't so concerned with batting averages or things of that nature, as much as he was of executing a sacrifice bunt, or executing a hit and run, or getting a guy over from second base—all the little things. I remember one time we were playing a ballgame in Baltimore, and it's raining. And it's the top of the fifth, and we're winning by three or four runs. Billy whistles, and I go over. He says, "Toby, I want you to go up there and strike out." So I went up there and struck out, Baltimore hit in the bottom of the inning, and then I'll be damned if the game doesn't get rained out. It was a five-inning ballgame, and we got credit for the win. And he says, "Toby, I'll remember that. Don't let that bother you." And I never did. Whatever he wanted me to do, I'd do it. Stats never meant a damn thing to him, and they never meant a thing to me. Just winning.*

Two of Billy's Twins, George Mitterwald and Charlie Manuel, learned that it wasn't speed that brought a runner in from second on a base hit—it was execution, and Billy taught them how to execute.

▶ **George Mitterwald:** *He thought I was a good base runner, even though I couldn't run that fast. I used to get a good lead off second base, and I never got picked off. When you're not fast, they don't pay quite as much attention as if you're a Rickey Henderson. So you can cheat a little bit more, and you have to do that sometimes, to score from second base on a line drive to left field or to right field. So he put that confidence in you, and when he was coaching third base, that's the things I remember from him. As a player in spring training in '66, '67, and '68, I listened to* *everything he told me. He said, "Come on, get off, get off, get off, get off, get off! You can get off more. Get off more!" And he let you know exactly what you could get off, and how much you could cheat, and the certain things that you could do to give yourself an advantage for some- body that wasn't quite as fast as somebody else.*

▶ **Charlie Manuel:** *Billy wanted the game to be played from a fundamen- tal standpoint. He wanted you to be alert, to take the extra base. He required you to get a good lead. He would jump your butt if you didn't score from second base on a single with two outs. He used to say, "That right there tells me that you didn't get off the base far enough." Billy was always pumping the right way to play baseball to me, and I mean that.*

▶ **George Mitterwald:** *There's another situation where there's two strikes and two outs in the inning, and if that hitter starts his swing, you're gone. You start running right now, because he's not going to stop his swing. And you know what? Sometimes that may let you score. And these were the type of things that he drummed into you day in and day out. He said, "Look, you gotta do this. Sometimes you gotta take a little chance. You might get picked off at second base, but you gotta be leaning sometimes, take a good jump and get it going, especially if it's the winning run."*

Casey Stengel had done the same with his Yankee teams.

▶ **Gil McDougald:** *What we were taught all the time, which Billy certainly would say, is base running. I mean, first to third was a must. When you're on first and a guy gets a base hit, a must. You must know how to run bases. You must know the outfielders' arms, you must know their positions, before the ball is hit. This is what Billy I'm sure taught every one of his clubs, all the players.*

So playing correctly and for the good of the team, and being will- ing to sacrifice personal glory for the collective group, was what Billy cared about. Billy told sportswriter Phil Pepe in February 1976, before his first Yankee spring training began, "I want to instill in these guys the idea of self-sacrifice. I want them to use the word 'we,' not 'I.' I don't want players who worry about getting the hit to improve their average . . . And if there's some guy who thinks he's too big for the team, I'll break him right down to size."[3] He meant it, too.

▶ **Willie Horton:** *Playing for Billy was the first time that I ever had a manager, whether Little League or professional baseball, who'd come up and just tell me something point blank. I remember when he first came to the Tigers, he came to my home. He came to Detroit to visit me himself, and he sat in my living room and told me what he expected of me. He told me that if I didn't put out, I was going to get a lot of splinters [sit on the bench]. It was a shock to me. I don't think no other manager would have said that. And that's the first time in my life I had anyone say anything like that to me. I was an established ballplayer, and one of the primary Tigers, and I never had nobody tell me, but it was the best thing that ever happened to Willie Horton. He just told me, "Willie, with all your ability, you can play this game. I'm here to get this God-given talent out of you. That's my job." I just looked at him. I didn't know what to say. Then after that, he said, "Well, let's go get [Tiger outfielder] Gates Brown and go play some pool."*

▶ **Toby Harrah:** *He tried to create that atmosphere that it was us against the world, and that brought everybody closer together. We played good as a team. We pulled for one another. You could not be a selfish ballplayer and play for Billy Martin. You couldn't do that, or you were going to have a miserable time. You couldn't worry about your stats, you couldn't worry about any of that stuff.*

Learning to play the game to win, even if you are a slugger, requires mental focus along with the physical exertion. If a ground ball to second wins you the ballgame, the winning player will want to deliver that ground ball. The guys who could and would do those things played for Billy. Take Fred Stanley. In a 1976 Yankee lineup led by Mickey Rivers, Thurman Munson, Graig Nettles, and Chris Chambliss, Stanley hit only .238. But he led the team in sacrifices, and that was just one way he contributed. He also moved the runners over so the big bats could drive them home and worked pitchers for walks so he could get on base. Billy saw Stanley do these things, and that's why he broke into that tough lineup.

▶ **Fred Stanley:** *I did the things that Billy wanted me to do. Take pitches, work the pitcher, get on base, and let the other guys drive me in. And things were working like that, so I was like his little pupil because he was trying to teach me some things, and I was responding to it. And you get excited when that happens.*

It was the same mentality that Billy pushed on all of his Oakland A's.

▶ **Mike Heath:** *It was a lot of hard work in spring training. We did a lot of things, and he taught us a lot. There were some little things that we did. If you were struggling with the pitcher, and you had a guy at third base, push bunt one. Instead of trying to get up there and hit him, push bunt one. If you can bunt, bunt him in!*

▶ **Mickey Klutts:** *We had our moments of failure, but it was all for the positive, even attempting a lot of things that we did. We would run on the opposing outfielders more than anybody I've ever seen. Anybody. It didn't matter who. We figured we could force these people to make mistakes. Just a regular base hit to right—I mean, we're going from first to third, we're going all the way. And it forces the outfielder to more or less tighten up knowing that. Force them to rush everything out there. It was just a philosophy of attack, and we practiced it a lot, too.*

Making Yourself "Unrejectable"

When you work relentlessly to improve yourself—from whatever starting point at which you find yourself—you become a professional, whether in baseball, marketing, sales, writing, auto mechanics, or teaching. Billy looked for ballplayers who took the time to really learn the inside-outs of the game by working on their own or with other coaches or players to improve their game.

Getting information from great coaches and players is more than just having face time. It's about really using your time effectively to work and improve. It's the same in business. Getting to the office at 7:30 A.M. and staying until 8 P.M. is great, but if the person in the next office is doing as much work as you and then some between 9 and 5, your long hours are a mask for inefficiency. How can you get better, increase your arsenal, and help your team?

Lenny Randle was one of Billy's young stars on the Texas Rangers. Defensively, Randle was playing second, third, and outfield on a regular basis for Martin. Offensively, he was the type of speedster Martin envisioned terrorizing other teams, in the same way in which he had used Cesar Tovar and Rod Carew in Minnesota, and later, Mickey Rivers in New York and Rickey Henderson in Oakland and New York. To help broaden Randle's skills, Martin arranged for him to work with Carew on his bunting technique underneath Metropolitan Stadium before games when the Rangers were in Minnesota.

▶ **Rod Carew:** *He had asked me if I would take some time with Lenny, and he said that Lenny had good speed, he was in the same mold as me as a player, and he was wondering if I would take the time to teach him or show him some pointers on bunting, and I said, "Yeah, if there's any way I can help another player to try and improve himself in a certain area of what he's doing, I'd be glad to do it." So we just went out there, and went through different steps and techniques in what I tried to do, as far as bunting went.*

The lessons made an impact on Randle, in part because Carew himself had years earlier taken Billy's advice and turned himself into one of the game's great stars. If learning to bunt had made sense for Rod Carew, it had to make sense for Lenny Randle.

▶ **Lenny Randle:** *Billy said to me, "Carew does 20 to 30 bunts a year. That's 20 to 30 bunts on your average. So that's going to win you games. Don't you want to do that?" "Yeah!" Who would say no? "Yeah." "So go see Rod. He'll be out in the cage." So Rod says, "We start with pepper. Bunting is just like pepper." And I'm saying, "You got a wand. That's not a bat." He says, " . . . Nah, you can have the same. I want to stay in the big leagues 20 years. So this is what's going to keep me here.*

I was a reject. Billy made me unrejectable. And this is how I did it. I bunted. I stole bases. I learned how to play second." He said, "I'm gonna hit. I'm gonna be the greatest all-time hitter. If you hit, you're going to play somewhere. If you bunt, you're going to play somewhere. If you can learn to do this art of bunting, you'll stay in the big leagues. It's like Leonard Bernstein doing the orchestra. My art is bunting. So 20 a day." I was a switch-hitter, so 20 on one side, 20 on the other side, just practicing. And when you could show bunt, it was like the whole infield and outfield was on their toes. When you do that to a game, it tells you something about your offense.

Carew was able to help Randle. Carew had had to learn those same lessons from Billy when he was still an up-and-comer in the late 1960s. In 1967, with Billy as his tutor, the 22-year-old Carew had been the Rookie of the Year, hitting a solid .292. But in 1968, with Billy off managing minor-league Denver, Carew slumped to .273. When Billy came back to manage the Twins in 1969, he reinforced in Rod the things the player had gotten away from, which were the very same things that would make him "unrejectable."

▶ **Rod Carew:** *I had had a good year in my first year as a rookie. I think I had hit .292, so it was a decent year that I had. Then he left. He had talked to me about bunting and using my speed to get on base and things like that the first year. But he left, and I started trying to do some things at the plate that I shouldn't have. I started trying to pull the ball, I started trying to put the ball in the seats. And I ended up having a tough year. So in '69, when he came back, he just asked me, "What happened?" I said, "I was just trying to hit with some more power." So he looked at me and he said, "Your game is to get on base, try and steal some bases, set up some run-scoring situations for the guys behind you. I just want you to go back to hitting line drives. Go back to bunting. And you'll have consistency." And lo and behold, I led the league that year for the first time.*

Many of the men who played for Billy years ago see the passion to learn the entire game eroding today. Today's players are stronger and more athletic than the players of 25 years ago, but they don't know the game the way the older players did. Also, today's players have contractual and financial security that often protects them from the threat of a trade or minor league demotion. Toward the end of his career, Billy saw what was happening, with players focusing on individual glory rather than team success, and it really frustrated him.

▶ **Fred Stanley:** *I think when I look at players, I think how mental mistakes are killin' this game. Now what happens is we get players comin' up to the big leagues that you cannot send down. They got big contracts, but they're not good players. They think they've got it made, and they don't have to work at their trade. That's the difference between now and then, because those guys back in the '70s and '60s were bustin' it because somebody could take your job. They worked harder at their trade. I think Billy started seein' some of these things coming in, and it was harder for him to swallow.*

▶ **Mickey Klutts:** *Used to be, when you came into the major leagues, you had to do most everything pretty well. Throw guys out. Run. Field. Hit. Hit the cutoff man. Play the mental game. But it's changed. That bothers me a little bit nowadays. I see the worst fundamentals in baseball I've ever seen in my life. Guys can't hit the cutoff man. It's an "I" game now. Billy couldn't manage some of these guys. He could not. I mean that.*

Making Players Believe in What They Did

Of course, there are many players today who, regardless of the money they earn, want to go all out and want to learn the total game. The key is to get that value system in them that transcends money and security. You need your staff not only to do what you say but to believe what you say is correct. Billy Martin understood this leadership fundamental. He not only drilled plays repeatedly so that actions became instinctive, he convinced players that the actions were the correct ones to take.

▶ **Mickey Klutts:** *He taught me how to think—well, all of us basically. He would manage and teach on the bench at the same time. He was con-*

stantly talking about the situation, and about two or three batters down the line. Constantly looking at the lineup and who they had on the bench, who was going to be coming up. Today, I can sit and watch a game, and I can tell you how they're going to pitch to certain guys, and where everybody's going to play 'em, and it just all comes as old hat to me, because he taught me. He just taught us how to look at the game as a real simple ballgame. He tried to teach everybody to think, and why we do things the way we do out there and the coaches do things the way they do, and he was constantly talking on the bench.

▶ **Charlie Manuel:** *He would be talking to us in the dugout, and relaying things to us, but in the meantime, he would be so focused on the game. I mean hey, look, when the game started, he stayed on that game nine innings, and I mean till it ended. As a matter of fact, a lot of the stuff I learned in baseball comes from Billy. Especially the way I talk on the bench, and I try to keep my guys interested in the game. All of that stuff I got comes from Billy.*

Billy explained everything. Then, if a move worked, the player understood the rhyme and reason. If a move failed, the player could at least understand the logic behind the attempt. The player begins to absorb the manager's overall philosophy.

▶ **Mickey Klutts:** *Our philosophy was to put as much pressure on the defense out there and to make them make mistakes, and to get them to think about more things than just the pitch and where they're playing in situations. In other words, they're [the opposing players] going to have to worry about everybody, and hit and runs, and squeezes, and bunt and runs, and everything. So, the more things they had to think about—and that included the opposing manager and pitching coach—the more trouble they'd be in. I had a couple squeeze bunts in those years, and I even saw [Tony] Armas squeeze a run in with one out. You could not tell what we were going to do.*

A philosophy is more than a laundry list of assignments. A philoso-phy is a firm conviction that naturally leads to certain behaviors that will bring that philosophy from idea to reality. If you believe in the philosophy of surprise, you'll want to be a better bunter, a better situational hitter, and a better base runner, so that you can surprise. You're not working on your bunting because someone told you that it would be a good use of your time; you are working on your surprising. You are working to contribute to the team philosophy. And when you see Tony Armas, the team's top power hitter, squeeze in a run and demoralize the opposition, you'll believe in the philosophy. This is why Billyball gained steam. It was a philosophy that inspired its followers to behave in the ways Billy wanted.

So as we have seen, to Billy, preparation for a lengthy baseball season had little to do with running laps in the hot Florida sun and much to do with creating mental and physical associations with particular sequences that would become automatic to the players once the season started. The best way to be ready is both to know how to get the job done in a specific way, and to want to get the job done in that same way. Automatic response comes from repetition and belief, and that's what Billy worked toward in his spring drills.

▶ **Jackie Moore:** *You do your drills right, and you work on 'em enough, and it becomes a reaction. You don't have to stop and think "What should I do?" And with the game continuous, it becomes an instinct. That's why Billy was successful, and that's how you win ballgames.*

You can make people do things for a while just by telling them to do them, but it's not until something starts to work that you get that belief. In 1965, Minnesota third base coach Martin and manager Sam Mele saw that first-hand, when they started their power-laden Twins team running wild on the base paths. Creating this change in approach took time, since the Twins players' vision of themselves didn't include aggressive running. After they started to see results, though, the team embraced the running game and ran themselves all the way to the World Series.

▶ **Sam Mele:** *We talked about running, running, running, and then, when spring training was halfway gone, they started to see it working, and* *damn it, it got infectious. They all wanted to run. Billy did it so many times, especially with a man on third. He didn't just have the guy take a lead, he had the guy look like he was gonna steal home when the pitcher was in his windup. Not halfway, but like he's charging, and damn, we won about three ballgames in the bottom of the ninth because the guy made a wild pitch. That was all Billy.*

Too many so-called leaders tell their followers what to do without ever taking the time to teach them *why* a new method is better than another way. The follower follows—maybe—but without full enthusiasm and faith. It follows that his or her effort will be half-hearted at best. And in a hypercompetitive world, half-heartedness will not work. As GE's CEO Jack Welch says, "Without everybody embracing what we want to do, we haven't got a prayer."[4] In one spring training game, Billy got a young pitcher to believe whole-heartedly when Billy's instructions proved most effective.

▶ **Mike Pagliarulo:** *We were in spring training in '88, and we were playing the Expos. We were kind of getting beat up a little bit, and Billy was wanting to work on some pickoff plays. And the pitcher, it was some young pitcher, he didn't want to do it. So Billy comes out screaming. Before he hits the white lines, Billy says, "Now listen to me, you son of a bitch, I want you to pick that guy off over there!" And he points to the guy on second base. He says, "I want you to put a pickoff play on right now, and pick his ass off! Do you understand what I'm telling you?" Well, the pitcher goes into the stretch, he turns around, and he picks the son of a bitch off second base! I couldn't believe it. I didn't know whether he picked something up from the base runner or what the hell was going on, but I mean, everybody in the park knew what he was saying, and the guy still picked him off. Little things like that happened all the time. That type of thing showed Billy's presence, and I liked having him on my side.*

As General Patton said, "You must get . . . instant, cheerful, and automatic discipline, so that when we the quarterbacks give the signal of life or death in the near day of battle, you will not think and then act, but act and if you will, think later."[5] When Billy put a sign on from the dugout, a player like Pagliarulo was going to do it. He'd seen enough evidence to have belief in the manager. He'd been taught, not just told, so his response would be automatic. Pagliarulo and others like him didn't follow orders to avoid a fine or a benching. They followed orders because they believed whatever Billy told them to do was right.

▶ **Bobby Meacham:** *What I remember about Billy that helped me a lot was that I thought when I came to the plate or when I was making a play, that I'm just going to do it this way. In other words, when I went out and played, I could just play. When there's runners on first and third and less than two outs, it popped into my head, "OK, push a bunt past the pitcher to get the runner over." Or when there was a double play situation—let's say there's runners on first and second—and it's a slow hit ball, they throw to me at second. Instead of going ahead and relaying it to first, catch the ball at second for the force and throw it right to third. Those are things that Billy would mention to me. They were good plays. So when I was playing, I was able to just go ahead and play. Billy wasn't a second-guesser at all. I remember him telling me, "I'll correct you once and then that's it." And I knew it wasn't just depending on how it turned out to do it that way again, but to do it that way all the time because that's the way you play the game. Sometimes it works, sometimes it doesn't. But he was very consistent and that's how you learn the most. Going out there without being afraid of anything and understanding what your manager needs and wants you to do. He was great at conveying that to everybody.*

Getting Rid of Distractions

With that true understanding between manager and player, there is no hidden agenda. There is a mutual respect and trust based on a shared belief in how to go about a job. The distractions are gone. Billy would do what he could to clear the plate for his players so that all they had to worry about was playing ball. He'd distract the press, he'd distract the owners. He'd do anything.

▶ **Charlie Manuel:** *I remember one time we went into Washington and we'd lost seven, nine, ten in a row. We had a 13-game lead at one time and it was down to like three or four. And he went in there and started a big argument through the press with [Washington manager] Ted Williams, saying Ted Williams wasn't as great as people says he was, that he walked too much, and all this stuff. But he just did that to take attention away from the fact that his team was losing nine games in a row. Or he would get in a big controversy with Earl Weaver. He always tried to upset the other team, especially if he considered them a big threat to us. I mean, he did that on purpose. It wasn't that he meant it or nothing like that, he did it just because he wanted to. He wanted to filter attention somewhere else and kind of get his team back in line.*

▶ **Toby Harrah:** *What Billy would do, that no other manager I played for could do, is he would take all of the pressure off of you as a player, which made it easy. It's the opposition to a certain degree, but a lot of pressure comes from the sportswriters you have to deal with every day when you walk in the locker room. And what Billy would do is he used to piss all the sportswriters off! Everybody was pissed! And Billy was always the focus of attention. When you walked in the locker room, you never worried about the writers ripping your ass. They were always on Billy. All you had to focus on was really playing baseball. Billy was the center of everything. It was Billy this and Billy that. That's the way Billy wanted it. Billy wanted his players not to have to worry about anything but playing. And that's what he was so good at. Like I said, it was kind of like us against the world. It was really Billy against everybody—Billy taking all the brunt of everything.*

Even a famous incident between Billy and Reggie Jackson had that effect. In 1977, Martin and Jackson almost came to actual blows in the Fenway Park dugout—in front of a national television audience—when the Yankees were in Boston for a June series, and Billy thought Jackson had loafed on a play. According to Fred Stanley and Mickey Rivers, the fight had the effect of distracting attention from the players.

▶ **Fred Stanley:** *What I think that situation did more than anything was it almost took the focus off each guy's individual performance and it placed it on "What's going to happen now?" "Who's going to do this?" "Who's going to do that?" All of a sudden it was like there was no pressure anymore, because what we were doing wasn't even center stage anymore. It was them! And all of a sudden, all we had to do was go out to play. It was easy!*

▶ **Mickey Rivers:** *The only thing you hear in the paper, they say, "Oh, Billy did this, Billy did that." Or Reggie. And that'd be it. No other guy got headlines unless the Yankees win. And that'd be the biggest point, we didn't have to worry about nothing. He backed the guys up. A lot of things happened, but it was squashed on account of him because he took care of the guys in that manner.*

Taking Care of the Details

Great leaders worry about every little thing that can go wrong and do so sooner than their competition. Billy was no different in this regard.

▶ **Jackie Moore:** *One thing that I always remember, all the years I spent with Billy, he always said, "Little things. Take care of the little things, and then all the big things will fall in place." He was a stern believer that you learn the fundamentals of baseball, do the fundamentals right, and everything will fall into place for you. And I have never forgotten that, and in my coaching career, I have tried to teach young players that I have coached that same process.*

Little things. Billy Martin had a tendency toward paranoia, and on the diamond, he saw something in every little action. On the field, he fed off of his paranoia in strategically brilliant ways. It wasn't a negative trait or feeling. The other team *was* out to get him, so he wanted to stay at least one step ahead of them. If there is one thing that baseball people agree on when they talk about Billy Martin, it's that he was one step ahead of everyone else in the game.

▶ **Mike Heath:** *He knew. He knew what he wanted to do, and he knew the tendency of other ballplayers. He knew a lot of things. I swear he was always five steps ahead of the other manager. He knew what type manager you go in and play, and what he was going to do. He was on top of things. He wasn't the modern-day guy, where now they have all the charts, and the computers, and this and that, and what he does when the count's 2–2. Billy don't care about that stuff. He really knew the game. He knew clubs, he knew players, he was good at knowing what the other teams and managers were going to do. He was very good at that. That's why he didn't need all the charts and all that stuff.*

▶ **Paul Blair:** *Billy was the kind of guy that didn't let anything get by him. He knew every phase of the game. He knew everything that was happening every single game. That, to me, is what a manager's supposed to do. That's your job. You don't let anybody pull anything over on you.*

▶ **Charlie Manuel:** *He could pick things up quick. You might not believe this, but for some reason, he could steal signs from the other teams. He could pick up leads—if it was a fast runner on first base and he took a lead—the things he did. He would look for things, and he could pick up real quick on things. He could really register in on seeing the game really quick. He would see mistakes. He'd see all the infielders move. He had a good field presence. Those are things that you have to do when you manage a baseball team, too. Those were things that Billy really taught me.*

Dr. Andrew Weil, a leader in today's integration of western medicine and alternative medicine, and the founder of the University of Arizona in Tucson's Program for Integrative Medicine, describes a concept known as "positive paranoia" in his 1972 book *The Natural Mind*. Weil writes, "It is important to distinguish between the two components of paranoia—the seeing of patterns and the negative interpretation of them—something few people bother to do . . . The pattern-forming tendency is an intrinsic function of the unconscious mind. When we allow it to impose itself on our perceptions, we see relationships between things that are not apparent to other people."[6]

Billy could pick up on those relationships. He understood patterns, even very subtle patterns, and the impact they would have on a ballgame and season. For instance, Billy taught Matt Keough a lesson about the importance of patterns once when the pitcher coasted through the final innings of an easy win.

▶ **Matt Keough:** *The worst ass-chewing I ever got from Billy in my whole life was after I won a game 7–2. First game of a series, I got a 7–0 lead in the ninth inning, and I gave up two basically meaningless runs and closed the game out. I came off the field feeling like I was Superman. And the clubhouse guy says, "Billy wants to see you in his office." I thought he was going to hug me and tell me how great I was, but he started just ramming my ass. "You no good piece of shit!" And I'm thinking, "What is wrong?" He said, "Those two runs you gave up in the ninth inning, they think they can play with us tomorrow!" He said, "That was brutal! You gotta close them out right then and there to make them come to the ballpark tomorrow and give up!" And I walked out of his office half stunned. But he was right. Because if I had closed 'em out in the ninth inning, and embarrassed 'em, they wouldn't have shown up the next day. And the next day they did beat us.*

Sometimes even *not* doing something is the result of conscious thought. Bobby Meacham, a great bunter, never squeezed for Billy, a manager who loved the squeeze bunt. To Billy's way of thinking, it made so much sense for Meacham to squeeze bunt that the other team had to be expecting it, so he could actually exploit their expectations to help a hitter who needed to capitalize on every advantage.

▶ **Bobby Meacham:** *I bunted a lot. He always had me bunt runners over . . . But yet I never squeezed with him as a manager. Never. And guess how many pitchouts I got when I was up at the plate with a guy on third? A zillion! So I was always hitting 2–0, 3–1, with a runner on third and less than two outs. That's why I drove in so many runs when Billy was managing.*

That's one little example of how Billy believed that he could force events to flow in a manner that would generate a win for his club. Martin believed that "Things don't just happen by accident on the field. They usually happen for a reason."[7] Billy even sought to take advantage of the playing field itself, depending on the strengths of his hitters, pitchers, or fielders.

▶ **Lenny Randle:** *Billy would go out with the ground crew to do stuff. He'd tilt the field so we could bunt and use our speed or he'd grow the grass higher. So he would deal with the ground crew early. A lot of people don't even know about that kind of strategy. He'd say, "The grass in Minnesota's thick, it's a good place to bunt, because they don't have fast infielders and their pitchers are sinkerball pitchers. So they have thicker grass to slow the ball up so it won't go through, so the infield can get it. So bunt on it."*

With Billy, the tiniest of details were exploited to gain an edge. At the same time, he always worried about what the opposing manager might try to do to him. One time in 1981, when he had curveballer Rick Langford pitching for his A's against the Mariners, Billy noticed that the batter's box looked odd. As it turns out, Seattle manager Maury Wills had increased the length of the box by a foot, so that his batters could move up and hit Langford's pitches before they broke. Rather than gain an advantage against Billy, Wills was hit with a two-game suspension when Billy pointed the box out to the umpires.

Because Billy was more active, more knowledgeable, and more thirsty for an edge than most of his peers, he did actually control games better than most. He could react to a situation, and it enabled him to operate without panicking and to quickly pull the trigger on an idea.

▶ **Bobby Meacham:** *One time, Billy wanted to walk a guy intentionally instead of pitching to him. But then he thought, "Maybe they'll squeeze with this guy, so I'll pitchout four times in a row instead." And so he pitched out once, it's 1–0. He pitched out twice, it's 2–0. Now they think, "Aw, he screwed up. We got Billy this time. We'll squeeze on this pitch here." He pitched out again, and the guy was coming home on a squeeze! He was gonna pitchout four times anyway and put the guy on,* *but he figured, "Why not just pitchout? Maybe we'll catch this dummy squeezing." And we get the runner coming home from third!*

Another time in Detroit, slugger Willie Horton was unable to play because of an injury. Rather than announce to the media that Horton was hurt, Billy instead created the impression that Horton was benched for insubordination. This way, the other manager still had to worry about Horton coming off the bench to hit.

▶ **Willie Horton:** *I remember a time during '72, I couldn't have played if I wanted to. He made big things that me and him were having problems. We sat and talked about that and laughed about it. I'll never forget that. I learned then that as long as they're thinking on the other side I could hit or pinch hit, the other manager's managing a little different. And I couldn't have played if I had wanted to!*

In Billy's own words, "As a manager, I like to stay on top of things. I want control over everything on the field . . . I wrote the form for the Yankees' scouting reports. I told them what I wanted to know, not what they wanted to tell me. The little things I want to know to get an edge. Will the other manager squeeze? Does he like to hit-and-run? On what count? With which players? Who's swinging the bat well for them? I like my scouts to scout the other managers as well as the players."[8] Because Billy worried constantly about the other manager, he prepared a little differently, and it may have enabled him to control the late innings better.

▶ **Jackie Moore:** *The matchups that he would see were going to happen by knowing the other club, by knowing the opposing manager, what pitchers that he had already used, or what pinch hitter he had already used were a big part of Billy's success. He could see what was going to develop in the last inning, in who was left on the bench, and so he could get the matchup that he wanted. There were never really any surprises. It was a sense throughout the way the particular game was developing, that he always had the right matchup at the right time. It's a matter of knowing your personnel, knowing what matchup you want,* and forcing the other manager to play his hand first. He was one of the best at this.

▶ **Ron Hassey:** You're watching a ballgame, and all of a sudden you get in the late innings and he already had the guy up in the bullpen being ready for any type of move that the opposing manager was going to do. He was ready for it. When you're playing against him, you're always looking for the trick play, the double steal. You had to be careful because he would do those things against you. Ninety percent of the teams won't do that stuff. But knowing Billy, he might do it, and he did do it.

Gathering and Digesting Information

Billy made his moves by feel, not by using numbers, formulas, or quantification. Because he lived the game, the moves were in his blood, and his mind was constantly digesting information he was picking up in late-night conferences with the baseball men of his time. The image of Billy as a good-timing, late-night imbiber is true, but it is important to consider that Billy usually was still caught up in the game even as he sat in a bar or pressroom drinking with cronies.

▶ **Mickey Morabito:** Back then in the league, most of the stadiums had these pressrooms, like in the old Metropolitan Stadium in Minnesota. After the game it became a bar. The Bard's Room in Chicago in Comiskey Park was another. The room on the roof they had up in Fenway Park in Boston. And after every game, win or lose, Billy would get dressed and walk up there, because there'd always be some old-time baseball people there. Chicago was the greatest. When [Chicago owner Bill] Veeck had it, it was the greatest after-hours bar in the world. They'd sit there till three, four, five o'clock in the morning, and because Veeck owned the team, he'd keep the bar open and tell the people to keep pouring. Billy would go up there with his coaches and they'd just talk baseball with everyone. It was incredible. Billy loved this more than anything else—sitting in a bar talking ball, especially with old-time baseball people. There were times on getaway day I'd have to go up just to drag him out, because we had to catch a flight. He loved talking about the game, talking about situations.

▶ **Ray Negron:** *Win or lose, after those games he would be in the press-room having his drinks, and everybody would be gathered around him. That's where he picked up a lot of stuff, from managers or coaches of other teams. He worked those coaches. Because you had to stop off there in order to go upstairs to the bus. So right away as they're leaving, they know Billy's there, so everybody would go see Billy, and everybody would be around him bullshitting. And Billy, he would volunteer a little to get a lot. He'd say, "This guy can't do this right now, he's not running now." And they think he's drinking too much. He'd say, "My right fielder's just not throwing the ball too good right now." And boom, they try to use shit against him. He did that a lot.*

▶ **Bill Reedy:** *I know scouts that would come to my place, when Billy was going to get in the playoffs, that were scouting other teams. They would come and give Billy a scouting report about the other team, because they all liked Billy.*

Billy's coaches remember the camaraderie and also the work that would get done in these late-night sessions, whether in bars, press-rooms, or on planes.

▶ **Jackie Moore:** *That was the way of baseball then. You didn't just play nine innings. We would all assemble in a bar or wherever. It was a 24-hour job. A lot of scouts that would be at the game or a lot of baseball people knew, "OK, this is where I'll find the other guys, and that's where we'll be talkin' baseball." A lot of your information would be one coaching staff or one manager talking to a club that just played the other club two or three days ago, just passing along the information. And that's part of the game nowadays that's lost.*

▶ **Charlie Silvera:** *He'd have his whole staff . . . There was always some-place to go. I was more or less his recording secretary. He'd come up with some sort of an idea. He'd say, "Charlie, put that down, we'll do that tomorrow." Sometimes I'd have a helluva time reading it after a couple of beers, writing in a dark bar, but you know, we got things accomplished.*

▶ **George Mitterwald:** *As a coach, a lot of times people say, "Well yeah, the coaches are going out and Billy, they're all going out drinking." But you know what? We were always talking baseball. In spring training, we were talking about the team. We were always together. We were through usually by 1:30, two in the afternoon, and we'd go out and we were talking about different things that we were going to do. Things that we should try. Who we liked, who we didn't like, who was looking good. And when you do that, when you talk about different things, and you get input from all different people, I think it just kind of opens things up. To me, it was a good feeling, because we talked about things. Billy was the final say, but he always listened to his coaches.*

In today's game, there is much more computer-generated knowledge coming from analytical bureaus and scouting departments. While there may be more information available, it isn't necessarily better information, especially in a "people business" like baseball where observation remains a vital skill. In the late 1970s, as computers started to work their way into baseball, much of the old school, including Billy, resisted. The intrusion of statistics into the game brought out the sarcastic side of Billy, because it ran counter to the psychological style of managing that he favored. Once in New York, when the heat was being turned up by ownership, Billy told a writer, "If you look in a computer, we should be ahead by 12 games. But the computer never played baseball, and neither did the guy who uses it."[9]

▶ **Mickey Morabito:** *Billy used to tell me when they started bringing the stats down, "I don't want to know that. I know what this guy can do against this guy." And he did. He'd remember at-bats two or three years ago, what this guy did against this pitcher, and he wouldn't have to quantify it. Right now, you look at managers in the dugout, they're lookin' at forms and charts. They've got these three-ring binder books with matchups. As long as I knew Billy, I never saw him pull out a book. There were some matchups that didn't work, and he still in his gut felt that this was what he was gonna do, because he just felt, "This guy can* *hit this guy. Don't tell me what the numbers are." So a lot of that was just a gut feel because he's been on a baseball field all his life.*

Stealing Signs

Billy also had a way of picking up the signs of the other teams. The age-old effort to steal signs has always been part of the game, and even as Billy tried to prevent other teams from stealing his signs, he was one of the better artists in stealing them himself.

▶ **Jackie Moore:** *He was good. He watched the opposing coaches and manager at all times, and that was an art back in those days. If you could get this little edge at a crucial point of a game, where the club had a guy at first base, and you knew their steal sign, you could pitchout and throw the guy out at second base. It was a way to win a ballgame. It was an art. A lot of clubs had good guys that could do this, and we changed our signs all the time, and the other clubs would change. But still, once in a while, you could pick something up and you might win a ballgame out of it.*

▶ **Sam Mele:** *He'd say, "Be careful, they're going to steal now," or "They're going to squeeze." I'd say, "Oh, you sure, Billy?" Then it would happen again and again. And it happened too often to be an accident, and he got to be damned good at it. He probably did it before with the Yankees, but he was damned good at it.*

Constant Awareness

To succeed, leaders must maintain constant awareness of the events around them. This includes keeping a vigilant eye on the competition. Intel's Andrew S. Grove, one of the most prominent CEOs of the past decade, is a man who approaches his job from an admittedly paranoid position. The same can be said of Billy. Grove wrote in his top-selling book *Only the Paranoid Survive*, " . . . when it comes to business, I believe in the value of paranoia . . . I believe that the prime responsibility of a manager is to guard constantly against other people's attacks .

. . I worry about competitors. I worry about other people figuring out how to do what we do better or cheaper."[10]

Grove also notes, "You need to plan the way a fire department plans: It cannot anticipate where the next fire will be, so it has to shape an energetic and efficient team that is capable of responding to the unanticipated as well as to any ordinary event."[11] Mickey Rivers reflects back on that ability to respond that Billy had helped cultivate in him, while Mike Heath recalls a situation where while playing against his longtime mentor, he tried to outclass the master, only to see his plan backfire.

▶ **Mickey Rivers:** *In situations, me as a player, and all our players, we know what kind of situation we was in. You got to know a little about the situation. He didn't tell us what to do. He'd say, "All right, now, look around your outfield." You look around the outfield, I see this guy in on me, I'll slap one over his head. Or he'd say, "OK, OK, I see this guy, he ain't going to move too good on third base. You can probably lay one down there. Watch him move. Make him come in on you." So I'll make this guy move on third base if I bunt. If I see a guy standing back on me, shoot, I know that's a hit for me, if I could get the ball down on the ground. You had to look at things like that. He'll let you be on your own, and that's what you like about a manager. And that was one of our biggest pluses. We knew as a team—individuals—what our jobs were. So we wouldn't worry about nobody else. We'd go talk to Billy, and he had the confidence with the guys. When the guys had the confidence, it would be easy for us to do what we had to do.*

▶ **Mike Heath:** *I'll give you a little example. Let's say you had two guys on, first and second. A guy hits a triple, both runs score, kind of ties the ballgame or you're one run up. The very next hitter, less than two outs, he would squeeze the very next pitch to get another run in. Well, I remembered all that playing for him, when he went back to New York. So this situation arose, I mean the same scenario. Couple runs score to tie the ballgame. Well, I pitchout the very next pitch, because the guy that was hitting was a good bunter. He didn't squeeze! I looked over at Billy, and he wagged his finger at me, "No, no, no, no, no, no, no." I mean, tell me? The guy knows! He knew. I didn't forget that.*

Billy summed up his overall strategy and philosophy by saying, "Don't let the little things get by you. That's the way to win. Details. Keeping track of the little things and not missing a thing that happens on the field."[12] Billy's attention to detail manifested itself as awareness.

▶ **Mike Pagliarulo:** *I think real good managers are able to see and hear better than anybody else. Billy could be at one side of the bench, and I could be talking to somebody down at the other side of the bench, and he knew exactly what I was talking about. I don't know how the hell he heard me, but he would scream out a remark about what I was talking about . . . I think it's more of a super awareness or a readiness that guys that are really into the game have. If there was something that went on out there—if I got a double play ball, guys on first and second, and I stepped on third base and threw it over to first—Billy would know the right foot to step on third base with. If I would come in, and I'd get the double play, he'd say, "Lookit, you coulda done it better this way." He was very aware. He didn't miss anything.*

One of Billy's goals was to get the opposition to lose focus. He would try to distract his opponents any way he could, just to try to get that edge, and he used little things to do it that others would ignore.

▶ **Dave Righetti:** *Curt Young was pitching for Oakland, and Curt Young used to start with both feet on the rubber. You're not allowed to start with both feet on the rubber. No big deal—nobody pays any attention to it. Billy did. And Curt Young had pitched pretty good little ballgames against us. So Billy disrupted him. Most managers don't want to do that. Most managers let things like that go and don't want to stir the boat, just try to win the game. Billy says, "To heck with that." First inning, . . . he got the umpire out there. The umpire's saying, "What are you talking about?" But you know what? It affected Curt Young. He's thinking about it, and it gives us an edge. He [Billy] would do what he could. If a guy had a penchant for beating us, he'd try to find a way to beat the guy. He'd do anything.*

Trying to Control the Flow of the Game

Billy also always tried to control the flow of the game—not let the other team do so.

▶ **Fred Stanley:** *He'd have our guys scream at the other players . . . Because if you can get a pitcher to lose focus, that was all Billy's thing. Concentrate on something other than getting the hitter out, for a chance for him making mistakes. We had some explosive guys, with Reggie and Thurman and Graig and Chambliss and even Lou [Piniella]. All of a sudden, the pitcher's in big trouble. And that was his focus.*

▶ **George Mitterwald:** *George Brett, in 1980, he woulda hit .400 if it wasn't for the Oakland A's, I can tell you right now. He hit .390, and I think he hit .217 against us for the year. Billy would find something that he thought might be a weakness, even in a great player like Brett, and he would do something to try to make him mad and get him going, just to get the edge. Billy just threw Brett nothing but slow curveballs. He didn't care who was pitching. He said, "Make him pull the ball!" And Brett used to get so mad. "You're throwing me these slow curves!" he used to yell at Billy all the time, kidding in a way, but not kidding too, because he wanted to hit .400. But that's the way Billy was.*

Billy used the exact same approach in pitching to the era's other great wandsman, his friend Rod Carew. Carew had made hitting a smooth, rhythmic science, and Billy was hoping to cause just that moment's hesitation in him that could break the rhythm.

▶ **Rod Carew:** *It was like a cat and mouse game when I played against him. He knew what I could do, so he was thinking of every possible way of getting me out. He said, "Don't throw him any fastballs, throw him slow breaking balls. Let's see what he thinks about doing with that certain pitch." And that's all he did. That's all he would have the pitchers throw me, and every now and then, they'd try to sneak a fastball by me, and I'd get a base hit. He would just go nuts in the dugout, and I would look over at him and smile, and he would just look at me and smile, like "You got me." I think with the slow breaking balls, he would* *tell guys, "Don't try and trick him. Just try and throw it right over the middle of the plate. Because if you throw it away, he's going to do something with it. If you throw it in on him, he's going to do something. If you throw it just right down the middle of the plate, he might just hesitate and think about it, 'Where am I going to hit this pitch?'"*

Much of Martin's theatrics with umpires also was intended to affect the flow of the game.

▶ **Lenny Randle:** *Strategically, Billy had umpires in his pocket before a game started. He knew the personality of umpires, so he knew how to set the tempo of the game. Most leadoff hitters and second hitters can set the tempo of the game, but Billy did that with his aura. You could just see the other manager and all of them waiting for the drama. Because when he went out, he wouldn't just go out and go over the ground rules, there was always something else going on. "Look, Fergie [Jenkins]'s pitching today. He's going to be nibbling outside. I'm not trying to say give him anything, but just don't squeeze anything. Just call the game both ways." It was almost like a boxing match. Even though they were the umpires, he was like the rules guy. He's planting seeds. Psychologically, he's setting them up.*

Billy was working to get his players every advantage he could, and the players definitely appreciated the effort.

▶ **Paul Blair:** *He didn't let any umpires get the best of him, because if they missed a play, he let them know they missed it. At the end of the season, umpires were more on their job, because they know Billy was going to be on 'em if they messed up something. So it kind of helped us down the stretch. I don't say we got a lot of calls, but they made sure the calls are right. And that's key when you are playing baseball, because if umpires feel that they can get away with something over the managers, they're definitely going to mess over us players. But Billy again, he would not let umpires mess with us. He would take up the fight. And we were all appreciative of the fact that he was definitely on our side.*

▶ **Frank Lucchesi:** *An umpire would miss a pitch, and some of the managers in the dugout might say, "Jeez, he missed that pitch." Billy would scream, "Hey! Looked like a good pitch! Bear down!" He never would hold anything in. That's the big difference. He'd let it out in an honest way. With the ballplayers, they figure, "Hey, he's sticking up for us."*

Said Martin, "There's very little new in baseball except what a sharp, alert manager can think of to get an edge. There isn't a great deal of opportunity for innovation in baseball, but every little bit helps."[13] In today's fast-paced, Web-enabled world, first-mover advantage is critical. Like Billy Martin says, you have to be aggressive, see the competitive landscape, and be prepared to act fast.

Notes

1. Randy Galloway, "Rangers Column," *Sporting News*, October 13, 1973.

2. Billy Martin and Peter Golenbock, *Number 1* (New York: Delacorte Press, 1980), p. 15.

3. Phil Pepe, "Yankees Column," *Sporting News*, February 21, 1976.

4. Noel M. Tichy and Stratford Sherman, *Control Your Destiny or Someone Else Will* (New York: HarperBusiness, 1994), p. 110.

5. Roger Nye, *The Patton Mind* (Garden City Park, N.Y.: Avery Publishing Group, 1993), p. 45.

6. Andrew Weil, *The Natural Mind* (Boston: Houghton Mifflin, 1972), pp. 170–171.

7. Billy Martin and Phil Pepe, *Billyball* (Garden City, N.Y.: Doubleday & Company, 1987), p. 3.

8. Ibid., pp. 22–23.

9. Murray Chass, "Yankees Lose, 3–2; Rosen Irks Martin," *New York Times*, June 1, 1978.

10. Andrew S. Grove, *Only the Paranoid Survive* (New York: Currency Doubleday, 1986), p. 3.

11. Ibid., pp. 5–6.

12. Neal Ashby, "Inside the Mind of a Manager," *Family Weekly*, July 17, 1977, p. 11.

13. Martin and Pepe, p. 23.

Organizational Dynamics

The Case of the Abysmal Athletics

When Billy Martin took over the dismal Oakland Athletics just before spring training 1980, the team had already taken on many nicknames other than the standard tag of A's. Clever scribes had labeled them the "Triple A's," the "Pathetics," and even "baseball's Boat People." Only 300,000 fans had bothered to show up to catch the team's embarrassing 54-win, 108-loss season in 1979. The baseball world was laughing at owner Charlie Finley, his losing ballclub, and the organization he had gutted. But when Martin took over, he saw a group of young players who were hungry, who had potential, and who were sick and tired of losing.

▶ **Mike Norris:** *We were all like a bunch of misfits. Didn't fit in where we were previously, or in my case, I had never gone to another team and couldn't get away, so I was just somebody sitting there waiting for an opportunity, too. But we were just all really wanting to prove that we were major league ballplayers. And I think, just getting that opportunity the way we did, we all were ready for it at that time in our careers.*

As usual, Billy arrived trumpets blaring, telling the press, "I'm going after a pennant . . . I'm not going to rebuild anything. You may not believe it now, but the Oakland A's will beat out the California Angels this year."[1] (The Angels had won the AL West in 1979.) On the first day of spring training, Billy told his players, "If you don't want to win, get

123

your stuff and get out. If you don't give your best effort, you're gone. But if you bust your hump for me, I'll bust mine for you."[2]

And he did bust, shifting himself into a hands-on teaching mode he hadn't had to use as much with his veteran Yankee clubs. PR man and traveling secretary Mickey Morabito had been close to Billy in New York, and he had joined him in Oakland. He saw a different side of the manager that spring, as Billy adjusted his style to his new organization and its needs.

▶ **Mickey Morabito:** *He did things I didn't see him do the last couple years in New York. I mean, he was on the field. He had a very, very young team. He had that great young outfield of [Rickey] Henderson, [Dwayne] Murphy, and [Tony] Armas, which at the time was probably as good a defensive outfield as I've ever seen. And Billy fell for young kids. He fell in love with this little second baseman we had, Jeff Cox. He looked and played like Billy played. He was scrappy. Those were the kind of guys he wanted out there. I think he kinda got those guys started from day one. He told these guys that they're not as bad as they were, and they're gonna surprise some people. And he kept harping on that, and sure enough, they were a bunch of young players that started making the improvement that they were due to make.*

When people think of Billy, they tend to think of the high-octane images. But his bag of tricks also included a finely honed sense of organizational dynamics, and this sense ultimately had more to do with Oakland's turnaround than any dirt-kicking or finger-pointing abrasiveness. Building a baseball team is like building a puzzle, and Billy Martin was the best at seeing how each of his 25 players, plus his coaches, could fit into a complete, winning puzzle. Billy didn't give his A's players talent. They had that. But he utilized that talent correctly. That was his art.

▶ **Matt Keough:** *One hundred and eight losses, and it was the same team. He could evaluate talent like no other. He went in, he found eight guys. He said, "Listen, I got a 40-man roster here. Eight guys are going to make me a winner or not." He picked the five pitchers and the three* *outfielders, and he built the team around them. Mike Heath was a big part of it too, because Billy basically shut down the American League running-wise with Mike. And he just augmented those with other players—the Fred Stanleys, the Wayne Grosses, the Mitchell Pages. All those guys. He just basically realized what his strength was, and the other guys were just going to be part of it, but he was going to win with the eight guys.*

By the end of 1980, Billy's first year in Oakland, the A's had finished in second place, posting a better than .500 record and winning 29 games more than the previous season. (Incidentally, the California Angels finished in sixth place.) The sense of gloom had been lifted and was replaced with a new sense of possibility. Sportswriter Red Smith summed up the accomplishment, noting, "With no important personnel changes, Martin gave the A's a new character, new spirit, new goals, new leadership, and a new style of play. Out on the coast, they call it Billyball."[3]

How did he do it? First, by molding the three outfielders. Rickey Henderson, Dwayne Murphy, and Tony Armas had each been groomed to play center, so Billy had to figure a new mix, depending on which could play another position. Murphy could only play center, so he remained there. Henderson could play left, so he went there. Armas could play anywhere, so he was assigned to right.

Next came getting the five young starting pitchers to throw strikes and get the ball hit to the outstanding young outfielders.

▶ **Matt Keough:** *They taught us how to pitch to our outfielders. And we learned. They taught us how to throw strikes, keep our pitch counts down. And we learned. We knew that Billy was trying to do the best he could, that when the ball got hit, somebody was going to catch it. And that was very difficult for anybody that played in '77, '78, '79 on that team, because we didn't have anybody that could catch the ball.*

Next came building the confidence of the young pitchers in their outfielders and in their manager's ability to position them correctly. In previous years, the pitchers had little confidence in the fielders. Now, they began to gain that confidence. And the pitchers knew Billy was teaching the outfielders.

▶ **Matt Keough:** *I cannot tell you what it's like to have Rod Carew hit a line drive down the left field line that's going to hit the chalk, and Rickey Henderson's standing there and catches it. Because Billy Martin knew Rod, managed him. He knew where he hit the ball. We had some of the most ugly defensive alignments, and you'd give up a line drive, and it would go right to a guy. And you would just come off the field going, "Jesus Christ, I've never seen this before." You would see balls that would get hit that would be base hits, and there would be a guy standing there. You know it's not an accident. It was all in his mind, like going onto a hard drive on a computer. So when pitchers see that, you say, "Wow!" You learn. One guy can do it for you, and that's a great burden not to have. Every time a guy hit a ball to a certain spot, he made a mental note of it, before there was spray charts and computer stuff that I do now. I laugh because it was already in his head.*

Next came getting the pitchers a few runs with which to work.

▶ **Mike Norris:** *He realized that we didn't have a big run-producing ballclub. But we had a lot of speed, so he utilized that. We had a few trick plays that would be able to get us one to two runs, maybe three runs with an error. Between Rickey, Dwayne Murphy, Armas, or Cliff Johnson, we would score three or four runs. And the pitching staff obviously weren't giving up more than three a game, and that's how we beat guys. But he came in and really showed us how to be able to manufacture runs. And that was an awesome thing to see materialize. See a guy get on, get bunted over, steal third base. He's over on third with one out. Fly ball to the outfield—boom—we got one run already. And that's a good thing to go out there, and you're already 1–0 after the first inning. Really helps the pitching staff out a lot.*

As the turnaround began, opponents started looking for an explanation. One explanation around the pressrooms for the dramatic improvement among the pitchers was that the Oakland staff was throwing the illegal spitball.

▶ **Matt Keough:** *Billy played that stuff up, because once again, he knew that if the hitters thought you had something—we used to laugh because all you had to do was put in somebody's mind that you were throwing a spitter and you could throw high fastballs by 'em all day long. And Billy used to play off that. Whether we did or whether we didn't was irrelevant. It was how you win the game.*

Next, Billy and his pitching coach, Art Fowler, had to build up the inner strength in the starters so that they could go all the way and finish what they started. Some of it was mere knowledge of how to pitch, but some of it was more.

▶ **Mike Norris:** *What happened was, we learned how to pitch to people that third time around the lineup. That's the whole key to why these kids today can't get through the sixth and seventh inning—they don't know how to get through the third time in the lineup. That's when the hitters have timed you. They know basically what you have by then. You've lost about five miles off your fastball, so now you have to be able to learn how to get them out on your own. Now is when you have to get a strikeout or a pop-up in the infield or something like that. Manufacture your own out. And we learned how to do that. And that would enable us to get to the ninth inning. And then it's just a matter of guts from then on. We knew we didn't have a great bullpen, so that was the fire that you lit up under yourself. And then at that point, you start taking pride in going nine. So it really became virtually almost a joke that we were going nine.*

▶ **Matt Keough:** *We just learned how to pitch in the air and to our outfielders, and we just learned never to look in the bullpen. But we all wanted to win, and he pushed for us in contracts and everything else so we didn't look at it negatively. If Rick Langford pitched a 14-inning complete game, I wanted to do it. And if I did it, [Steve] McCatty wanted to do it. And if McCatty did, Norris wanted to do it, and it was just a nonending type of thing.*

Finally, Billy worked with catcher Mike Heath so that Heath could serve as an enforcer to keep that intensity level up.

▶ **Mike Heath:** *He always told me to talk to the pitchers. The communication is the biggest part. He'd say, "You gotta push some of these guys. You gotta learn their psychological makeup and make 'em pitch, because so many of 'em just get content." He'd tell me, "You have to go out there and chew a little ass every once in a while to get 'em going."*

It is hard to grasp Billy's accomplishment with the A's in this day and age of free agency, when team owners simply go out and offer huge salaries to lure star players. But back in 1980, in a different baseball era, Billy Martin went out and built an entirely new A's organization without any money or any new players. He built his team by encouraging the young players that were already there with his unique leadership talents—and the team won, the team played an exciting brand of ball, and the team drew fans.

▶ **Mickey Morabito:** *It was great. I think the people wanted something here, and the media wanted something. He just added instant credibility to the team. That year was just kind of an amazing year. Billy basically took the same exact team that lost 108 games in 1979 and all of a sudden we played .500 that year and challenged for the division lead most of the year. The same group all of a sudden just overachieved in 1980!*

Martin brought the best out of each player through one-on-one psychology and disciplined group instruction. At the same time, he pulled the entire organization together in a way that gelled and produced wins.

Managing by Using the Talent at Hand

As a manager, Billy Martin looked at what he had, not what he lacked, and he found a way to win. If he had speed, he used speed. If he had power, he used power. If he had strong relief pitching, he used strong relief pitching. Often an organization has glaring weaknesses that are easily identifiable. However, because of budgetary constraints or any other number of problems, the talent the leader seemingly needs to solve the organization's problems is not available. For Martin, the solution meant utilizing the resources he had. In other words, Billyball meant making the most of the talent at hand by using psychology, by generating excitement among the people who were there, and by pushing those people to their limits.

Earl Weaver, the famed Orioles manager and Billy's arch rival throughout the 1970s, considered Billy's realistic approach to guiding players as his top skill as a manager. According to Weaver, "Billy's teams don't have any particular style. That's why he's so good. Look at the teams he's had in Minnesota, Detroit, Texas, New York, and now Oakland. The first thing you notice is that no two of them are alike. Martin always looks at his talent first, then manages accordingly."[4]

For example, Billy brought the 1980 A's from last place to second in one season by unleashing their great speed on the base paths and their scrappy attitude. His club swiped 175 bases for the year. Eight years earlier, Billy had won the AL East title with an aging Tiger team that stole only 17 bases the entire season! Said Billy, "One basic rule for any manager is to manage according to his personnel. A good manager doesn't try to adapt his personnel to his style of managing; a good manager changes his style of managing to suit his personnel."[5] Billy was always able to change his style and get results.

▶ **Mickey Morabito:** *To me this is the greatness of Billy. Today, a manager gets pigeonholed. But Billy was amazing. You could never pigeonhole Billy, because he took what he had. If it was a veteran team, he was able to relate and manage a veteran team. If it was a team of kids, he did some things a little bit differently to motivate those type of players. To me, that speaks volumes, which I don't think gets as much credit as it deserves. In this day and age, I think every manager gets pigeonholed in being a specialist. I mean, "Well, I can only manage a veteran group," or "I'm only good with kids." Billy just made do with whatever group he had. He made them better.*

▶ **Ron Hassey:** *Some managers can't change. This is the way they do it, they've always done it this way, and they think that's the right way. Billy could change. In Oakland, he did a lot of things because of the type of team he had. He managed the team the way his players were. Sometimes you have to change your thinking and your philosophy on how to manage because your team is a different type of ballclub, and he did those things. And he did it outstanding in Oakland. In New York in 1985, I think he sat back more. He knew he had Rickey [Henderson]. Rickey was outstanding that year. He got on base and it was like a double—you knew he was going to steal. He got things rolling for us. Billy really didn't have to do much offensively, just maybe setting that lineup differently a little bit here and there, like moving [Don] Mattingly into the second spot, or [Mike] Pagliarulo, moving him around a little bit. As soon as he took over that ballclub, we started moving.*

▶ **Buck Showalter:** *I think a lot of people come in and ask players to adjust their style, which I think's a mistake. I hope I don't have a style. I hope it's depending on what type of players I have. It better be, because it's about the players. When someone comes up and says, "What kind of manager are you?" well, if I got eight bruisers that can hit the ball where the grass don't grow, we're going to play a long-ball game. If we don't, then we're going to get some rabbits that can run. Ideally, you'd like to have both, but it doesn't happen that way much.*

Billy had to adapt in New York as well as in Oakland. In 1985, Billy managed the Yankees to a 97-win second-place finish, juggling a pitching staff of only two legitimate starters—Ron Guidry and 45-year-old Phil Niekro—with renowned flake Joe Cowley, a wide cast of middle relievers, and ace closer Dave Righetti. He had to understand who could do what on any given day in order to help win each game, because he didn't have the type of staff where he could just roll out a great starter for seven innings and then hand the ball over to Righetti to finish up.

▶ **Dave Righetti:** *What'd we have, three guys? Cowley, he won 12 games. He was thin in the brains, so we didn't know how long he was going to* *last! But if I'm not mistaken, there's probably three of us in the bullpen that pitched 100 innings in 1985—me and Fish [Brian Fisher] and [Rich] Bordi, and that's unheard of. I was the stopper, now the stopper throws 50. But he let me pitch. If I tied a ballgame up, I stayed in until it was over one way or another. So I'd go two, three innings for him. He'd done that the first day he came to the team in '85. Guidry was in a bases-loaded jam in Texas, nobody out, sixth inning. "Rags, get in there." "What?" I ended up throwing four innings. I loved it! I absolutely loved it! But everybody thinks of it as too early. I could care less what it was. I wanted to win.*

In today's competitive world, being short-staffed and under-budgeted is a way of life, and it's not going to change any time soon. It's as if all of today's business managers are taking over their own version of the 1980 A's or handling the 1985 Yankee pitching staff. We need to respond the way Billy did: by seeing the pluses and making the very best of them, and for the time being, ignoring the minuses.

Billy Martin never belittled the players he had. He built them up. Imagine if Billy had gone to Oakland and, instead of working with the 2–17 Matt Keough to help him win, openly longed to have Catfish Hunter with him again. He certainly wouldn't have turned his A's around that way, by wishing for a staff he didn't have. Said Billy, "One of the secrets is knowing what your players can do. That's what it takes to win. I don't ask guys to bunt who can't bunt. I don't ask guys to hit and run who don't make contact."[6] And he didn't ask guys to be Catfish Hunter who weren't Catfish Hunter. He just asked them to be as much as they could be.

▶ **Buck Showalter:** *He's a winner. They used to say about Bear Bryant [the winning college football coach], where I grew up, and I felt the same way about Billy—you always felt like he could take his and beat yours, then take yours and beat his. I think . . . that there were a lot of ways he tried to show you could win baseball games. To have that statement they always make—"You're only as good as your players. Good players make good managers. Bad players make bad managers"—I think Billy kind of broke that excuse. You can make chicken salad, if you're willing to try to figure out a way to work to your players' strength.*

▶ **Mickey Klutts:** *It's just the way he would constantly motivate. His job as a manager was to bring out strengths in everybody and to stay away from weaknesses. That was his job. If you had a weakness, he was going to keep you away from your weaknesses, however he could on that ballclub. And every player has weaknesses—everybody. Even a Mike Piazza has weaknesses.*

▶ **Jackie Brown:** *He was a good judge of talent, I thought, and I always felt like he knew what you were capable of doing. He expected more out of Ferguson Jenkins than he did out of Jackie Brown. He expects you to do what you're capable of doing, and that's all he asks you to do. That was what always amazed me about him. He did not expect Jackie Brown to go throw shutouts. He expected Jackie Brown to win games 4–3 and 5–4. And that's what he told me. He expected Fergie to win some games 1–0, but he expects Jackie to win the 4–3 and 5–4 ballgames. That's just the way that he went at it.*

That's what it takes to win at anything, including business. Exploit the strengths you have, and make your personnel feel good about those strengths. Try to put your staff members in situations where they can succeed, and protect them from situations where they will fail. Don't cry about the holes in your organization. Don't continually let your staff know how great your last place of employment was or how strong the last department you managed was. That only demeans your current staff and gives the impression that you don't really want to be there. Billy Martin, in any of his non-Yankee managerial jobs, could easily have dwelled on his glory days playing and managing the Bronx Bombers, but he didn't.

▶ **Tom Grieve:** *He might on occasion talk about his days with the Yankees. He talked about it enough to where you knew what he felt about it, but he didn't spend the days going, "Now, when I was with the Yankees . . ." He didn't do that at all. I mean, if he did that I think he would have lost a lot of respect of the players. It's like, "Hey, if the Yankees are that great, why don't you go work for them?" No, he didn't do that.*

When faced with a challenging new situation, go headlong into your new task. Work to fill the gaps in your organization by finding or develop-

Early 1950s: As a member of five Yankee World Championship clubs, Billy Martin earned a reputation for doing the "little things" necessary to win, such as breaking up double plays. He's shown doing just that in this game against the Chicago White Sox at Yankee Stadium. *(Billy Martin, Jr., Collection)*

Early 1950s: In 1951, Billy Martin met Mickey Mantle, the country boy from Oklahoma who would go on to smash 536 home runs as a New York Yankee. The two immediately became best friends, and were as close as brothers right up until Billy's death in 1989. *(Billy Martin, Jr., Collection)*

Early 1950s: Whitey Ford (far right), was the third member of the Yankees' legendary Three Musketeers. He, Billy Martin (center), and Mickey Mantle (left), partied their way across Manhattan and America, racking up big-league bar tabs along with their championships. *(Billy Martin, Jr., Collection)*

1953: Charlie Silvera, Billy Martin, and Lonnie Logson of Portland Oregon—along with an NYPD horse—celebrate the Yankees' 1953 World Series win and fifth consecutive World Championship. For the Series, Billy batted .500, set a record for most hits in a six-game series with twelve, and won the MVP award.

(Billy Martin, Jr., Collection)

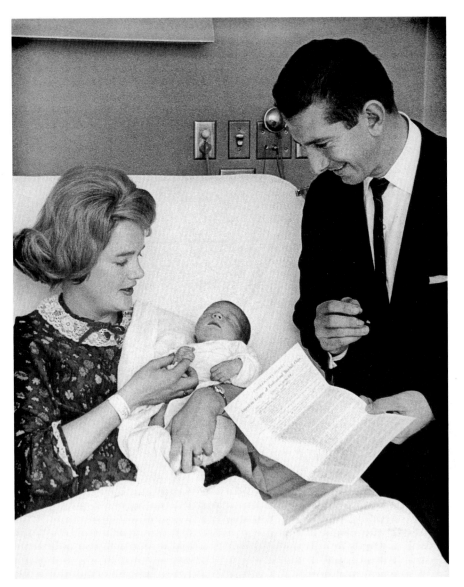

1964: Billy Martin's years playing, scouting, coaching, and managing for the Minnesota Twins organization from 1961 through 1969 represented the most stable period of his family life. In 1964, Billy and wife Gretchen became proud parents of a son, Billy Joe, who was immediately inked to a Twins contract by his proud dad.

(Billy Martin, Jr., Collection)

Late 1960s: When Billy Martin launched his managerial career for the 1969 Twins, his years of learning as a devoted player, scout, and coach were about to emerge in the form of an aggressive, war-like style of play that very much reflected the man himself.

(Billy Martin, Jr., Collection)

1969: No matter where he managed, Billy Martin's pinstripe pals were never too far away. In this photo from the Twins spring training camp, Billy visits with the Yankee Clipper himself, Joe DiMaggio, a fellow Bay Area Italian-American who had befriended Billy during the latter's rookie season of 1950. *(Billy Martin, Jr., Collection)*

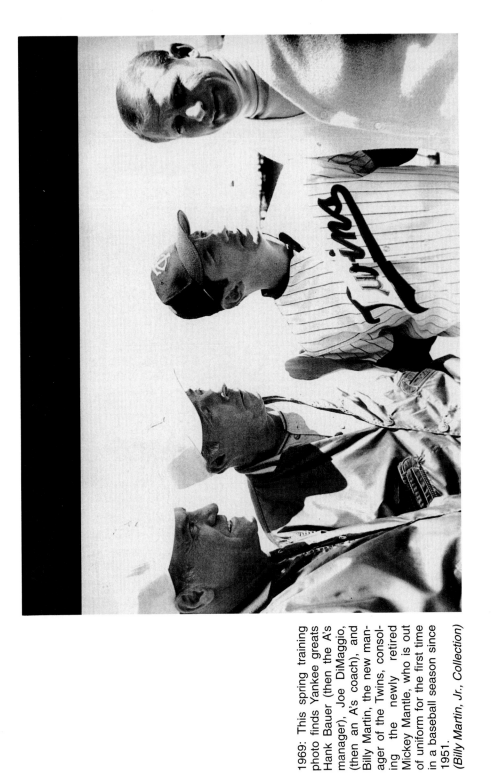

1969: This spring training photo finds Yankee greats Hank Bauer (then the A's manager), Joe DiMaggio, (then an A's coach), and Billy Martin, the new manager of the Twins, consoling the newly retired Mickey Mantle, who is out of uniform for the first time in a baseball season since 1951.
(Billy Martin, Jr., Collection)

1969: Twins rookie manager Billy Martin shows the strain of a tough loss. Through the years, Billy's players continually marveled at just how much he *hated* to lose. A man of many insecurities, winning gave Billy the self-worth and recognition he craved.

(Billy Martin, Jr., Collection)

Guest Consignor, "Mickey Mantel" at Garret - Wynne Angus Sale, December,,'65 From Left to Right.- Horace Garrett., "Cy" Winkler., Billy Martin., Bedford Wynne and Wayne Goodnite.

1965: Billy Martin's father-in-law, "Cy" Winkler, made his living as a cattle agent. In this photograph, Mickey Mantle (third from the left) has shown up to help move some product at the Garret-Wynne Angus Sale. Billy, fourth from the left, saw himself as a cowboy, and in 1979 would open "Billy Martin's Western Wear" on New York's Madison Avenue.   *(Billy Martin, Jr., Collection)*

Late 1960s: This photo shows Billy, Jr., Twins manager Billy, Sr., and his wife, Gretchen, hanging out by the pool in Florida while attending baseball's winter meetings.

(Billy Martin, Jr., Collection)

1969: Five-year-old Billy Martin, Jr., was a fixture around the Twins' Metropolitan Stadium when his dad moved into the manager's office in 1969. Here he's seen bringing some heavy lumber out to his proud father, who was busy cavorting with members of the White Sox coaching staff.   *(Billy Martin, Jr., Collection)*

1969: This Family Day photograph shows Billy Martin with his second wife, Gretchen, and five-year-old son Billy, Jr., on the field at Minnesota's old Metropolitan Stadium.
(Billy Martin, Jr., Collection)

1970: He was known as "Billy the Kid," and in many ways, Billy Martin never grew up. He always related very well to kids, whether in groups, or one on one (as shown above), and gave freely of his time and resources to them. Only days before his death in 1989, Billy gave a reading of *'Twas the Night before Christmas* to 2,000 underprivileged children in Tampa, Florida.   *(Billy Martin, Jr., Collection)*

1971: Members of the Yankees Dynasty of the 1950s meet in St. Petersburg, Florida, during the spring of 1971. From left to right are Billy Martin's mentor Casey Stengel, former teammate and Tiger coach Charlie Silvera, Billy, and former teammate Hank Bauer, then managing the Mets' AAA club at Norfolk, Virginia.

(Billy Martin, Jr., Collection)

Billy Martin had a soft spot for children, and throughout his life, he did what he could to put smiles on the faces of the kids with whom he came in contact, and willingly used his name to assist those in need, like the disabled boy in this picture.

(Billy Martin, Jr., Collection)

1972: Though he's remembered for his on-field intensity, Billy Martin was a practical joker who loved to horse around with his players. Here, the manager of the 1972 AL East champions has probably witnessed one of his infielders taking a fungo where it hurts. *(Billy Martin, Jr., Collection)*

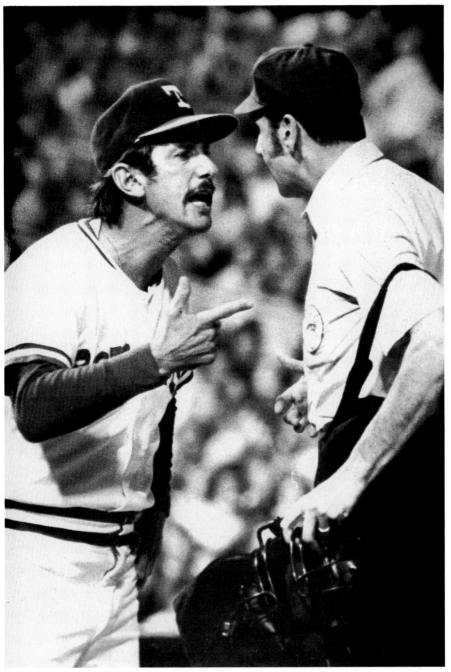

1974: In 1973, the Texas Rangers lost 105 games, so when Billy Martin came to town talking pennant, few believed him. Yet his charismatic leadership immediately sparked the Rangers to second place with an amazing 86-win season, earning Billy the first of four Associated Press Manager of the Year Awards.

(Billy Martin, Jr., Collection)

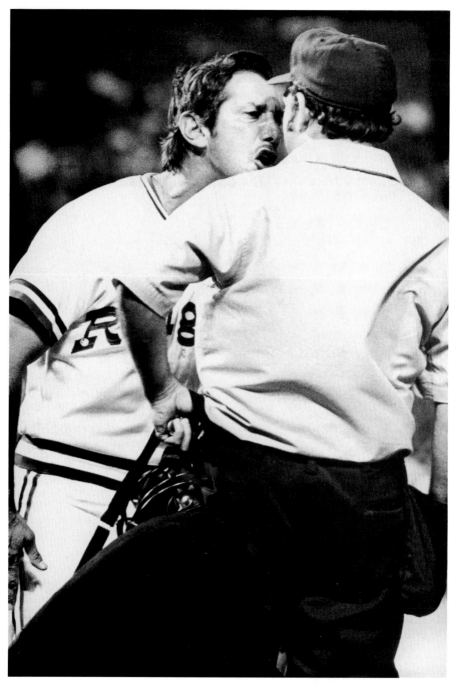

1974: Billy Martin probably got the hook for this argument in a game at the Rangers' Arlington Stadium. On one occasion, managing in the Watergate era inspired Billy to "wire" leadoff man Lenny Randle so that Billy could prove that the "men in blue" were "out to get him." *(Billy Martin, Jr., Collection)*

1976: When Billy Martin took over the managerial reigns of the Yankees, he immediately added his former teammate, the one-and-only Yogi Berra, to his coaching staff. Talk about an experienced guy to have by your side—to this day no one has played in more World Series games than Berra. *(Billy Martin, Jr., Collection)*

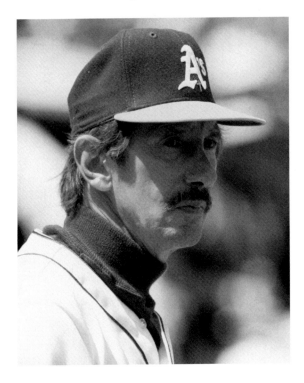

Circa 1980–1982: In 1980, Billy Martin installed his swashbuckling brand of bare-knuckled baseball into his hometown Oakland A's. By 1981, Billy had a team that had lost 108 games in 1979 playing in the AL Championship Series versus—who else—the New York Yankees.

(Oakland A's)

1976: Billy Martin enjoys a moment in his true home—the Yankee Stadium home dugout—during the pennant-winning 1976 season. By the look on his face, he's probably just painted Orioles skipper Earl Weaver into a corner.

(Marty Appel Collection)

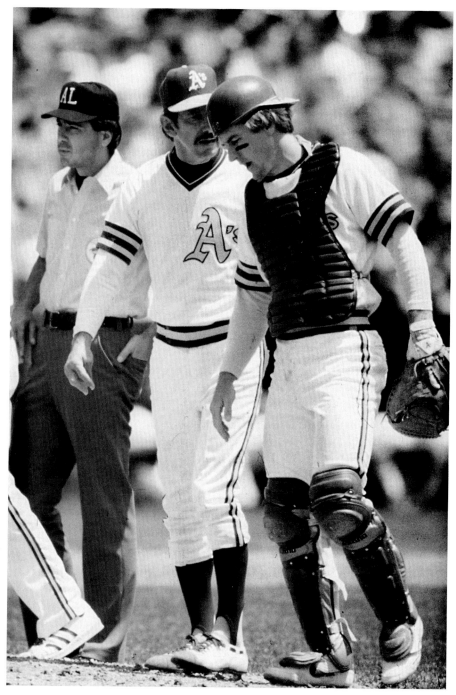

Circa 1980–1982: Billy Martin and catcher Mike Heath talk about staying aggressive. Billy first managed Heath with the 1978 Yankees, and enjoyed watching the young backstop stand up for himself in a memorial brawl with Carney Lansford of the California Angels, recounted in these pages by Heath. *(Oakland A's)*

1982: While fans enjoyed the theatrics of Billy Martin's legendary arguments with the "men in blue," his players appreciated his willingness to stand up for them, to pay attention to details on the field, and to do anything necessary to win that day's game. And when his A's won, Kool & the Gang's "Celebration" blared from the Coliseum speakers! *(Oakland A's)*

Billy Martin's A's were cast in his image—aggressive, scrappy, and ready to fight at the drop of a hat. As they battled their way out of the cellar and into pennant contention, they enjoyed some celebrated brawls, particularly with their California rivals, the Angels.

(Oakland A's)

Billyball was centered around five then-unknown starting pitchers—Mike Norris (shown above with Billy Martin and catcher Mike Heath at the Coliseum), Matt Keough, Rick Langford, Steve McCatty, and Brian Kingman—who through a combination of their own talents and Billy's confidence-building leadership, became big winners and "overnight" sensations until a series of injuries ended the party in 1982.

(Oakland A's)

Here at the 1982 home opener in Oakland, Billy Martin and Angels manager Gene Mauch prepare to do battle yet again. Billy prided himself on knowing the strengths and weaknesses not only of the opposing players, but of the opposing managers, too. And he always believed he could find a way to beat them! *(Oakland A's)*

Even though Oakland was home for Billy Martin, his heart was in the Bronx. He returned to manage his beloved Yankees in 1983, and also skippered the club in 1985 and 1988. In 1986, the Yankees held a "Billy Martin Day" celebration, and retired his familiar uniform #1.

(Marty Appel Collection)

 BILLY MARTIN

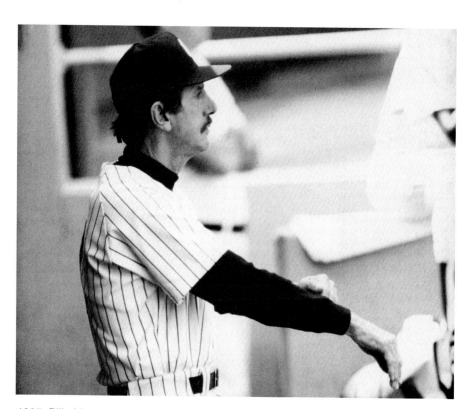

1985: Billy Martin giving signs from the dugout. Regardless of the off-field turmoil that seemed to be a constant in Billy's life, he was always hyperalert and hyperaware in the dugout, looking for any opportunity to take the offensive, to make something happen, and to gain an edge for his team. *(Marty Appel Collection)*

In 1986, the New York Yankees retired Billy's uniform #1. Two of Billy's long-time pals, Bill Reedy (far left) and right-hand man and pitching coach Art Fowler (center) join Billy for the celebration. *(Billy Martin, Jr., Collection)*

It's no surprise that a player nicknamed "Rambo" would be one of Billy Martin's favorites. Former Yankee slugger Mike Pagliarulo credits Billy with teaching him to stand up for himself and to speak his mind during their seasons together in 1985 and 1988. *(Mike Pagliarulo Collection)*

From left to right: Yankees owner George Steinbrenner, Billy Martin, Jr., and Billy Martin, Sr., at a late 1980s gathering. While George and Billy weren't always smiling for the cameras, their creative tension did spark the Yankees to prominence with an AL Championship in 1976 and the World Championship in 1977. And, of course, things were never dull. *(Billy Martin, Jr., Collection)*

Judge Eddie Sapir (right) of New Orleans was Billy Martin's trusted agent and friend for many years. In this late 1980s picture, Billy tells Judge Sapir that he's no doubt due for another raise. *(Billy Martin, Jr., Collection)*

ing the talents you need, but don't cry over the shortcomings and problems you face while your competitors are working. That's just wasting precious time. It's important to remember that Billy had arrived in Oakland a has-been in the eyes of much of the baseball world. He had been moved out of his Yankee managerial job twice, and though only a few seasons removed from celebrating the 1977 World Championship, he was considered largely unemployable. Oakland was no dream job for Billy, but he turned it into one through his hard work and positive attitude.

Creating Positive Energy

As a leader, Billy had a lively, strong, and infectious personality (especially during the first days of any of his managerial stints), which infused ballclubs with energy. It was his club against the world, and for "Billy guys," a sense of fun, family, and winning was prevalent.

Having a Good Time

There's no doubt that Billy was having a good time with the A's, and he helped everyone around him to share in that good time. The positive atmosphere he helped to create carried through to the players and to the coaches. It was a rebirth full of positive energy.

▶ **Mickey Morabito:** *It was refreshing. There was no pressure, and that's what I thought was great. There was absolutely no pressure on Billy. He was just enjoying it. I mean, I'll be honest with you, I think 1980 was probably my most fun year in all of baseball. I mean, all the three World Series I had in New York, even the World Series I've had here in the latter years in Oakland, but I had more fun in 1980. And from a work standpoint, 1980 was probably the worst year I've ever had because we traveled 100 percent commercial flights. We didn't have one charter. That is almost unthought of in the way teams travel today. We were on commercial flights every night. We were flying the day of the game a lot. We'd have to stay over in the city after a night game and leave early in the morning to fly that day to get to our next game. And we were changing planes—I mean, it was unbelievable. And somehow we had a great bunch of young guys, and Billy and the staff were great. We all liked each other. We hung out together. [Team owner Charlie] Finley was* *cheap, and he wasn't going to spend money on charters, but we had fun with it. And maybe because of that we all kind of came together.*

Instilling a Sense of Family

The 1980 A's had an energetic purity that fresh starts allow, and they had that togetherness that tends to define many great sports and business teams. They shared common experiences of adversity and success, and they were together on the planes, in the clubhouses, and in the bars.

▶ **Mickey Klutts:** *It was minor league travel at its best! Being in Oakland, the only place we could go was east other than L.A. and Seattle, but oh yeah, we stump jumped all over. We started out, we were a bunch of orphans looking for a father. And to me it was just great. I'm in the big leagues. I don't care what team or how much I'm getting paid! It was fun. We were a little family.*

▶ **Mike Heath:** *Yeah, well, that was a team! And this is where I get back to the guys today. It's "I." I think that's the big difference, guys back then, [we were] more of a team. We discussed things on the plane. You might have a beer or two on the plane, play cards, you start discussing the game, and that's how you learn. You learn how to play the game and learn from your mistakes that way.*

▶ **Mike Norris:** *I think the greatest asset he would have—and it's no secret that he drank—but we all would be in the bar after the game. A baseball player's mentality is when he's on the field, he talks about winning. When he's in the bar, he talks about baseball. So out of 25 guys, there'd be 20 guys in the bar talking about baseball. Then at the same time, he knew where everybody was. So he was very congenial with that, and then we'd be learning baseball. We'd go over that game that night, or we'd form some strategy for tomorrow. Every time, we'd always go to bed with a positive note. Very often the hotel bar is off-limits to your team. Most of the time, that's where the manager goes and has his cocktails, and the bar is off-limits. Well, it wasn't for us. That kept us from running around New York City and Chicago all the time. We got a lot of unity behind that.*

▶ **Jackie Moore:** *The combination of that young club with talent, a lot of speed, and Billy taking over with a breath of fresh air and confidence, they were kind of meant for each other. And you could tell that they were having fun. It wasn't the old club that you'd play in a four-game series where you expected if you didn't sweep them, you'd at least win three out of four. They were a different type of ballclub. I went there in 1981, and this continued. What a refreshing atmosphere they presented. And the players were together. It used to be, game's over, you get on the bus, and everybody's saying, "Hey, what are you doing?" "We're going to eat here." Heck, it'd be most of the ballclub go to the same restaurant or wherever we'd go. And you expected this. No one was left out. That was the beauty of it. It's just a big family.*

This is not to say that you should lead your entire organization into the nearest bar to share a few drinks. However, it is important to foster a sense of unity and shared purpose in your organization—something at which real leaders are masters.

For Billy, who at some level still longed for that feeling of family he experienced in his glory days as a player, the A's were like stepping back in time. Of course, Billy had always tried for that "big family" quality as a manager, even during times when there was so much pressure on him that he might be excused for missing something. In 1977, in the midst of the Yankee soap opera swirling around Billy, team owner George Steinbrenner, and players Reggie Jackson and Thurman Munson—which thoroughly dominated the back pages of the New York City tabloids—Billy still found out about an incident that happened to Yankee infielder Mickey Klutts and took action to help him. At the time, Klutts was a young rookie whom you'd think might be the last person on Billy's mind, given the pressures around him.

▶ **Mickey Klutts:** *One night I got robbed of $500 out of my hotel room at the Sheraton. I came in, and I just said in conversation to someone, "Hey, somebody ripped me off." Well, of course I wasn't making much money, and I didn't have much money, but to make a long story short, it somehow got around to Billy, and Billy called George without me knowing it and said, "Hey, the kid, somebody ripped him off 500 bucks." After*

the game, there was a letter on my stool to me from George. It said,
"Don't let New York get you down." And there was 500 bucks in it. And
he just paid me back, and it had been initiated by Billy. I found out later
from one of the guys, Billy said, "George, pay the kid."

Years earlier, in his first managerial job, Billy had even bought Charlie Manuel his first suit. Again, you don't have to buy clothes for your
employees, but maybe you can help generate more of a team atmosphere in your office or on your team by building that same sense of
togetherness. It can make a big difference, no matter what your budget
or your weaknesses. Rather than worry about what you need, exploit
what you have. Be creative. And show your personnel that you care
about them as employees and as people.

Helping Young Teams Understand What's Important

Billy's famed outbursts mostly occurred with young teams needing to
learn the lesson that losing is unacceptable—especially losing ugly.
Mickey Morabito, who traveled west with Billy from New York to the
A's, saw Billy put a different face forward for a team that he felt needed
to understand the importance of winning.

▶ **Mickey Morabito:** *One of the things that I saw him do—this might be*
weird for me to say—was actually get mad more. He'd come in after a
loss and scream and yell. A lot of times not screaming and yelling at the
players, but just screaming and yelling in general that we lost a tough
game. And I think it was just so the guys can see that, "Hey, we lost the
game and that shouldn't be acceptable. We want to win." I think right
now you walk into a lot of clubhouses in baseball after a game and it's all
the same. Guys run up to the spread and eat their food, and they answer
their questions, and they leave. I mean, I would challenge you to walk
into some clubhouses and tell me if that team won or lost that day. You
just don't see a lot of emotion. And I think that was the one thing that I
saw Billy do that year. Not so much railing on players, but just basically
getting upset after a loss. Slamming your door. Screaming in general,

maybe screaming at his coaches, so the players can hear it. I think the guys watched that, and I think that taught them that Billy wasn't going to accept losing, and maybe they shouldn't accept losing either. When you lose 108 games like they did in '79, you get numb to it. You lose a game, "Yeah, I expect to lose." They say this is true and I believe it is: "Losing breeds losing, and winning breeds winning." And I think he just wasn't going to let these guys feel comfortable with losing a game. I think they needed to see that reaction from him as a manager.

Billy's outbursts in Oakland were nothing new. He'd done the same thing in Texas. Tom Grieve was a young player on the Texas turnaround team back in 1974, and one night after a tough loss, he found himself alone at the clubhouse spread when Billy walked in.

▶ **Tom Grieve:** *We came off. The food table was right in the middle of the clubhouse. And to get to my locker, I had to walk right past the table of food for after the game. Obviously, it was a tough loss, so you don't turn on the music and start having a great time, and I certainly wasn't planning on doing that. But as I was walking to my locker, I paused at the food table to grab a small plate of food before I went to my locker, and he happened to walk in right as I was doing that. And I was the only one there. And I hear him screaming, "Ah, stick your head in that f—ing food table! If I played like this team, I wouldn't be hungry after the game. But yeah, go ahead, eat that food. Stick your face in that food!" So I'm kind of looking around, going, "Oh shit, I'm the only one here at the food table." You know, he wasn't mad at me personally—I just happened to be the one at the food table. So I put the plate down and went back and sat down, and Billy went in his office and everybody was kind of laughing about it, because they knew he wasn't mad at me, but I happened to be the poor guy that happened to be at the food table. Now he didn't go over and tip over the food that day, but he made it uncomfortable after a game that you lost. Then the funny thing is, when you got dressed and left the ballpark after that, he was fine then. If you were in the hotel bar, he'd come up and buy you a beer. He said something to me the next day about that, he said, "Hey look, that was not intended at you, you just happened to be the one that was at the food table."*

Billy was just communicating his message his way to players who were new to the big leagues and needed to learn the difference between acting like champions and acting like any other club. With a veteran team, Martin typically kept his distance and played down his "in-your-face" tendency. The men who had been through the battles knew what it took mentally to win, and he respected that knowledge and generally left them alone. For instance, Ron Hassey, the catcher for the veteran-laden 1985 Yankees, saw a very different Billy in the club-house than the one running the young Rangers and A's teams.

▶ **Ron Hassey:** *He always talked about the type of ballclub we had and I think, to tell you the truth, the club that we had that year made it easier on Billy. Because when you have a [Dave] Winfield, and a [Don] Baylor, a [Willie] Randolph, and a [Ken] Griffey [Sr.]—gosh, we had so many good players that year. And when they started to hit, I mean, everything fell into place. I think the veterans motivate each other, and I think Billy just kind of stepped aside and let it happen. I mean, he wasn't really a guy that stood up in the middle of the locker room yelling and scream-ing. I never saw it. I never saw him tip over the spread, stuff like that— I never saw anything like that from him. I've seen it from other man-agers, but I never really saw it from him.*

The Use of Hierarchy

Billy created hierarchy on his teams as a means of keeping players focused. Billy sometimes used players whom he felt were dispensable to keep the other players focused and motivated.

▶ **George Mitterwald:** *One of his theories was, "Hey, when you got a base-ball team, you got 25 players. Fifteen of 'em are going to love ya, five are going to hate ya, and five of 'em are undecided. If those five can be on the side of the 15, then you're in good shape. If they're on the side of the five guys that hate ya, you're in deep trouble."*

The method may have been one of the least attractive but still effec-tive methods of Billy's leadership. If you were one of the keys to the team's performance, you could do what you wanted, as long as you maintained your performance. In the middle were some regulars, key utility players, and pitchers. Some of these players were integral parts of the team, either on the field or in the clubhouse, so Billy worked to keep them pumped up, involved, and feeling important. However, if certain players did not have much of a role on the club—and there were sometimes two or three "misfits" on a team—he would ride them pretty hard to show others what life could be like if they didn't play hard.

The main purpose for this entire hierarchy seems to have been to keep the stars and average players motivated. If the average guys could elevate their performance to the star level, they would get special treatment, but if they would sink to the misfit level, it would be bad news. And for the stars, there was only one way to go. It was an interesting incentive program.

▶ **Mike Norris:** *I think his methods of managing were quite effective, unique . . . I think the ability that he had to . . . take five of his superstars, let them do what they wanted to do, then take two or three guys that were the 24th, 25th guy on the roster, make examples out of them, where the other 15 guys wouldn't screw up. So the Armases, the Norrises, and the Hendersons pretty much did what they wanted to do, but he let us know that if we screwed that up, we were going to get that privilege taken from us, too. And then, there's two or three guys down there—the worst pitcher on the team or the utility infielder—he used to stay on those guys and just ride 'em. And so these other guys, the 15 guys he needed to go out and play every day—that's how he kept them in line. 'Cause nobody wanted to get on his shit list, but then you always wanted to do good so you could maybe be like those four or five guys that got treated like kings.*

▶ **Dave Righetti:** *There was a definite faction on the teams. You either were a Billy guy or you weren't. There was no in between . . . It made it hard sometimes. It would split the team sometimes. He had about three or four guys on every team that wanted to shoot him in the back of the head because of one reason—he wouldn't play them. He didn't believe in a deep bench if they weren't guys he thought could help.*

As manager of the club, Martin's control was, for the most part, limited to making out the lineup card. Salaries were determined by ownership. Incentive clauses were determined by ownership. However, it was still Billy's job to motivate the players. Through hierarchy, he encouraged players to optimize their abilities. Stars had to play like stars to maintain their exalted positions. If he felt that they weren't putting in the effort he demanded, he used whatever leverage he could on them. Players could fall into this category if Billy thought they weren't contributing 100 percent. For the most part, Billy had two destinations for players, depending on their performances: the exalted stratosphere of the stars or the list of players he had no use for and wanted to move. For the players he had no use for, life was tough because not only were they going to sit the bench, they were also going to take the brunt for some of his anger and frustration as a means of motivating the rest of the club. The approach was by no means meant to be endearing, especially to the players at the end of the bench, but Billy used the tension effectively through the years to keep his teams progressing.

Removing People's Uncertainty and Building Their Confidence

Uncertainty undermines performance, especially in inexperienced people. Billy removed the uncertainty that plagued young players by letting them know what their roles were going to be on his team. By telling a player "You're my man," he gave him confidence to go out and play aggressively. With that confidence, players became more focused on the moment: "Hit the ball." "Throw strikes." "Field the ball." Not "I'd better get a hit this time up or my butt's gonna be on the bench" or "I'm headed for the bullpen if I don't win this game."

Often, poor performance is not the result of any deficiency in skill. Instead, fear, uncertainty, and a lack of confidence in oneself keeps us from getting to where we want to go. All employees, but especially young employees, want to know *how* to contribute and *what* to contribute.

It becomes easy to praise or critique performance if there is a frame of reference for both the player and the manager to review. Billy was good at installing confidence in the young, unproven player by explaining that player's role to him.

▶ **Tom Grieve:** *Billy, with his ability to motivate and to get the most out of the team, really allowed everybody to do as well as they did. To me, his best quality was the ability he had to get the most out of every player, and he spent a lot of time kind of nurturing that. I can remember I was playing only against left-handed pitching, so I was going to get 200, maybe 250 at-bats a season. So Billy spent a lot of time going around to the players during the season and during spring training saying, "Look, I know you probably feel like you should be playing more, but this is the role that I have for you, and you are a guy that's very important to the ballclub. I need you. So when you're not playing, keep your head in the game, do your extra work, so that when your time comes when I do call on you, you'll be ready to play." He just had a real good way of easing that kind of a thing with all the players.*

He took this quality with him to New York in the late 1970s and during later stints in New York in the 1980s, where he had more veterans, and sometimes, what could be perceived as too much talent. Finding roles for a club full of good players—all of whom could play everyday on other clubs—is a tough job.

▶ **Fred Stanley:** *Well, he tried to get everybody so that they felt that they were part of the club, and that they would be used, and they had a worth to him. And if there were changes to be made, it was made so we picked up somebody that would really help us. When we picked up Jim Spencer, it was so we could have a left-handed hitter right off the bench who could hit some home runs and play a dang good first base. So whoever happened to leave our club, it wasn't because he was a bad player, it was because we were going to get a better one. And Billy was able to convince everybody that "Just because you don't play today, that doesn't mean anything. You'll get back in there." And keep going. He did believe in platooning to a certain extent, he didn't do it with everybody, just a couple guys. But he would get at-bats for people, and try to put 'em in positions where they could succeed.*

▶ **Lenny Randle:** *I don't know why, but he just talked to me different. I wasn't in fear of him, I just respected him. He just knew people, period. He just said, "Look, here's what I expect from you. You're going to hit .270 to .300. You're going to steal 30 to 40. You're going to pick it, you're going to play these positions, and you don't try to go beyond that. You don't have to be Mickey Mantle. There's only one Mickey Mantle." And that's what a lot of managers don't get today. They try to push guys without positive reinforcement. They don't do it. They get too personal, rather than productive, rather than, "You're better than that." You chew somebody out, but you're telling them they're better than what they were. And that was a compliment.*

When Billy Martin arrived in Oakland for the 1980 season, he quickly let his players know what their roles were to the team. Billy wanted to create a semblance of order to replace the chaos of 1979. He named his starting rotation more than two weeks in advance of the opener, giving a huge boost to his uncertain hurlers. Billy noted, "These guys felt like they had been pushed around, but now they have their pride. That's the important thing."[7] An article from the time portrayed Billy with his arms draped around the shoulders of pitcher Matt Keough, saying that despite a 2–17 record and a 5.03 ERA in 1979, he was confident of 15 to 20 wins from him in 1980.

▶ **Matt Keough:** *In 1979, I get hurt, I have a horrendous year. I come into spring training the next year with Billy Martin, thinking I have to bust my ass to get a job. But he walked up, day one, and said, "Matt, you're going to be one of my top three guys in my rotation. Don't worry about it. I'm going to get some guys that catch the ball for you, and we're going to score some runs, and you're going to be fine. You'll win." And that was the end of it. And I just walked off the field after day one going, "Jesus Christ. I thought I was going to have to come in here and survive. Now I'm important." I went out there and had a year—I wish I was born ten years later—250 innings and a 2.92 ERA with 20 complete games. I'd be a billionaire now. The bottom line was, he told me the truth.*

The value of a strong vote of confidence for a 2–17 pitcher is immense when it comes from a man with big-time credentials as a player and a manager. And so Billy's prediction came true: At season's end, Keough had a 16–13 record and a 2.92 ERA.

Teammate Mike Norris came out of spring training as the number five starter in a five-man rotation, but he quickly established himself as the ace of the staff. Norris had first come to the big leagues in 1975, but injuries and front-office manipulations kept him from ever getting a true chance to pitch regularly. In 1979, he had gone 5–8 with a 4.81 earned run average.

▶ **Mike Norris:** *I was definitely ready, but I needed an opportunity to go pitch every five games, which is what I wasn't given the opportunity to do prior to Billy coming. I kind of bounced around from 1975 till Billy got there in 1980. I left spring training that year as the fifth starter, so my job really wasn't safe, but my first start of the season was against Toronto, and I lost 1–0 in ten innings, and proceeded to have a pretty good temper tantrum when I lost the game. And Billy looked at that quite admirably. I came out of the bathroom after tearin' it up, and from that day, he said, "That's my number one starter from now on." So having a little likeness of him didn't hurt, the competitive nature, and the hating to lose.*

Norris blossomed into a star, putting up a record of 22–9 with a 2.54 ERA for the season. Billy was hard on Norris, and pushed him to take the game very seriously. The two had several incidents that Norris recalls today with laughter.

▶ **Mike Norris:** *One time on the airplane, we had gotten beat by Seattle about 17–3. We just got clobbered. One of the pet peeves with him was, if you lose, act like you lost. Don't get on the bus acting like you won a ballgame. So after the game was over, we got on the airplane, and you know those little white headrests that you have on the airplane? I took one out off the back of the headrest, and made a mask out of it, and paraded up in first class, and walked in front of him. Boy, he almost had a heart attack, and he cursed me all the way back to my seat. And he said, "When you win 20 games, then you can do something stupid like that. But until then, sit down in your seat and shut up!" So when I won my 20th game, you know what I did!*

Here, Billy again made the point that losing was unacceptable, and so Norris, as one of the leaders of the team, shouldn't have been joking around after such an ugly loss. He expected Norris to take some pride in himself, and to set a better example for the rest of the team. It was all part of the teaching process. A year later, in 1981—after Billy's amazing A's broke out of the gate with 11 straight victories—Martin's legendary Yankee teammate Whitey Ford analyzed the A's pitchers: "Billy has a staff of good, strong-armed young pitchers, but you must remember that they were pretty average in 1979. It took Billy to motivate and weld them into a winning unit. He did it by instilling confidence in them. They were down on themselves. Billy gave them pride."[8]

It had been no different in Texas, where Billy had established a pitching rotation for his 1974 club of newly acquired superstar Ferguson Jenkins, unprovens Jackie Brown (age 30, ten career wins) and Jim Bibby (age 29, ten career wins), and Steve Hargan, a former winner at the big-league level who had not won a game in the major leagues since 1971. He also continued to develop Steve Foucault into the team's primary reliever.

▶ **Jackie Brown:** *It was Ferguson Jenkins, Jim Bibby, myself, and Steve Hargan. And Steve Foucault. It was like the first month of the season. And he called us five in his office, and he said, "Guys, as long as we're winning, you're in the game. And Fookie, if I have to go to the bullpen in a win, you're the one that's going to pitch. You better get ready." Well, that's exactly what we did all summer. All the four guys got innings, he put us on the mound, and for some reason, I can't explain it, we all had good years. I think a lot of it was the confidence Billy showed in us.*

Jenkins had a stellar year with 25 wins, and the four unproven pitchers came through big, knowing that their roles in the rotation were theirs to lose. Billy had made that clear to them, and it gave them the confidence to go pitch.

▶ **Jackie Brown:** *Fergie had a great year, Bibby won 19 games, I won 13 that year, and Steve [Hargan] won eight. I couldn't tell you another num-*

ber in my career except that year, because that was really the big year for me. That was the year that I felt like I proved that I could pitch in the big leagues. I remember what us four guys did, and if he went to the bullpen in the seventh inning, it was Steve Foucault, if we had a lead. He might have got as many innings as the starters got. He was the guy that Billy went to.

The Case of Dave Righetti

Dave Righetti had been the Rookie of the Year for the Yankees in 1981, pitching for Gene "Stick" Michael and Bob Lemon, but in 1982 he got off to a 5–5 start with a 4.23 ERA and even landed back in the minor leagues temporarily. It was a season of confusion for Righetti, who saw three managers and five pitching coaches come and go, some brought in just to work with him.

When Billy came back to New York in 1983, he knew what kind of arm Righetti had, and he made things simple again for the pitcher. With Billy, Righetti didn't have to look over his shoulder anymore or think about this mechanic or that mechanic. He just had to throw the baseball.

Righetti remembers 1983 with Billy very clearly, because Martin helped him to reestablish his career at the level at which people expected him to perform. The funny thing is, Righetti had already earned a job in Billy's Yankee starting rotation three years earlier. Only Billy's famous October 1979 barroom fight with a Minnesota marshmallow salesman and subsequent firing by Steinbrenner days later kept Righetti from first joining the rotation in 1980.

▶ **Dave Righetti:** *Most of that stuff is pretty vivid, because it was so important to me. In '79, I came up and played for Billy. Billy was aware of me from the beginning when I signed with Texas. And then when I get traded over to the Yankees, and I ended up pitching for him, he loved me. After the 1979 season—and I'll never forget it because managers don't call rookies in except to say, "Here's the ball" or "Your ass is in trouble"—he called me in . . . He had [Ron] Guidry with him, and Guidry was real quiet, and at that time I was still leery around Gator, you know? And he says, "Hey, Gator, what do you do in the off-sea-*

son?" Typical Guidry: "Hunt." That's it, one-word answer. Billy says, "Righetti, you hunt?" I said, "No." He said, "Start hunting." And he says, "How much throwing do you do?" And Gator says, "None." He says, "Well, don't throw either." He was basically telling me, "Do what this guy does. Here's a good guy to follow." And that winter he gets in a fight with a marshmallow guy in Minnesota, so I got no job. He believed in me, and here he is giving me the ball the next year with [Luis] Tiant, [Ed] Figueroa, Tommy John, Guidry, and whoever else George is going to buy. He's going to take a chance on me. He wants me on the team and I'm only 20 years old. So I'm feeling pretty good, and I got this guy who's supposedly so hard in my corner. I loved him. I'd go through the wall for him. So that kind of led up to 1983. The first day, Billy and Art [Fowler] say, "Here's the ball. Go win 20 ballgames." They don't tell me how to pitch, nothin'. That was all he said, and he never said another word to me about it.

Martin liked Righetti and wanted him to succeed, and he knew that the kid just needed stability so that his ability could take over. When Righetti pitched a 1983 Fourth of July no-hitter against arch-rival Boston, striking out Wade Boggs for the final out, Billy was very proud.

▶ **Dave Righetti:** *When I got fortunate enough to do that, he loved it. He called my parents. He had me on the phone. You know, I see the pictures of him in the old films, and see him in the dugout—I can see he was just a nervous wreck! And I know he felt like it was his own kid who did it. I know how much he really liked me. And he wanted me to do well, and I felt the same way about him. I was trying to give him everything I had. That was kind of a neat story for us together.*

Giving young, hungry staff members roles to perform that are clearly defined and within their abilities is a crucial aspect of getting the most out of a team, whether for a ballclub or any other organization. For Billy, that pattern was repeated over and over, from Jackie Brown in 1974 to Matt Keough in 1980 to Dave Righetti in 1983. These players all needed a boost of confidence, and they got it through Billy. He believed in them, and he let them know it.

Asking for Sacrifices for the Good of the Team

The leader's job is to create roles that are achievable for the staff, to build up their confidence in their abilities to perform those roles, and to make them believe in the correctness of their roles within the context of the entire organization. That isn't always easy, especially if a person may be well suited for one role but needed even more in another role.

For instance, Tom Grieve was a young player for Billy's 1974 Rangers who was good enough to play every day, and eventually did play every day. At that time, however, he was platooned. Rather than sulk, he had a good attitude about the role, in part because of how Billy was turning the entire team into a winning unit.

▶ **Tom Grieve:** *I always looked at being platooned as a regular job, even though you weren't playing every game. You still felt like you were a regular on the team, and you felt like a big part of the team. And the team was pretty good. We were winning, and it was exciting, and there was more fans, and so never was that anything that anyone considered complaining about. We were happy to finally be playing on a good team and everyone had a great deal of respect for Billy, and so if that's the way he felt the team had the best chance to win, then everybody was all for it.*

Platooning is one thing, but moving from a starting role to the bench is even tougher. In 1977, just before spring camp broke, the Yankees acquired shortstop Bucky Dent, relegating 1976 regular Chicken Stanley to the bench. The trade crushed Stanley, who had prepared himself to play 150 games in 1977, and who thought that he had finally achieved the true "regular" status he had worked for since first coming to the major leagues in 1969.

Martin was a fan of Stanley's. He had given him his first starting job in the big leagues, and Stanley had delivered for him. To bench him for Dent had to be difficult for Billy. Still, he had to do what was best for the team by playing Dent, and at the same time, he had to keep Stanley's spirits up so that he could now contribute to the team as a utility player.

▶ **Fred Stanley:** *You know what, he came up to me in the airport—this is when Bucky first joined the club. He put his arm around me and said, "You know, I will always want you on my club. You're going to get playing time, and sometimes it happens for the best. Keep your chin up, and you'll get to play." Because I was pretty depressed. I mean, you're going from the World Series, the dramatic home run by [Chris] Chambliss [in the bottom of the ninth in the last game of the AL Championship Series], and it was just a fairy tale for almost everybody in that organization. And the next year, we were going to complete the cycle, we were going to win the World Series, there's no question. And when I went to spring training, my whole focus was that I was going to be that guy to help 'em do that. And when Bucky showed up, I saw my playing time diminish greatly. And you know what it is? You start to feel sorry for yourself for a while, because you're thinking, "Jeez, what did I do? What more could I have done?" But George just wanted an All-Star at every position, and it was his money, and I probably would have done the same thing. Billy just brought me aside and said, "Listen, it's something that happened. You can't control it. Let's just try to work through it."*

In a team meeting just before camp broke, Billy spoke about sacrifice, and looking directly at Stanley, said, "You may not think so now, but you're going to end up rooting for Bucky Dent harder than for anybody else on the club. And when that happens, when everybody's rooting hardest for the man in his own position, we'll know that we're a team."[9]

This wasn't just talk for Billy. Remember, when he was a player himself, he had rooted for Gil McDougald even as Gil played over him at second base, so he wasn't just blowing smoke. Billy knew from his days in the Bronx that amazing ballplayers like Hank Bauer, Gene Woodling, Andy Carey, and Moose Skowron had to wait their turn to play regularly or take part in Casey Stengel's legendary platoons. He also knew that the guys on the bench still rooted wholeheartedly for the guys playing in their positions.

Billy still wanted his players to align themselves with the team, even though free agency was giving the players the power to move from team to team for larger playing roles and even larger bankrolls. Stanley made the transition in 1977 and stayed with the Yankees through the 1980 season. Then, he joined Billy in Oakland for two more seasons and more playing time.

▶ **Fred Stanley:** *You know what he had me do? He would come over to me, and he'd say, "OK, I want you to watch their manager. And I want you to pick up their signs. And you let me know if you think you got a sign." And you know what? He kept me in the ballgame, because I was always trying to steal signs. I was always trying to do something. And he'd say, "What do ya think?" I'd say, "I think he's going to pitch out." We just had a situation where he kept me in the game. Then Yogi [Berra]'d come down to me in the seventh inning and say, "You might want to start getting ready." So I'd run up the runway, run into the clubhouse, do my stretching, run down, get my heart pumping a little bit, and about 80 percent of the time, I'd be in that ballgame. So he kept me going, he kept a lot of guys doing the same thing.*

The lesson here? Even when things aren't going your way, you can stay involved. Maybe that's easier said than done, but it can be done, and a good manager can ease the transition for his or her workers.

Building Team Chemistry

Lou Piniella is one of the best managers in baseball today, with a 1990 World Championship to his credit with the Reds, and several postseason appearances at the helm of the Mariners, including a trip to the AL Championship Series in 2000. Piniella was already a veteran outfielder when he first played for Billy Martin, but on that first Billy team in 1976, Sweet Lou learned something new about competition.

Said Piniella, "I . . . learned that a team can win without great individual stars. A ballclub wins when each player does what he can to the best of his ability . . . You . . . need each player contributing his own unique abilities to the entire ballclub . . . Billy taught me about team chemistry. It's not important how the individual statistics measure up at the end of the year, but how the team standings end up—if we're number one, nothing else matters."[10]

▶ **Fred Stanley:** *Everybody pulled for everybody. Like today, you go on the plane today with the players. They all got their laptop computers, they're all locked into this other stuff. There's just not a lot of camaraderie. Back in those days, the music was going, Mickey Rivers was wearing one of the stewardess's aprons, and he was serving dinners. It was crazy! Guys went out and had fun together. Now it's entirely different. You still have to have good players to win. There's no question you have to have stars to win. But it's the chemistry to get those stars to play every single day. And you can't have nine, you gotta have 25.*

In his own unique way, Rivers echoes Stanley's sentiments, describing how the chemistry of the 1976 Yankee team took hold.

▶ **Mickey Rivers:** *We just got Willie [Randolph], with Dock Ellis comin' over. But see, Pittsburgh wasn't playing Willie, so we had to work that in. Startin' out, we had to work that in, kinda slow. Working slowly. Things are going well. Now I'm getting the chance. Roy [White]'s just a quiet guy, anyway. Roy liked to win. He liked to see guys go out and do what he do, and hit like that. So I had no problem with guys like that, that were that caliber, but the big guys—Catfish [Hunter], and Chris [Chambliss], and [Graig] Nettles—I kind of had to mingle in with them guys. I liked to have fun. I got over there, and the first one, Sparky Lyle, he's a go-getter. He's the one, "Oh, come on, Quick." He's a fun guy, he likes to play tricks, tie your shoelaces together, burn 'em, and all that. So I say, "Well, initiate me." So that went on for a couple of days. I'm getting adjusted to playing now. I got together with a couple of guys, and now we getting hand in hand with the guys so we can communicate a little bit better now. OK, I told 'em, I say, "Look, this is my point now, I'm a base runner. I'm not going to hit no home runs for ya, so now you know, so we'll have no miscommunication with each other." Billy talks with the guys. He said, "We just got to get together with him." So, we got to a point, we had a couple arguments, but we ironed it out, everything went well. Now, to this point now, we're doing good, the team's playing good. We're winning, the team's winning in 1976, 'bout 14 games ahead with a couple weeks to go, and I think we ended* *up winning by at least 7½ games. But now we all together now. We had the big guys. They wanted to play. We had Oscar [Gamble]. We had Carlos May. Guys like that, they didn't care. They didn't mind other guys playing. We didn't have no animosity between the guys about the guys going out there, because they know Billy make the lineup. You know that '76 season was a great season. We had guys that really played. We were kind of dominant.*

Billy believed that only the manager—the one individual who worked directly with the players on a daily basis—could understand how to create the chemistry, and only the manager should have the authority to make decisions on how to use the personnel. This firm belief led to many of Billy's fights with the front office. Yet Martin always contended, "Many general managers are brilliant men. But they know the players mainly from their statistics, and there's more to a baseball player than his stats: his mind, his heart, his character, the way he travels. Only the field manager knows him that well."[11] Billy knew his players because he got close to them.

▶ **Mickey Rivers:** *People don't understand. People said, "Man, lookit all this y'all had going on." But the key thing was that we won. We was winners. We was champions. And that's all on account of Billy . . . Even guys that didn't like him will tell you, "Well, he was a good manager. He knew how to get the best out of the guys." I've seen guys who hated his guts, but when he put them in there, they got the job done. And they couldn't understand how he did it. I was just talking to a couple guys: "Aw man, I did this." And they feel good about themselves later on. And they couldn't understand. He put 'em in the right spot. We changed guys. Sometimes we'd take someone out and put [Jim] Spencer in to hit against the left-hander. Come on—Spencer don't hit against no left-hander. Left-handers don't hit against left-handers. And Vida Blue come in there. Boom! Put Spencer in there. Boom! Spencer gets three hits. You know, it works out. Strategy. And that was a big key. He knew something about the guys. And knew when he talked to the guys, he tell 'em exactly their role that they'd be playing.*

▶ **Fred Stanley:** *He had a feel for the way it's working. He could feel the way the momentum's going, how to change it, and how to keep these guys motivated. He had a personal way. He'd touch you. He'd grab your arm, he'd say something to you. He'd come out and take ground balls with you, and talk to you. You don't see managers do that any more. When was the last time you ever seen a big league manager walk out and take ground balls with your second baseman or shortstop?*

▶ **Toby Harrah:** *Billy Martin didn't call a lot of meetings. Billy Martin didn't do a lot of things of that nature. He motivated through association, through seein' you at the park. He'd come out and take ground balls at second. He'd come out with me at shortstop and take ground balls, and we'd be talking about things. He'd take throws from me. He'd come around the cage and he'd talk to me about my swing. He talked about base running. And he really taught you how to play the game.*

In knowing his team's talent from up close, Martin knew what he needed to do to win. Billy never used players in one certain way just because that was how they were "supposed" to be used. For instance, just because relief pitcher Righetti was "the closer" didn't mean he could pitch only the ninth inning. If he was the pitcher best suited to stop a sixth-inning rally, he came into the game.

▶ **Dave Righetti:** *He wasn't trying to prepare for the next day or any of that. Billy tried to win the game that day. And I felt the same way, no matter what happened to me. As a reliever, the writers were all over me, "You're in the fifth inning, the sixth inning. You're pitching, you're not saving the game." I'd be trying to tell them it doesn't mean anything.*

In New York, where Billy always had a potent offense, he wanted to bring in a pitcher—no matter who he was or what his supposed role was—to put out the fire so that the offense could take over. Once, in a 1977 do-or-die AL playoff game with the Kansas City Royals, he brought in closer Sparky Lyle in the *fourth* inning. Lyle, a great competitor, stopped the Royals dead in their tracks for the next five innings, and the Yankees won the game.

▶ **Mickey Rivers:** *He brought Sparky in the fourth inning. Come on. Who does things like that with the best reliever and stuff like that? That's what I'm saying, he knew the guys and the individuals. And that's what helps.*

Chemistry is the key for any team of any kind to function properly, and Billy understood that fact very well. The manager who sees personnel on a daily basis often is best suited for knowing who is ready and who might be poised for a bad day. The clue might come from looking in their eyes, from watching how they look moving about the clubhouse, or from watching them get loose. Billy paid attention to these and other factors. He had that awareness.

▶ **Lenny Randle:** *He saw, "How can I get the best ability out of each guy for X amount of days? Can I get 150 games out of this guy? Or can I get 20 games out of this guy? Or can I spot this guy 80 games, and then maybe he'll burn out? Can I put this guy in for a whole week and let him get his confidence up, and then when he gets tired and goes 0 for 12, take him out, and then let him get himself back? Should I bring this pitcher in and let him get his confidence?" He just strategically knew how to bring in a guy. He knew about guys' hobbies. He could go around the locker room and know guys' habits—what books they read, what's in the locker, girls, whatever.*

A great example of Billy's understanding of chemistry can be seen in how he built on the exciting turnaround of his 1980 Oakland Billyball squad going into 1981. He didn't go out and try to land big-name free agents, as was the trend. Instead, he tweaked his roster just a bit. He looked to complement the aggressive, young players he had won with in 1980 with a little veteran wisdom. He needed to strengthen his bench, his middle infield, his clubhouse, and his bullpen.

▶ **Mickey Klutts:** *When he went to the A's, all he acquired was this young team, and it was a challenge to him. But then you looked in the outfield, you got [Tony] Armas, [Rickey] Henderson, and [Dwayne] Murphy. "My God, wait a minute, I can build something here." So he acquired a Joe Rudi off the bench . . . In '81, we had Jim Spencer, Rudi, and Cliff John-*

*son on the same team. He acquired these big veteran hitters off the
bench to help those young guys. If he had to pinch hit for somebody,
he's got somebody coming up.*

The veteran names Klutts rattled off—Rudi, Spencer, and Johnson—
had all been strong hitters in the big leagues. Perhaps more importantly, they had all played major roles on World Championship teams.
The middle infielders Billy acquired in his time in Oakland—Fred Stanley and Davey Lopes—had also played for World Championship teams.
Billy was trying to find the pieces that could turn his second-place team
into World Champions, and that meant adding winners who would be
happy to play a role on his Billyball team, not guys who were going to
upset the solid foundation already in place. With these types of veterans, he was getting more than players. These men were basically
player-coaches for him—in effect, mentors, if you will.

▶ **Lenny Randle:** *He always kept some veterans around him. If they weren't
playing, then they coached. Like [Willie] Horton, or Frank Howard, or
[Jim] Fregosi, or Stanley. So when he had [Cesar] Tovar and those guys,
he has veterans who could work with all the outfielders or the infielders.
Billy'd say, "You can be another Tovar." And I was going, "Tovar? Yeah?"
I mean, it was kind of like, how could you lose with all that help? Here's a
guy that's going to teach you how to play second, teach you how to play
center field, steal a base, intimidate another team, piss a pitcher off. I
mean, everybody had a role. And off the field, Cesar had a role, too:
"Tonight, I got you. I take care of everything. Billy told me to take care of
you. Let's go." And I was like, "What the hell?" You know? But you didn't
ask. You just went along. And it was a plan. Billy knew that some guys
would get mad, upset, or whatever. They had to relax. You still have to go
off the field and play billiards, whatever your habits are. Bowl, go to a
club, dance, whatever it was. And show up at the park. And do your job.*

Making the Difficult Decisions

Hard choices often must be made to fix a failing organization, and it's
the leader's job to make those choices. To do the job well, the organiza-

tion has to be put first, above the welfare of any individual, with no exceptions. When Billy turned a team around, he worked to put his organization in place as quickly as possible. Popular veteran players, current stars, and at times, even promising youngsters were discarded for the betterment of the team. They weren't necessarily bad players, but they weren't the right fit. Then, of course, there were team "cancers" that Billy got rid of, too—players who just didn't understand what he was trying to do and who presented obstacles for the organization as a whole.

▶ **Charlie Silvera:** *Some guys don't understand what the game's all about. They get on the field and they don't know how to operate. Those are the losers, those are the people you have to get out of there, and Billy would do that. He'd go to the owners and say, "This guy is a loser. We have to get him out of here. He's a whiner." There's winners and losers, and the Yankees didn't tolerate losers.*

▶ **Toby Harrah:** *Well, you know, myself, having been in baseball my whole life, some ballplayers it's not there to get. And then, some ballplayers it was. And Billy had this ability to know the players that it was there, and the ones it weren't, he'd get rid of.*

Billy was named the manager of the Yankees for the first time on August 2, 1975, inheriting an uninspired third-place team from Bill Virdon. By the end of the season, the Yankees remained in third, and many observers felt that the team was still uninspired—a perplexing fact considering that Billy was already renowned for his ability to shake up staid, stagnant situations.

But what Billy was doing at that time was watching. He was by and large allowing the players to go their own way during the last months of the season so that he could identify the ones he wanted to keep and the ones he wanted to trade.

▶ **Marty Appel:** *The team didn't do all that well for the rest of '75, and Billy kept saying, "Don't hold me accountable, because I need to mold a team from the beginning. You wait and see when I have them for a whole spring training."*

▶ **Ray Negron:** *The way he ran the 1975 season, he was already seeing what was going to be happening in 1976. And that was the most incredible aspect of Billy Martin. Billy had already started to formulate what he needed to do for the 1976 season. He was already making a list of players that he thought would help the Yankees. He would give Gabe [Paul, the general manager] a list of players all the time. He always had a pad, he was always writing stuff on his desk as far as what he wanted to do. Whenever he had a shot at looking at the other teams, he always took advantage of that. He saw Willie Randolph during the playoffs, and he dug him right away. He had asked Gabe Paul about him. And Gabe Paul, who was a great GM in his own right, had his own list going on. So that's in essence how Billy was trying to work it for the following year. He knew who was going to be there, who wasn't going to be there. That was the brilliance of Billy. When he took over that club, he knew that that particular club that he had wasn't going to be the club that was going to win an American League pennant the following year.*

After the 1975 campaign ended, Steinbrenner, Paul, and Martin traded talented and popular Yankee players Doc Medich, Bobby Bonds, Pat Dobson, and others for then-unknowns Willie Randolph, Mickey Rivers, Ed Figueroa, Oscar Gamble, and the controversial Dock Ellis. More than a few eyebrows were raised. Bonds, for instance, was among the most talented players in the game, with speed and power from the top of the order. Only a year before, the Yanks had traded favorite son Bobby Murcer to the Giants to get Bonds. Now, Bonds himself was being traded for Rivers.

Still, the new players, it was believed, were right for the turnaround, while the departed players were not. The Yankees, who had not appeared in a World Series since 1964, suddenly traveled to the Fall Classic in 1976, 1977, and 1978, proving Martin, Paul, and Steinbrenner to be correct in their aggressive moves. But initially, the changes were jarring. When Billy arrived in Florida for spring training in 1976, more than one-third of the team he had taken over at the end of the 1975 season was gone.

But it was not a matter of just changing the personnel. In addition to the new players came a new attitude around the clubhouse. In short order, Billy had instituted a sweeping culture change in his organization. He later recalled, "It was an overhauling job from the basic foundation . . . The last two months [of 1975] I was an observer. I didn't like the execution on the field and I didn't like what was going on in the clubhouse."[12] But in the spring of 1976, Billy had full control of his new team, and he had the strength of character to get the veteran players' respect and to enforce what he wanted to see done on the field.

When the 1976 season opened, the Yankees came out of the gate strong, and they never looked back. The Yankees absorbed the attitude of their manager in spring training and took it with them out onto the playing field all season.

▶ **Fred Stanley:** *We were on a roll, and we were comfortable, and you know what happened? He instilled this cockiness. When we walked in there, they [the opposing team] knew that they were in for a fight, no matter where they came from. If they came to Yankee Stadium, they knew that this club that was on the field, that was wearing those pinstripes, was for real. And when we went on the road, we drew good crowds, because they not only came to see the Yankees play, but they came to see Billy, because Billy put on a show.*

In the business world, executives hired to run turnaround corporations often face the same situation that Billy found in 1975. For instance, in the early 1980s, Jack Welch was creating a new GE by selling off aging manufacturing businesses in favor of service businesses. Welch was criticized throughout the business press for his actions, especially when he sold GE Housewares, the division that made small appliances, in 1984. As Noel Tichy and Stratford Sherman write, "Housewares had become a lousy business, but nostalgic GEers didn't care . . . By attacking such a vivid symbol of the old GE, Welch had, in effect, declared war on his own employees."[13]

Did Welch want to be the enemy among his own employees? Of course not. But he knew, as the one person looking at the entire corporate picture within the context of competitive realities, what many employees could not see: GE Housewares had to go. And making the difficult decision, Welch had to respond in the way that ultimately was best for the organization—even for those employees who detested him for it.

As a leader, you must put personal and emotional feelings aside, be able to withstand strong criticisms both from within and outside the organization, and remain unerringly focused on the goal that necessitates the moves.

▶ **Ray Negron:** *When Billy Martin put his ballclub together, he didn't give a damn what the player was, he wanted to put together the best team possible. If that team was 25 black guys, it was going to be 25 black guys, or 25 Hispanic guys, or 25 white guys. He was going to give the owner in that city the best product possible.*

Even though tough decisions have to be made, there should still be room for compassion. One of the toughest trades Martin ever made was in Texas, when he dealt two pitchers who had done a great job for him—Jim Bibby and Jackie Brown—to Cleveland for future Hall of Famer Gaylord Perry. Brown—whom Billy loved—was the 30-year-old veteran who had become a winning big-league starter for Billy in 1974. Bibby was on the rise and would enjoy a very solid career. While the trade was deemed best for the Rangers at the time and was supported by Billy, it crushed him too, because he loved the effort Jackie had given to him, and also, because he knew very well that he was moving Jackie further from his Oklahoma home.

▶ **Jackie Brown:** *I'll never forget when I was traded in '75. Billy Martin called me in the office. He trades me and Jim Bibby for Gaylord Perry. Now Gaylord Perry's a Hall of Famer, won 300-plus ballgames. You're going to have Ferguson Jenkins and Gaylord Perry on the mound back-to-back, two of the best pitchers in the game. And when he called me into the office to tell me that I had been traded to the Cleveland Indians, Billy Martin cried. He did not want to trade me, because he liked Jackie Brown as a human being, and he liked the effort that I gave him every five days. Billy actually cried, and he said, "You don't know how bad this hurts me, but Jackie, we've got to make this club better." And he promised me that day, he said, "You will be back in this organization."*

See, I'm from Oklahoma. I'm playing pretty much in my backyard. Texas was like home to me, and he knew how I felt about that. And at the same time I think he liked Jackie Brown. Most people never see that side of Billy Martin. He promised me that night, he said, "You'll be back in this organization." And I came back as pitching coach in '79, '80, '81, '82. Brad Corbett, the owner, brought me back, and he said, "Billy promised you you'd be back here, and you are." It's kind of special. I wish I could sit here and use big words and great things that would read good. I'm not good at that kind of stuff. But my heart is big enough, and for Billy Martin, it's as big as anyone's.

Building a Staff of Coaches You Can Trust

A leader needs to build a complementary staff of trustworthy individuals capable of teaching his or her methods to the entire organization. Good assistants not only share and spread the leader's message but also build upon the leader's weaknesses to minimize the impact of those weaknesses. All leaders are flawed, no matter how good they are, and Billy certainly had his weaknesses. So Billy looked to a coaching staff that would be supportive of his philosophies, yet have their own complementary skills as well.

Billy wanted loyal coaches who knew what it took to win, whom he could delegate authority to, and who wouldn't upstage his authority, which he felt was very important symbolically.

▶ **Buck Showalter:** *Billy would delegate authority and was a better listener than people thought he was. He'd listen to the people he trusted, and those that were loyal around him, and knew that they were only looking out for what was best for him and the team.*

Billy's coaches worked as his "fingers"—that is, as extensions of him. His coaches—most notably Art Fowler and Clete Boyer, but also Jackie Moore, Charlie Silvera, Yogi Berra, Dick Howser, Elston Howard, Frank Lucchesi, and George Mitterwald—knew what he wanted done and had his trust. Many of Billy's coaches were ex-Yankee winners with a baseball education similar to Billy's.

Charlie Silvera, the catcher who played in the shadow of Yogi Berra during his career with the Yankees, was part of World Championship teams in 1949, 1950, 1951, 1952, 1953, and 1956, and he had known Billy going back to their days in the Pacific Coast League in the 1940s. Charlie roomed with Billy and Hank Bauer at the Concourse Plaza Hotel in the Bronx when Billy first came to the Yankees in 1950. When Billy was named manager of the Minnesota Twins for 1969, he added Silvera to his coaching staff. Talk about loyalty. It turns out Billy and Silvera had made a deal years earlier as young bench warmers with the Yankees.

▶ **Charlie Silvera:** *Well, this goes back originally to when we roomed together at the Concourse Plaza Hotel in the Bronx, right up from Yankee Stadium. Billy wasn't playing. I wasn't playing. So we'd sit around, do a lot of talking, and we made a pact that if I ever got a job with the Seals, and he with the Oaks out here, not even thinking major leagues, that either one would be our coach. So it ended up that he got the Twins job, and by God he called me. Now this is 19 years after we made this pact. He called me, and I ended up a coach with him there in Minnesota, Detroit, and Texas.*

Martin, having spent over three seasons as a third-base coach with the Twins, knew Silvera would bring that Yankee bloodline to the Twins, and from there, he looked to mold Silvera into the type of assistant he felt he needed.

▶ **Charlie Silvera:** *I came from the Yankees, and listen, I was there eight and a half years, and I was on seven pennant winners. I knew what it was to win. I didn't play much, but I was there. And I knew what it was to go to the other way. I went from the Yankees to the Cubs, and they'd sit around and say, "Jeez, we're going too good, something's gotta happen." So Billy said, "I'm going to mold you. It's going to take you time." He says, "It's altogether different now. Don't be afraid to tell 'em what to do, because these guys'll shit all over ya. You gotta be tough on 'em, because they'll say, 'Yeah, yeah, yeah.' You gotta keep reminding them to do this, do that. Finally, you remind 'em enough, they'll say, 'Well, maybe I better do it.'"*

As with his players, Billy was tough on his coaches. He could be intimidating, and he certainly called the shots. At the same time, he didn't want his coaches to be yes men, and they could certainly give him their opinions freely, as long as they didn't undermine his leadership.

▶ **Frank Lucchesi:** *Billy wanted the coaches to do a good job, but there's one thing I found out knowing Billy all these years: Never, never make a suggestion to Billy in front of people . . . I would get more out of Billy when I was alone with him. A lot of people didn't know that.*

▶ **Jackie Moore:** *Billy was open. We knew that we could give our opinion. He didn't want all of us to agree—if we didn't believe it, not to agree with it. We all knew that Billy had the final decision or the final say, but he was open to your opinion. He wasn't looking for a yes guy, he wasn't looking for someone just, "OK, whatever you think Billy, I think that way, too." And he expected a lot of his coaches. A lot of people say he was tough on his coaches. He expected his coaches to be part of Billy Martin. As he said numerous times, "You guys are my fingers. I can't be every place all the time. When I'm not there, I expect you guys to be in charge and do things right."*

▶ **George Mitterwald:** *He may yell and scream at you at times, but if you had a strong feeling about a player and you voiced it to him, he would listen to you. And chances are, if you really felt that a guy deserved to be on the ballclub, he would be on the ballclub. I mean, he could be intimidating at times. I got intimidated by Billy a lot of times, and I used to get mad at him sometimes as a coach, because he used to take things out on us sometimes unmercifully. If a player screwed up, and it was one of my guys, he might chew me out for three hours. But you know what? I knew that he was trying to make me better to get through to that player that, "Hey, you can't make this mistake again." And chances are, they didn't do it again if it was a mental error.*

▶ **Willie Horton:** *Billy's the type of person that, to me, hired a coach to support his team, his players. Your job is to help him develop the play-*

ers and to support them. Your job is to make that player's job easy so he can go out and perform. He hired people around him that had experience and knowledge that could do the job. That's what I learned from him, and I've learned to do that in life. As a matter of fact, I was telling my son that yesterday in our company. I said, "How you're going to grow, you get people that can do this thing better than us. And don't fear that." That's what he had over a lot of other managers. I think you see a lot of good managers, but look at the coaching staff. You want people that can do that job just as good or better as you can.

The Case of Art Fowler

Billy's best coaches served important roles that went beyond their baseball skills. Art Fowler, Martin's pitching coach and right-hand man during most of his managerial stints, had a reputation for serving only as Billy's drinking buddy. Yet on every team he coached, Fowler had two vital roles. First, he had Billy's respect and could offer his opinion to him without fear of the consequences, and very few people had Billy's respect in this way. And second, he was a buddy and adviser to the pitchers.

▶ **Willie Horton:** *Art Fowler—he brought things out of pitchers, man, I ain't never seen done. Because he comes straight and he tells you the truth. He might say it a little different, the way he talked from down home, but shit, you listened to ol' Art, he'd bring something out of you.*

▶ **Ray Negron:** *Art was a very decent baseball man. Art got entrapped from the standpoint of being Billy's drinking buddy. When you fall into that circle, you were his drinking buddy, and not a baseball man, which is b.s., because he wouldn't be working for Billy if he wasn't a good baseball man. Art was a disciple—total Billy guy. Really understood what Billy was all about. He really truly dug Billy. Respected his baseball ability, his knowledge of the game, and most importantly, he knew Billy's loyalty. He knew what loyalty meant to Billy, so in turn he knew he would always be loyal to Billy . . . When it came time to talk from the technical aspect of the game, Art could do that. Art was a decent pitcher himself, and he knew talent.*

Art was also a great confidant for Billy. Art was able to speak with Billy and help to calm him down. All leaders, as previously stated, need assistants who complement their weaknesses, and Art, in helping to keep Billy relaxed, served a crucial role. When Art wasn't around, Billy was much more vulnerable to making back-page headlines.

▶ **Charlie Manuel:** *Well, I think that he really liked Art Fowler, because not only did he think Art could get guys to relax and have fun and laugh, but he'd been around Art before and he knew him, and he trusted him. He was good to Billy. I think Art was a no-threat guy to Billy, and at the same time, he could bounce things off of Art, and Art was a good listener. I think Billy trusted him about things so much, that's why he was so close to him.*

Art was also a very funny man. Humor was important to all of his teams, Billy knew, because of the tremendous intensity and pressure that his demands created for ballplayers. They needed some release. Art was friendly with the pitchers, protecting them from Billy, and he kept everybody loose. For almost 20 years, Fowler played good cop to Billy's bad cop, and many very successful pitchers swore by him.

▶ **Dave Righetti:** *He would never let Billy mess with the pitchers. As hard as Billy supposedly was with the pitchers, he didn't badmouth 'em. Not in front of Art. Never. Art wasn't a teacher. He was more of a head guy, in telling you how easy it is. "This is easy, just go out and do this and that. That's it. Don't worry about it." He was one of those guys you just liked seeing every day. He was old school.*

▶ **Mickey Morabito:** *The A's staff was a situation, again, where Billy would tell you to give Art the credit. Art was very helpful with a guy like Keough and a lot of those pitchers, because he was their buddy. And that was the kind of a pitching coach that Billy needed. He didn't need somebody really to be the mechanical guy, teaching or whatever. Billy's pitching coach had to be a buddy, somebody that the pitchers could actually sit there and get on Billy about. And Art was great with that staff at that time.*

▶**Mike Norris:** *Art, to me, relaxed me. He was quite comical. That was probably his best asset . . . There wasn't a whole lot that he taught me. But he kept me loose, and if you know me, I think that's the best thing that he could have done for me, was just keeping me loose. And so, I'd be very loose, and let things go, and that's how I was effective.*

▶**Matt Keough:** *There were times where Art Fowler would come out to the mound, and he would say things like this: "Now I don't know what the hell you're doing, but you're making Billy mad as hell. So change." And leave. I mean, you have to laugh, right? But there's a method to the madness, because Art was never allowed to say anything to us that Billy didn't tell him to say. So if he did that, it was coming from Billy. And what Billy was trying to do was just loosen your ass up. One time we had an exhibition game in '81 after the strike, and I was pitching against the Giants. The game meant nothing; it was an exhibition game. Before the game, I said, "Art, what do you want me to do?" He said, "God damn it buddy, this game don't mean anything, just go out there and throw strikes." I threw like 27 straight strikes to start the game, they had about six runs. He comes walkin' out, he says, "What in the hell are you doing?" I said, "You told me just to throw strikes." And he said, "Well Jesus Christ, buddy, mix in a ball." And walked off the field. So they always could do that, and Art could always be the buffer between Billy and the pitchers. But we always knew that Art was still loyal to Billy.*

Leaders need to find complementary catalysts, just as Billy did with Art Fowler. Trust, shared values, and added skills are among the keys to strong working staffs. Share the glory: You can't do it all by yourself. Billy's coaches were deeply loyal to him and knew he would be there for them, too.

▶**Jackie Moore:** *I spent years with Billy Martin. Billy Martin was always very loyal to me, and I was always very loyal to Billy. And there was a mutual agreement there that, in our nature of business, when I was fired, well, Billy was a guy that I could come to and I knew that I'd have a job,* *because of the years that we had spent together and the loyalty. There was a never a question about that—I just knew he would do it.*

▶ **Charlie Silvera:** *The traveling secretary in Detroit, he said, "Boy, you and Fowler are really loyal to Billy, aren't you?" I said, "Well, by God, he's kept us working. He brought us back from the ashes." And we were loyal too. And we took a lot of crap, but we came from the Depression era. Most people don't understand. We had nothing. I went to a Jesuit high school. You took orders. You went in the service. You took orders. So now you learn how to take orders. You learn how to be loyal to something. The only loyalty they have now is the dollar bill. They don't know what loyalty is. That's a word that most of 'em never heard of. But Billy, he was a hardscrabble guy, and what the heck, I'm standing up for him. I tell you what, he was tough, because he wanted you to succeed. He was tough on his coaches. He'd say, "Now, lookit, if you guys don't do the job for me, that makes me look bad. So go out and do your job."*

Through his understanding of organizational dynamics, Billy got everyone on his team to do his job.

Notes

1. *Associated Press*, March 18, 1980.
2. David Grunwald, "Battlin' Billy Martin Ignites Baseball Fever in Oakland," *Family Weekly*, August 17, 1980.
3. Red Smith, "Billy Martin: Pilot of Year," *New York Times*, October 6, 1980.
4. Thomas Boswell, "A's Prove It—Martin's Great Manager," *Boston Sunday Globe*, May 9, 1981.
5. Billy Martin and Phil Pepe, *Billyball* (Garden City, N.Y.: Doubleday & Company, 1987), p. 16.
6. Maury Allen, *New York Post*, May 9, 1978.
7. Grunwald.
8. Will Grimsley, "Awful Lot of Stengel Managin' Amazin' A's," National Baseball Hall of Fame file, April 20, 1981.

9. Ed Linn, *Inside the Yankees: The Championship Year* (New York: Ballantine Books, 1978), p. 56.

10. Lou Piniella and Maury Allen, *Sweet Lou* (New York: G.P. Putnam's Sons, 1986), p. 151.

11. Joseph Durso, *New York Times*, December 10, 1980.

12. *Utica Observer-Dispatch*, August 1, 1976.

13. Noel M. Tichy and Stratford Sherman, *Control Your Destiny or Someone Else Will* (New York: HarperBusiness, 1994), pp. 104–105.

Chapter 5

Leading Your Organization

Being named manager gives you a certain amount of authority, but it does not make you a leader. Leaders need followers. Leaders gain followers by displaying competency and by creating excitement for the task at hand. Billy excelled at both of these things.

A vital key to understanding the leadership of Billy Martin comes down to one word: loyalty. Billy Martin knew how to give loyalty to his players, and that was perhaps the greatest key to his earning their loyalty in return. Despite his tough-guy image, Billy Martin really had very few requirements of his ballplayers. Basically, he demanded 100 percent commitment to the team, and he demanded that players follow his instructions on the diamond. If players gave that commitment, Billy would do anything for them, and he was genuinely concerned with their welfare.

▶ **Paul Blair:** *This is what I'm trying to do with my guys. What I try to do is . . . let them understand that I care for them. And this is what Billy did. There is no question that he fought for us players. He wouldn't let George [Steinbrenner] come in to mess with us at any time. He'd take the heat. He'd be the buffer. And this is what I try to do to my boys. I want them to understand that any problems they have, if I can help them with it, please come to me and let me try and help them. And that's the way Billy was. So that's what I'm trying to take away from Billy.*

Establishing Your Authority

Billy Martin demanded that he be the only leader on his team. He fundamentally believed that as the leader, he needed authority, and so he fought very hard to prove to his players that he was running the show. Billy wanted his players to do many self-sacrificing things for the good of the team, so he needed to have them believe he was the leader, accept his baseball values, and follow his instructions. Without that authority, optimal execution of his diamond agenda was an impossibility, because his players would be moving this way and that, following the baton of more than one conductor.

▶ **Buck Showalter:** *My first recollection of Billy was how he carried himself. There was just a certain aura about him, that he was in charge. I think he drove home that responsibility with me of what being in charge comes with, as far as making decisions. He was very passionate about the Yankees. That's something that burned very deep inside. Billy had a zest for competition. I think of the great confidence that Billy's clubs played with. A lot of it had to do with the persona he brought to those clubs.*

In today's big-money era of sports, the baseball manager constantly has to defend the integrity of the team against the power of the bottom line. That requires trust. A player who suspects he is on the bench because a lesser player with a bigger contract or a more powerful agent is being nudged onto the diamond by the owner can create dissension and make the manager look like a puppet. The game and the team concept become a sham. The manager has to ensure that the game maintains its integrity.

Not all players will be happy, especially the ones who are not playing much. But as long as the entire team believes that the manager is attempting to put his best combination onto the field to win each game, the manager's leadership retains its viability. Billy fought very hard to maintain that show of authority, especially during his five Yankee stints. He believed it was absolutely critical to winning, and other managers agree.

▶ **Buck Showalter:** *I think it's important that the players know that the manager has a certain hammer, and that he's going to make the decisions and someone else's not going to dictate to him. The only thing that's going to be dictated to him is by your actions. If I play well, I'm going to play. The greatest accolade a manager can pay a player is putting him somewhere in the order. And once you take that hammer of being able to make out the lineup away from the manager and the players know that, then you might as well fold the wagons, because it's over. If they know that you don't have complete say-so over those things, it's hard not only to get their respect, it's also hard to make them accountable. Because they know, "Hey, it's no big deal. This guy's just a figurehead."*

▶ **Mike Pagliarulo:** *Every player can feel that. Whether the press thinks it or not, whether the fans believe it or not, or whatever is written or said, the players know who's calling the shots . . . Billy was calling the shots. It's a really good thing knowing that this guy's going to go up to bat for you, even though you might be stinking it up. I felt bad when Billy wasn't the manager after '88, because I really liked him. I enjoyed being with him, and he was on my side. And I would have done anything for him, too.*

▶ **Charlie Manuel:** *When he got named manager of the Twins, in that spring of '69, I made our ballclub. He put me in right field and left field, and he played me a lot. And I started hitting, and I had a tremendous spring. That same year, if you look, he kept not only guys like me, but he kept a lot of rookies. I think Billy picked his team for talent, ability—pluses—what the guys can do, if he can run, throw, hit. He just didn't let who the guy was, or because he'd been in the big leagues, influence him on picking his team. He picked the best guys that he thought for his team, because I know that he did not have to keep myself or [Graig] Nettles or [Rick] Renick. He picked us because that's who he thought was his best players.*

The Case of David Clyde

Billy ultimately lost his job managing in Texas over a player issue. The club was trying to establish a following in Texas, and in 1973 (when

Billy was still with Detroit), while losing over 100 games, the Rangers' front office management utilized a gimmick just to increase the gate. That gimmick was David Clyde, the number one draft choice in all of baseball and a kid fresh out of high school. Clyde was a left-handed pitcher and a tremendous talent who figured to be a star someday. But he was not ready to pitch in the major leagues.

Whitey Herzog, manager of the 1973 Rangers, loved Clyde and was eager to have him go to the minor leagues to get some seasoning and confidence, but the Rangers' owners had others ideas. They knew that if they put him on the mound right away, fans would flock to the park. But was Clyde ready to pitch in the major leagues? Was he the best guy for Whitey and, in 1974, for Billy, to put on the mound on a given night? No. And in Billy's world, there was no way that this could happen. This violated an absolute with Billy. It was an affront to the game and to his leadership, especially since Billy's 1974 Rangers were winning and attracting fans on the merit of their play, not on the merit of a gimmick.

Clyde got off to a good start in 1974, with a 3–1 record, but things faded from there, and Martin and his coaches wanted to send Clyde down to the minor leagues. The new Rangers management, led by owner Brad Corbett and Billy's former Yankee teammate, Dr. Bobby Brown, disagreed. Whereas Martin was brought to Texas and given a free hand by previous owner Bob Short, Corbett's team chose to exert more control. The Clyde situation, among other events, helped pave the way for Billy's eventual ouster in mid-1975.

▶ **Charlie Silvera:** *One of the reasons we were let go was the David Clyde thing. Billy said, "Well, we gotta do something about David Clyde. He's deteriorating. His habits are not good anymore. What should we do? Should we send him out, or should we keep him here?" He asked me first. I said, "Well, I think you ought to send him out. Send him to Sacramento, give him a couple starts out there. Bring him back and let him open up against the Yankees." All the coaches agreed, then the front office didn't, and so he stayed. He opened against the Yankees and went less then two innings before a full house. And from then on, we were gone.*

Bobby Brown went to desperate measures to try to get Billy to toe the line in order to help him keep his job. He even brought in old teammate Gil McDougald from New Jersey to try to talk to Billy.

▶ **Gil McDougald:** *I remember, Doc Brown asked me to fly down to Texas when Billy was managing. There was a left-handed bonus player, a pitcher, that they signed right out of high school. And the Texas ballclub wanted Billy to pitch him. "No way! No way will I pitch that kid." Now, the club is trying to draw people, right? They're trying to stimulate a hometown kid. In the meantime, Billy is extremely mad at the guys up above. So Bobby says, "Gil, if you don't fly down and try to talk to him, I'm going to fire him." I says, "Fire him, because hey, you know Billy. He'll say, 'Gil, you're in all this b.s.?'" I said, "The minute I try to make sense to him, his back goes up." I said, "Bob, I'll come down. I'll try to talk to him, but Bob, don't expect anything." So I told Bill, I said, "Bill, how many times do you have to get fired? You're always trying to prove that you're smarter than somebody. Why don't you prove that they're dumber than you by going ahead and pitching the guy? Why is it a big deal? It's only one game you gotta pitch him." He said, "No way!" I said, "Oh, well. Nice try." But I tell you, that's the truth. And then they eventually fired him.*

As a footnote to this story, Clyde wound up the 1974 season with a record of 3–9 and a 4.38 ERA. He played in one game for Texas in 1975, then resurfaced with Cleveland in 1978 and 1979. He left baseball after the 1979 season with a lifetime record of 18–33—no doubt having suffered for being in over his head and caught in the middle of a disagreement between the on-field and the front-office management. Had either Herzog or Martin had his way, Clyde's career *may* have unfolded differently. As in other businesses, a short-term bottom-line focus can exact ugly consequences on the rank and file.

Doing What Needs to Be Done

Billy's obstinacy was not smart as it pertained to his job security. But from the standpoint of being loyal to the game and loyal to the players on the team, his actions made sense.

▶ **Buck Showalter:** *Billy certainly wasn't afraid to stand up for things that he felt was right. One thing, you wish that Billy had picked his battles a little better. Billy fought every battle! He didn't pick his battles. I've learned that you've got to pick the battles you can win and are worth winning. If you're constantly doing that, you're in a constant state of battling, because there are a lot of people who haven't walked this walk and don't know. And you can't explain it to him. Whether it be media or people in the organization that have never played a game or gone through a season, you just can't explain to them what goes on down here until you've been through it.*

In 1983, with the Yankees, Billy faced the unenviable task of benching free-agent acquisition Steve Kemp, a proven RBI man with Detroit and the White Sox, in favor of then-unknown rookie Don Mattingly. Kemp had signed a five-year, $5.5 million contract with the Yankees, and during spring training had led the team in home runs, RBIs, and batting average. However, in the fourth game of the season, he injured his shoulder badly, and it impacted his swing. While he was still able to play, he slumped miserably, and Billy slowly but surely replaced him in the lineup with Mattingly, whose confidence grew with the playing time.

In 1987, Billy recalled, "I remember when I took a lot of heat because I wanted to play Mattingly over Steve Kemp . . . But you could just see that Mattingly was a natural hitter and an outstanding defensive player, either in the outfield or at first base."[1] Of course, Mattingly caught fire, and by the time he stopped hitting, his #23 was retired in Yankee Stadium's hallowed Monument Park. Kemp, because of the injuries, never regained his true form for the Yankees or anyone else (although he managed to hit .291 as a part-time player in 1984).

The fact that a highly visible owner like George Steinbrenner had paid so much money for Kemp naturally put pressure on the manager to play him. And at the same time, Kemp was a very good player and presumably would have come out of the slump with enough at-bats and time to recover properly from his injuries. Yet Billy had a player on the bench in Mattingly who was ready to go *today*. And in New York, the team was expected to win *today*. As games go by and the free agent doesn't hit, the manager has a responsibility to the other players to put somebody in the lineup who will get the job done. Billy had to do what needed to be done.

The media tried to read too much into the Kemp-Mattingly situation, using the years of history between Billy and Steinbrenner to insinuate that Billy was benching the star to spite the owner. But that really wasn't the case this time.

▶ **Dave Righetti:** *You gotta remember, not only did Kemp basically lose his hitting eye, no question about it, but early in the year he cracked a bone in his chest. He wasn't healthy. He wasn't able to do things. And he's a line drive hitter that hits the ball in the gaps, which is not right for Yankee Stadium. Billy didn't sign Steve Kemp. He loved his hustle and all that, but he didn't fit. It's not what we needed. So I think that was the problem. He didn't just play Donnie to spite George and take Kemp out. Donnie was just a little better. He was a better fit.*

Protecting Your Authority

The leader must always protect his or her authority. As Billy himself put it:

> "Players have to believe in the manager's authority or they can't do their best. The manager isn't always right; nobody is. But somebody has to make decisions, and the manager is the one—and if the players don't have the conviction that your decisions are mostly right, they can't carry them out wholeheartedly . . . a lot of the time, you have to make a player do something he doesn't want to, for the good of the team . . . You can't do it if the player thinks, 'Why listen to him? He's not the boss. He may be gone next year. I'll do it my way.' When that attitude takes hold, teams don't win . . . For a team to win, a manager . . . has to have authority, above all, because none of the other things can happen if the players don't have confidence in the manager's judgment, and in the fact that it is *his* judgment, not someone else's, that counts."[2]

Martin would go to unusual lengths to protect his authority. Detroit slugger Willie Horton once watched Billy quit his job as manager of the Tigers when club General Manager Jim Campbell lectured Billy on how to manage Horton with the slugger sitting right there in the room with them. During spring training, Billy had made a mistake regarding Horton, and the next morning, Campbell called a meeting with Billy and Horton to discuss the situation. Horton recalled what happened next.

▶ **Willie Horton:** *Mr. Campbell said, "Lookit, Billy, I don't want you to say anything. Willie, I don't want you to say anything. Billy, not only to Willie, but to all the other players, you've got to communicate." Well, Billy jumped up, and there's fire! He had a pipe that Mr. Campbell gave him years ago, and he threw it across the desk. He said, "You take your pipe and your team. You don't tell me how to run my ball team." And at first I didn't understand it, but I did understand it after. See, that's the man. When you gave Billy a job, that was his team. When I thought about it, it's true—all he was talking about was respect. You never say that in front of a player.*

Billy knew he had made a mistake with Horton, but that was not the point. The point was that Campbell was showing that he had power over Billy, which in Billy's mind could only undermine his leadership role with his player and with his team.

▶ **Willie Horton:** *He came back and told me that he was sorry himself, as a man. Nobody in this world ever knew but me and Billy. But he told me that the only way you have leadership is if you have control. He admitted he was wrong to me, but said if he had to admit it to the team, he wouldn't do it, because he would lose control. I took what he told me, and I learned character from him. He gave me so much more value in life to live, and he's part of me in what I'm doing today. I carry myself as a strong individual.*

Billy's players generally saw a leader in Billy that they were excited to line up behind. They believed in his abilities fully, which is so important in enabling a leader to establish and keep his or her authority.

▶ **Toby Harrah:** *The thing about a lot of managers you play for, they do things and you're kind of questioning whether they're doing the right thing. When Billy Martin made a move, everybody knew that it was the right move. Nobody ever questioned what Billy did. If Billy told me to run through that window, I'd just take off and run like hell and go through it. And that's the kind of loyalty I had toward Billy. All I know is, I never really felt scared playing under Billy. I felt confident. I just felt like Billy was our leader, he set the tempo, and you just felt like one way or the other, with Billy managing the ballclub, we could win— no matter who we were playing. For me anyway, I believed in him that much.*

Billy got his players behind him because his baseball judgment was sound. He also earned their respect through his attitude. Players knew where he stood, and they could either accept his program or reject it entirely.

▶ **Dave Righetti:** *Outside of being philosophical, I liken it to Patton. Supposedly his GIs hated his guts, but they trusted him to lead them and they'd win. If they went in it aggressively and went in it with him, they might come out on top and win. That's the way I always felt with Billy. To me, that's a leader, regardless if all the guys believed in him, because then you're talking about a cult hero. I never minded people being a dissenter, and with Billy there was no fence sitters. I think he brought that out of guys. You were either with him or against him, and I think in that way, that is a leader, because he makes it a definitive answer: "Here it is. I'm the guy, and if you want to win, go with me. We're going to win." If you don't want any part of that, obviously, you'll find a way not to be there. I think that's just as much a leader as anything else. In professional sports, that's all that matters. You were definitely trying to win games, and he brought those guys out. The cream would come up, there wasn't any hiding.*

▶ **Bobby Meacham:** *Billy was just one of those guys. You know when you're with a guy who just won't back down? When you go play a game, or play a season, you want to be with somebody who's gonna watch* *your back and fight with you till the end. And that's how Billy came off. If you did things his way, if you did things the right way, he's gonna fight for you and with you till the end. And that makes you just wanna go to war with the guy. Whereas Yogi [Berra] was more of a "I know the game and we're gonna play the game the right way" guy, but you didn't really feel like he was gonna fight for you if you had a brawl or something. Billy, you knew was gonna be right next to ya.*

Accepting the Responsibility of Leadership

The leader must also accept the responsibility of leadership—something Billy always did. Billy earned loyalty by standing up for his players and by siding with them in most of their disputes with the front office. Even the press, never totally enamored of Billy Martin, recognized his willingness to fight for his players and to be his own man.

Wrote *New York Times* reporter Murray Chass early in 1977, "Martin is the kind of manager who will back a player all the way down the line if that player has done a job for him. This trait has led to some of the differences between him and Steinbrenner."[3] Wrote another *Times* reporter, Dave Anderson, months later during the 1977 World Series, ". . . what George Steinbrenner may not realize is that because Billy Martin is what he is, Billy Martin might be the best manager for the best team money can buy. George Steinbrenner would prefer a manager who will follow orders. But players seldom respond to a manager who is a puppet for an owner . . . Players usually perform best for a manager who is his own man, not the owner's man."[4]

▶ **Dave Righetti:** *You knew who the leader was. You knew it wasn't George, see? He's the ultimate boss, but you felt like Billy was almost on your side and not the organization's. He was all Yankee, but he was pro-player, pro-uniform, and pro-field. If there was a rain game or something like that, he was pro–calling that game off. He didn't want people getting hurt just to get a gate. He was all about winning ballgames and protecting his players. There was nobody like Billy.*

▶ **Mickey Rivers:** *Billy took care of the guys, because if George was going to come down and have something to say, we'd talk to Billy. He'd say, "Look, I'll take care of you idiots. I know what I'm doing, so you let me do the talking. If I say something you don't like, we'll talk about it later." So he argued for the players. We knew where we stand with him, because we already went over this, before George even got to the meeting. So that's why the guys like him, because he stood up for the guys. He'd say, "OK, I'll fine you $500." Boom. We'd give him $500. Couple weeks, there's your money back. You know what I'm saying? That's what it took. That what it took. And that's why the guys played for Billy. That's why he got the best out of the guys, because the guys believed in Billy.*

Billy's actions often had the effect of pulling the team unit in closer to create an "us versus them" mentality. So without making anybody a better hitter or fielder, he strengthened the power of the team. "Them" might be the umpires, management, rowdy fans, or the media on any given day.

▶ **Toby Harrah:** *He really kind of, for me anyways, created the atmosphere that it was you against the world. It was you against the press. It was you against the fans. It was you against the other team. And that's what was special about Billy.*

If you violated the closed circle or in Billy's mind showed what he considered to be disrespect, he'd come at you right away.

▶ **Dave Righetti:** *Steve Kemp, who's a good friend and a funny guy, made one mistake. I think he talked to Joe Falls of the* Detroit Times *or whatever the heck it is there. And in the paper, they asked the inevitable question, "Who do you think was the better manager? Sparky [Anderson]? Or do you like Billy?" Oh God! 'Cause he played for Sparky for like seven years. And I guess Kemp said, "You know, they're both great, but maybe Sparky communicates with his players a little bit better." So . . . Joe Falls's Sunday column in Detroit was great. It's almost the whole front page, and it's filled with quotes and stuff. And so that was in there. Billy* *saw it. All his friends saw it . . . But anyway, we're stretching on the floor in the locker room in Detroit, which is real tiny, and my cubicle was behind this little corner behind the manager. And I could hear Billy talking in there and coming out. And Kemper's right there on the floor below him. He goes, "Hey Kemper!" "Yeah, skip, what's up?" "How's this for communication? You ain't f—ing playing today!" And that's no bullshit. And he took him out. I think Mattingly played and never came out. That's pretty much a true story. But poor Kemper, everything bad happened to him.*

▶ **Bobby Richardson:** *Well, he was a battler. And I mean, just like Reggie Jackson. It didn't matter who it was, if you did something that he felt wasn't quite right, he'd challenge you. And he surely wasn't afraid of anything.*

Recalled Graig Nettles before the 1983 season, "Billy is the only manager we have ever had who stands up to George. He is the only manager who will fairly make up his mind about me and then decide whether I can still play or not . . . In the past other managers have said, 'We've decided to do this.' And when they say 'we,' they mean George and I have decided. Billy says 'I,' not 'we.' Billy knows what I have done for him in the past, and he knows what I can do for him."[5] With all of the managers whom Nettles had played for in more than ten seasons with the Yankees, he had a pretty credible sample set from which to draw his conclusions.

Billy's willingness to stand up for his beliefs helped a player like Nettles because it gave him one less thing to worry about. The ability to focus on the job at hand, without having to worry about management doing the right thing, is critical in baseball or in other businesses. Have you ever worried about criticism from a superior who you felt lacked the expertise to truly assess your contributions? The stress from that feeling can break down focus and poorly impact performance. When a leader seems to understand your contributions and needs, it secures that loyalty and bond. Billy had a sense for both the needs and abilities of his players, not just in general, but on a day-to-day basis, and his decisions were made accordingly.

, let me ask you this: Who do you want me to bring out of
at's better than you were at the time?" Well, argument's
as nobody out there that could come in and throw the ball
the time. That was flattering, but it was also to the point:
to win a ballgame.

y was in that dugout, he was focused on winning the
hat the owners, writers, or fans were thinking. And he

e: Billy, he'd been fired. I don't think he ever thought about
. The only thing that mattered to him was winning, and he'd
ay he thought that he could to win. Whether it was a psycho-
antage, whether it was taking a chance that didn't make sense
o-called baseball people, he didn't care. If he thought it gave
nce to win, he'd do it, and if it looked like it was something that
second-guessed, then big deal, "Let 'em come and second-
e."

Russa: The old adage is, "Manage from the gut and don't watch
tt," and I think you have to do that in order to be successful.
s a very instinctive manager. He wasn't afraid to make a move in
out.

arrah: I remember, I had one of my better years, I drove in 90-
hing runs under him, and I think I drove in seven or eight runs just
ueeze plays. He loved the squeeze play. The reason he liked the
ze play is because it can really disrupt the pitcher, it disrupts the
se. It pisses everybody off, because here's a ball that maybe travels
or four feet that wins the game for you. And Billy was great at using
queeze play. He never was like a lot of managers I've seen today. They
"Well, we just need that one extra run. We need to get that extra run
et the five-run lead." These guys squeeze in the third inning of a ball-
e, and I think, "Billy Martin would just puke if he saw guys squeezing
he third inning of a damn ballgame." Billy would do it in the ninth, with
game on the line. He would do it when it took balls. Half the managers

▶ **Dave Righetti:** When we had an off day, we got it. Before, when he wasn't the manager, George would steal the off day from ya. It never happened when Billy was around. George didn't understand that kind of stuff. I don't know if he does to this day. I'm sure all these guys gotta show up, do everything exactly the same. All the stuff nowadays you hear about, Billy didn't care about all that crap. Just be ready for the game. You don't all have to be out there at 3:30 in the afternoon, for crying out loud, for a 7:05 game. So to him, it was just play ball, show up on time, and just play hard. And that was it, that was really it.

What was amazing about Billy Martin was that he not only would go to the wall for stars like Dave Righetti, Graig Nettles, Thurman Munson, Mickey Rivers, Sparky Lyle, and Catfish Hunter, but also for reserves. He had heated disputes with front offices in Detroit, Texas, and New York over utility players being sent to the minor leagues or being released. Why? Partly because he wanted a say in who stayed and who went, a say he bristled over not having. Partly because he might see some contribution a player makes to the team—like a veteran clubhouse leader like Elrod Hendricks—which is actually more important to the overall functioning of the team at any given time than a "better" hitter or pitcher might add. But mainly, Billy wanted to show his players that he'd fight for every last one of them if they'd been loyal to him.

▶ **Mike Pagliarulo:** Being a young player, and having Billy Martin as your manager—people certainly had their opinions, but Billy would fight for his guys no matter what. If you were dead wrong, Billy would go out and fight for you. He didn't care. And that's what he did. I've seen him do it. I've seen our guys screwing up. Billy didn't care—it was his guy. And if he liked you, no matter what you did, he was going to fight for you. He must have been a great teammate when he played. He must have been just a great teammate. You want guys like that to fight for you no matter what. That's being a team. That's teamwork. And that's how I felt. He would do anything for his players. All these little things, if you were one of the players, he took care of you. And if he liked you, he gave you everything you needed to be as good as you can be.

Billy would just do whatever it took to help his players.

▶ **Mickey Rivers:** *He always made sure his guys are feeling good about whatever he had to do. And he'll back you up, too. Thurman was so sore. I'll tell you how bad Thurman was, Thurman used to play on his knees— he couldn't get up. He [Billy] would go to George, "All right, George, we need a masseuse." We'd get about three. "Look, George, we need a sauna." Sauna, boom. Get a sauna. "Hot tub." Boom, we'd get a hot tub. We had everything you could have for that team, what you'd call a modern-day clubhouse. We had everything we needed. He was looking out for the guys, and that's why the guys like him. We was one of the first-class teams. Everywhere we went, we could stay first-class, and do everything first-class. And that's why it had an effect on the guys, that's why we was winning.*

George Patton ran his tank training school at the Army Staff College in Langres, France, in 1918 in a similar fashion, always looking after the welfare of the men. He said, "When the first men of the Tank Corps came to Langres we had hot coffee for them. One of them, later commissioned, said to me after the war that this act had a profound effect."[6] That's why Patton was winning.

If you have become a leader, be sure to remember what it's like to be in the trenches. If you give a little without being a pushover, you can build loyalty and bring your group closer together. Billy did just that, even when it meant standing up to the team owners.

Ignoring the Naysayers

Sometimes leaders have to ignore the naysayers—those who oppose or criticize your actions. For Billy, naysayers could come from the ranks of team ownership, of fans, or the media. Billy learned to ignore naysayers while coaching third for Twins manager Sam Mele in the mid-1960s, when the two implemented their running game and saw it criticized heavily.

▶ **Sam Mele:** *We had a [Harmon] Killebrew, a [Jim] Lemon, a Bob Allison—the big long ball hitters. They struck out a lot and clogged the*

---

bases a little bit. And so in sp give a damn how many guys 'em score on a single, even if Keep them running. Keep them not bitching about it up in the st. getting a lot of guys thrown out. talked about it. That's what we're the outfielders—or infielders on a b going to have to hurry their throws. do it. We figure that's best for the infectious with the players all year lor 'em home. Guys make a bad throw. S halfway up the line. If it was a swinging

Billy remembered Mele's support that Mele told him, "Don't listen to any to all that criticism. I know what you'l You just keep right on doing what you anybody."[7] Later, Billy passed Sam's mes:

▶ **George Mitterwald:** *Billy used to say, "A lot but to me it's first-guessing because whe exactly what I'm doing. It may not turn out th is the way that I can beat the odds, and this i it." But people didn't realize that.*

But by learning to block out the expecta on his own goals, Billy grew as a manager.

▶ **Matt Keough:** *He just figured out where he could lievable. All of a sudden, where did these 20 co from? People were saying, "What is he doing?" We is he was winning. I asked him one day, when I p game in Toronto, and Ron Luciano, who was wol Game of the Week at the time, he had me fried after was out of gas. But I asked Billy the next day, "How ca 14 innings? I mean, don't you know they're going to*

He said, "Mat the bullpen th over. There w like I was at We're trying

When Bil game, not w had guts.

▶ **Tom Griev** being fired do it any logical ad to most him a cha would be guess m

▶ **Tony La** your bu Billy wa the du

▶ **Toby** some on s squee defer three the s say, to g gai in the *today don't have the balls to do it with the game on the line. To execute the squeeze play, you have to have balls as a manager, and not really care about being second-guessed. And Billy didn't give a shit.*

▶ **Charlie Silvera:** *I'll tell you what, he had more balls than any man I've ever met in my life. And he wasn't afraid to squeeze at home and steal home. And it was exciting! There was a method to his approach, sort of a shock treatment. Get out and get ahead. Let them know that we're going to do things to keep on the attack. He had his own way of doing things, and he sort of revolutionized managing.*

Dealing with the Media

As stated earlier, leaders also have to contend with external naysayers. For Martin, that meant in part the media. External concerns are ever present for leaders, and his inability to deal consistently with the media in a positive manner was perhaps one of Billy's major flaws. Billy struggled with the media throughout his career, especially in New York. Phil Pepe, who covered Billy throughout his career and liked and admired him, regrets Martin's behavior around the New York press, not only because he oftentimes considered it wrong but also because it hurt Billy and contributed to his firings.

▶ **Phil Pepe:** *It bothered me that Billy could very often be short and rude and nasty to baseball writers. He wasn't that way with me or Moss Klein, another writer traveling with us. If you were a regular on the beat covering his team, and you showed that you appreciated him, I mean, there wasn't anything he wouldn't do for you. And I'm talking about anything, not only as a writer, but also as a person. And yet his reputation with writers was terrible, and it was well deserved that it was terrible, because he mistreated writers badly frequently. And I witnessed this, and it bothered me so much because I said to myself, "Billy, why do you have to be that way? Why do you treat people like that?"*

Martin prided himself on being a baseball expert. It was his life. As such, it was tough for him to be questioned by people who hadn't walked the walk, and he was unwilling or unable to bite his tongue when they said what he considered to be amateurish things. Add to that his volatile emotions and his paranoia of the press's power over him—especially in New York, where the competition for a scoop on Billy ran high—and he didn't always do what might have been the smartest things politically.

▶ **Billy Martin, Jr.:** *Dad didn't care. He wasn't going to play those games with those guys and suck up to them. Where there's a side of me that supremely respects that, there's also a side of me that says it's certainly not the smartest thing he ever did. He could only go so far before his snapping point, and then, look out. I've sat in his office, and I've heard a writer ask him a question, where dad just gave that "are you f—ing kidding me?" look. It would just totally discredit you in front of everybody. He'd look at the reporter and say, "Did you ever play baseball? I mean, Little League? Anything?" And where do you least want to be ridiculed? In front of your peers. He would just hammer them. His office could be just packed full of reporters, and he would just stop and pause and stare, and you could just see him seething.*

▶ **Marty Appel:** *That provocative edge. I can see him in his office, in his sweatshirt with his uniform shirt off. It wasn't easy in there. Somebody was always on the verge of asking a question the wrong way. And so there was a tension in that office, even though he seemed to be sitting back and relaxed and smoking his Sherlock Holmes pipe, and making the occasional little joke, there was always a tension in the air that some writer, inexperienced with this drill, was going to say something that was just going to explode.*

▶ **Phil Pepe:** *I've thought about it a lot through the years, and I've come to the conclusion that it was very difficult for Billy to sit there after losing a game and have to explain why he failed. Every day when your day's work is done, how would you like to be questioned about your failures of that particular day? Billy just couldn't tolerate it. And again, he came from an era when that wasn't necessary. Casey Stengel didn't have press conferences every day, win or lose. In those days, the writers rarely went to the clubhouse. They wrote about the game. You didn't have to explain why* *this strategy failed or why that strategy failed. And he never could deal with it. He just couldn't deal with being second-guessed.*

The Case of Reggie Jackson

Showing loyalty to the players became more difficult for Billy and all other baseball managers after the advent of free agency during the winter of 1976. In the Yankee situation, for example, the team had gone to the playoffs and World Series in 1976 for the first time since 1964 led by a tightly knit 25-man unit. The leaders of the team—Munson, Nettles, Chambliss, Piniella, and Hunter—all played for the team first and willingly followed Billy's command. They were stars, but they were great team players, too.

After the 1976 season, Billy sought to add another team-oriented star to the club, right-handed outfielder Joe Rudi, who was available in the first-ever free agent draft. From a baseball standpoint, Rudi made sense, because he would add a needed right-handed power bat to the lineup.

Instead, the Yankees acquired Reggie Jackson, the charismatic slugger who, like Rudi, had been a crucial part of three World Champion Oakland A's teams of the early 1970s. Jackson was an intelligent athlete who played the press to his advantage and would sell tickets for the Yankees just by showing up. From a box office and baseball standpoint, Reggie looked great to George Steinbrenner, and of course, on that score, he was right beyond his wildest dreams. Presumably, Jackson would make the Yankees even stronger.

Unfortunately, Jackson wasn't a great fielder and struck out too much. And unlike the team players who had led the Yankees to the title the year before and Joe Rudi, he was a man who was not about to suppress his personality for his new teammates or manager. These weaknesses were glaring to Billy, who was more focused on the dynamics of his club than ticket sales or the back page of *The New York Post*.

▶ **Phil Pepe:** *Billy liked Joe Rudi, and he begged George Steinbrenner to sign Joe Rudi and not Reggie Jackson. Billy was from the old school, from the time when players weren't getting those big dollars, and I think he had* *a tough time dealing with the escalation of the salaries. Especially since his idol was always Mickey Mantle. Mantle was a guy who was humble, was a team guy, played hard, played to win, played hurt, and was Billy's best buddy. And all of a sudden, here was Reggie. Reggie was the symbol of the new Mantle, and I think that it bothered him. "He can't shine Mantle's shoes, and yet look, we have to treat him like an equal of Mantle's? He makes all this money? It's just not right." Billy never wanted Reggie on the team. He kept saying, "He's not a Yankee type." And I think what he meant by that was he was too for himself. Reggie used to like to boast and brag. And so, they got off on the wrong foot right from the beginning.*

The players who had won for Martin in 1976 were wary of Jackson's attitude from day one and also were bitter over the paycheck an outsider was getting when they were the ones who had led the club back to first place and into the spotlight. Billy, who prided himself on being a player's manager, sided with the men from the 1976 club.

▶ **Phil Pepe:** *Billy made his biggest mistake the first day that Reggie Jackson arrived in training camp in Fort Lauderdale. Billy completely ignored him, and Reggie ignored Billy. Billy says, "Well, he should have come in to me. I'm the manager, he should have come into my office." And Billy's probably right. But Billy, if he was the smart management guy that everybody thinks he was—or that he should have been—he would have swallowed his pride, I believe, and he would have gone over to Reggie and stuck his hand out and said, "Hey, big guy. I'm glad you're with us. Great to have you here." From that day on, there would have been no problems with Reggie. If he had only treated him like the star Reggie believed he was—and was. And the reason he didn't do that, I believe, is because he didn't want to make it seem like he was toadying up to Reggie, because the other players on the team would have resented it. They won for him the previous year, and he didn't want to make this new guy be the big star. But George was right, Billy was wrong. Reggie, yeah, he was full of himself, but because he loved the spotlight so much, he produced so well under its glare, and I think he gets a bum rap, because he was a guy who really wanted to win. He was a winner. He was a guy who could put people in the seats, which was important to Steinbrenner. He* *might not have been the team player or the complete player that Rudi was, but he was a better fit for New York and for the Yankees. Billy just couldn't see that and didn't accept it.*

But was Billy's handling of Reggie a mistake? If Billy, the ultimate team guy, went out of his way for a player who was all ego right off the bat, then wouldn't Billy have been making a mockery of his own 1976 leadership and his 1976 team—a team built on that core concept of team chemistry, team camaraderie, and no "stars"? It was a difficult situation and there were some major egos involved, and ultimately, Billy didn't want to have to coddle Reggie.

Instead, Billy wanted Reggie to coddle the team, so to speak. Billy batted Reggie fifth in the lineup when Reggie preferred to bat in the symbolic power spot of fourth. Billy benched Reggie against several of the tougher lefty pitchers around the league, even though other lefty sluggers like Nettles and Chambliss played. Billy substituted defensive great Paul Blair for Reggie late in games, and in fact, he preferred not to play Reggie in the field at all. He expected Reggie to accept all of this willingly, but Reggie mostly felt humiliated by the moves. Graig Nettles recalled:

> "New people on a ballclub should try to blend in before they let their personalities show. Reggie came on strong right from the start. It got him in bad with a lot of his teammates, because he was so outspoken right from the beginning. That first week Thurman and Lou and I were looking at one another wondering, 'What's this guy all about?' We had won the year before. We didn't need him and his flamboyance in order to win again . . . And what made our relationship with Reggie worse was that Reggie and George were buddy-buddy . . . We would wonder, 'Is this guy a player or is he front office?' . . . I know Billy felt very strongly about that. Billy likes to be numero uno, and he didn't like Reggie coming in and hogging the spotlight."[8]

As Piniella recalled it, "The spring of 1977 at Fort Lauderdale's Yankee Stadium now seems a blur of Reggie Jackson adventures . . . Reggie never tried to defuse the attention. He talked, and talked, and talked, always about himself, always about what he would contribute to the Yankees, always with the press hovering over him as if he were the only Yankee who had ever achieved anything in the game."[9]

▶ **Fred Stanley:** *I think in spring training, I think everybody was waiting to see how this was all going to play out. See, we got in a fight with Baltimore in '76 when Dock Ellis popped Reggie in the head with a pitch. So we were a little apprehensive, because Dock Ellis was still on the club. And we had some problems in spring training, because Reggie and Thurman didn't get along. We had problems because Reggie was doing some other things that were drawing attention to him. Reggie's a darn good player. And Reggie is Reggie, and everybody would understand that's been around him what you're talking about. Reggie had a flair for having the media attention on him, and before that it was Thurman and Billy. Thurman was almost MVP of the World Series, I mean he did everything. Thurman was a very great player in '76. And when Reggie came on, the spotlight changed a little bit, because Reggie was a guy that would look for an opportunity to talk the press. Whereas Billy and Thurman, they talked to 'em, but it wasn't their main objective. And I think that bothered Thurman, and I think it bothered Billy.*

As any baseball fan from the era well knows, spring training was just the start of the Yankees' adventures with Reggie. In fact, Billy spent the entire season trying to restore a team chemistry that was severely disrupted by Jackson's presence and the new era he represented. The disruption almost cost Billy his job many times in 1977, and ultimately did cost him his job in 1978. It was a tremendous test of leadership, one that Billy handled his way.

▶ **Marty Appel:** *This is sacrilegious, but there were days when I used to wonder whether he would just as soon lose with Reggie just to spite George, to say, "We won the pennant without this guy, now look what you've done." There were days that I wondered, not that he was losing on purpose, but I wondered if that style change sort of fit Reggie's pres-*

ence and then he could say, "Hey, I would have won this thing without Reggie. I did it last year."

Finally, everything came to a head on a hot day in Boston in June 1977. With a national television audience watching, Billy went after Reggie in the Fenway Park dugout after Jackson, playing in the outfield, seemed to dog it on a little pop fly that Jim Rice hustled into a double. Fred Stanley was on the field that day, and he had gone to the mound when Martin emerged from the dugout immediately following the play to change pitchers, and more interestingly, to change right fielders. Stanley, Mickey Rivers, and Ray Negron recall what happened.

▶ **Fred Stanley:** *At the time, we thought the ball should have been caught, and we would've been out of trouble. That really would have helped, an extra out. And all of a sudden, a run scores, Rice's on second. Plus you're in Boston, so there's the atmosphere. It was a pretty intense moment.*

▶ **Mickey Rivers:** *When the ball hit down there, Reggie, he didn't try to hustle at all for the ball. And the guy still was running around the bases, Jim Rice. And then he threw it in sidearm, and the guy scored a run. I said, "Oh, man." I see Billy come to the top of the steps. He started hollering! Reggie's saying, "Why'd you do that? Why'd you do that?" [Dick] Howser and Yogi [Berra] come closer. And they still hollering. And when Reggie got to the dugout, that's when the big scene started coming.*

▶ **Ray Negron:** *You want my interpretation? That day, I'm sitting next to Billy, when all of a sudden that ball drops in right field. One of the players said, "He loafed on it, Billy." And Billy got pissed right away. And he says, "Blair, get out to right field." And Blair's like, "Oh shit." He was at the end of the dugout, he says, "You sure?" "Get to right field. Tell him to get his ass in here." Blair's running out to right field, and Reggie, all of a sudden he notices, and he's gesturing, "What are you doing out here?" hoping probably that he's going out to the bullpen. And Blair says, "I'm in here." So when Reggie started coming in, and he started* *taking his glasses off, that's when I ran to the other end of the dugout, because Reggie started screaming right from the third base line. He was already screaming at Billy, "What the f— are you doing?" When he got to the dugout, he called Billy an old man. "What the f— are you doing, old man?" "Old man?" And Billy went nuts. He went ballistic. He went, "Whaaaattt?" And all of a sudden, as he starts to charge Reggie, that's when Yogi and Elston [Howard] grabbed him right away. With Reggie, he didn't really need to be held, because Reggie wasn't going to fight. He just wanted to mess with him, because he felt messed with. And his manhood had been tested in that situation. The first thing Reggie said was, "You embarrassed me in front of 50 million people?"*

Was the brawl premeditated by Billy? Not likely. However, it is likely that Billy knew at some point that some crisis would have to occur to resolve the situation and to determine who was managing the team— Billy, at $70,000 per year, or Reggie, with the then-astronomical five-year, $3.5 million contract? The players knew all along that something had to give on the club.

▶ **Mickey Rivers:** *See, that was a matter of time. This is what all the guys were talking about. It was going to come to that point, no matter what. It should have come to that point early, and they would have been through with it. But it had to come to that point. But we told Billy from the start, "You let him have too much rope, then you're going to hang yourself with it. Then you ain't going to see it." And that was the day it come to that point. I saw the ball. He [Jackson] was just lackadaisical out there in the outfield. The guy kept running. He knew it. And the guy scored the run. I could see it coming. Everybody could see it coming. It was a matter of time.*

The dugout brawl was seen as a sign of Martin's instability by some, but it's likely that a private closed-door meeting with Reggie probably would have had no impact on the slugger. Public embarrassment was a certain way to get through to the image-conscious Jackson. The fact that Reggie immediately pointed out to Billy that "50 million people" were watching shows that Billy had gotten his attention.

And underneath it all, Billy had more than Reggie on his mind through his very public act. From the perspective of almost all of his players, Billy was showing his loyalty to them. And they were loyal to him as well.

▶ **Mickey Rivers:** *That was the turning point, because before that, we'd ride on the bus, but Reggie could drive his Rolls. Billy wouldn't say nothing. "Ah, that's OK, I gave him permission." Nobody'd say nothin'. But the guys know the difference. And we'd say, "Oh, Skip, you know one time it's going to come down to this." And then when it come down to that point, [we'd] remind him, "Remember what we told you before, you started this way with him, and then . . ." And we told him like that. After a while, times got a little better, but we told him it was going to come to that point. If all of us went on the bus, we'da been better as a team. But wait till it come to that point. But see, nine out of the ten guys were with Billy. Because they know Billy was going to be behind 'em 100 percent.*

Billy himself has said of the event, "I knew the other 24 players were looking to see how I was going to handle this, with Reggie being a superstar and having the big contract. I thought if I did what had to be done, that would bring George down on me. But if I let it pass, I would lose the other 24 players . . . I knew what I had to do."[10]

▶ **Fred Stanley:** *Every manager handles different situations differently. Some managers would have waited until Reggie got in the dugout and then taken him out. Billy was a very emotional, fiery, "whatever happens, happens" manager. And at the moment, that was what he decided had to be done. And like it or not, it set. I tell you what it did, when we were in the clubhouse after the game, everybody was sitting around waiting to see exactly what else was going to happen, because we knew that Reggie was really upset with this deal. And we knew that Billy was not going to back down, and there was going to be some fire. And so they finally got Reggie out of there before things got crazy.*

Eventually, the team gelled again, including Reggie, who was awesome down the stretch. The Yankees got down to business in August and September and won the division title.

There was one more high-profile, though more diplomatic, incident between Billy and Jackson in 1977, when Billy sat Jackson during a do-or-die American League playoff game. With the season on the line, Billy benched Reggie in favor of the lighter-hitting, stronger-fielding Paul Blair. At the time, Billy said, "This is nothing you enjoy doing, but if I didn't do it for the ballclub, I shouldn't be managing."[11] Jackson, to his credit, kept his thoughts to himself, stayed in the game from the bench, and delivered a clutch pinch hit.

▶ **Paul Blair:** *It was a shocker, but it wasn't a shocker, because he just showed that, "Hey, I believe in you, you can go do your thing." Billy did that all year round. I think he kind of saw me throughout my career with Baltimore, and I did do a lot better job in key situations when the game was on the line. I seemed to raise my level of play for some odd reason. He seemed to feel that in me, and it was such a good, good feeling, because I remember when he told me that morning at breakfast that I was playing right field. He said, "I told George I'm putting you in right over Reggie." And he said George told him, "That's fine, but you better win." Well, it was just nice that a man showed that kind of confidence in you in that kind of a situation.*

Recalled Piniella, "Billy expected a low-scoring game and wanted defense. It was the ballsiest decision any manager ever made in a big game in my time . . . We were shocked. Billy never said anything to anybody about it. He was the manager."[12]

Believe it or not, both Blair and Jackson got big hits in a ninth-inning, come-from-behind rally to propel the Yankees into the World Series. Or in the understated words of Paul Blair, "I guess it turned out real good."

More than 20 years later, free agency has turned the game of baseball inside out. In many cases, players have the upper hand over the team manager. Back in 1977, Billy knew what was coming, and he didn't like it. He may have been wrong in some of the things he did to Reggie, but he didn't back down.

Billy earned the respect of his players by always doing what he believed was right for the team—by showing that he cared for the team first—even if it cost him his job. At the time, Phil Pepe wrote, ". . . it took a man of strong will and character to pull them through all the turbulence and turmoil, the controversy and contentiousness."[13] If Billy had not done a perfect job in those turbulent days of 1977, it was still an outstanding job of leadership in uncharted waters.

Putting Yourself in Your Followers' Shoes

As leader, you have to put yourself in your followers' shoes and never forget what they are going through. You need to have respect for them as people. There must be give and take. Billy pushed his players extremely hard on the field, but he was usually pretty easygoing after the final out was made.

▶ **Buck Showalter:** *Basically, if you're going to expect to be treated with respect, you had to respect the game and respect the Yankees, and do the things that he wanted you to do. But there was a certain leeway you were given if you did these things. There was a certain trust that you earned by doing that. He would then trust you. His trust didn't come easy—I mean, it wasn't something that he threw around easily. It had to be proven on the ballfield. It's not earned anywhere else. Not through a bunch of popping your gums, or talking, or anything else. It's done through actions.*

For Billy, that leeway might be letting a veteran skip batting practice if he wanted to on a given night.

▶ **Mickey Rivers:** *We didn't have to take no batting practice if we didn't want to. Billy didn't care, as long as we get the job done. The guys say, "It don't make no difference, Skip. We know our job. We going to win." Anyplace he went, he got the best out of the guys, because he knew how to talk to the guys, and the guys could understand him. He knew how to communicate with the guys, on their level. We know where he was coming from. If they have any problems, talk to him now, don't wait. Don't try to go out there and tell the paper this and that. He'd say, "If you have problems, come see me." And that's why the guys didn't*

have the problems, 'cause he'd come to the guys steady, and "we're
going to do this way."

That respect also carried over to the nightlife. In the 1970s, the
boys-will-be-boys nightlife was still a big part of the game, but Billy
didn't care too much about what his veteran players were doing, as
long as their behavior did not affect their play. His own escapades in
the 1950s with Whitey Ford and Mickey Mantle were of course
legendary, and to his way of thinking, had never stopped the Yankees from winning the World Series every year. So Martin was
tolerant.

▶ **Ray Negron:** *He didn't get in nobody's way, and we had a wild bunch of*
f—ing guys. And these were older guys, and he wasn't going to put in
no f—ing rules on these guys. Just, "Hey, respect me. Respect me." You
knew when Billy wanted something, you did it. That's all. Were we wild?
Absolutely. Did we have fights? Absolutely. Did we get up people's
asses? Absolutely. Did we play ball? Abso- f—ing -lutely. And did we
win? Truly absolutely. You wanna run a nursery school and have great
guys in your clubhouse and all that shit, be the f—ing Cleveland Indians,
and never get to the f—ing dance. OK? Simple as that.

Martin was often right there in the bar with his players, a violation
of one of baseball's age-old rules, and a rule that if followed would have
kept Billy free of trouble a couple of times. But Billy liked being around
the players, and he thought the rule was a foolish one. Said Billy, "That
was the old rule, but it wasn't my rule. I never sat down with my players, buddy-buddy. But I sit at the end of the bar and send them over a
round of drinks. Why should I treat them like men on the field and then
like boys off the field?"[14]

▶ **Rod Carew:** *Even if he ran into the players in a place, he was the kind of*
manager where you didn't have to get up and leave. Most managers
would say, "When I walk into a place, if you're there, I want you to go."
But he would just come over, he might buy you a drink, he'd sit down,
he'd talk to you, laugh and joke, and have a good time. That's just the

way he was. He's treating you as a grown person and will allow you to be yourself. One thing he used to always tell us was to be careful. Be careful on the way home. Not get into any trouble. We used to laugh because, here's a guy that didn't back down from anything, saying, "Don't let these people get on your nerves." And he did.

▶ **Fred Stanley:** *Billy still was a player, even when he was a manager. I think Billy loved the idea of putting that uniform on, going out there and seeing if he could do it. I think Billy challenged himself physically as a 50-year-old man would challenge himself to go out and do those things. He challenged himself off the field. It was always a game for him, it was always a gladiator approach. I think that's the things he did really well, and that's the things that got him in trouble.*

▶ **Toby Harrah:** *With Billy, it wasn't like once the game was over, that that was the end of Billy Martin for the day. No. You'd run into Billy on the road. You'd run into him in bars. You'd run into him in restaurants. And it was always like, when you're on the same team with him, you're like family to him.*

The players gave loyalty to Martin because he made it clear to them what was important to him and what was unimportant. He remembered when he had been in their shoes, and he had that empathy for them that actually helped him to secure their loyalty.

▶ **Mickey Rivers:** *You go out there, step on that field, you give him 100 percent. We goin' out there, we goin' to bust our butts. And after that, shoot, we'll go out. You know what I'm saying? He enjoyed it. He enjoyed people. We had a good time with Skip. And he took time with the guys; he'd sit down and talk.*

▶ **Mickey Morabito:** *He treated men as men. I mean, these guys aren't kids, this isn't college. These guys are all married, they're all old enough to be out there on their own. You know back then in the '70s when Earl Weaver was managing the Orioles, Earl wouldn't let the players in the hotel bar. He'd say, "That's where I drink, I don't want them in here."*

And they'd have to go to other places. And Billy, we'd talk about that, he'd say, "Ah, let 'em be in there, that way if they get in trouble, we can put 'em in an elevator and get 'em in their room." Rather than have to go out somewhere else where they have to get back in a cab and find their way back to the hotel. That never bothered him.

Billy knew that the respect he showed his players was going to help him because it fostered the loyalty he craved, and it promoted a familylike atmosphere. He knew it worked, saying, "Be honest with players and let them be men. If I show my players loyalty, they'll give me loyalty in return."[15]

Setting the Goal at its Highest

When Billy Martin arrived in a new city to manage, he inevitably began by saying, "I didn't come here to lose." He immediately began to talk about winning a championship, creating expectations of players—and *in* players—from the outset, even if the new organization was a supposed loser.

In 1965, years before he managed his first big league game, Billy shared a basic philosophy with *Sporting News* reporter Max Nichols, saying, "First place is the only way to think. I don't see how you can get anyone worked up by telling him that if he works hard and plays well, he might finish fifth."[16]

Years later, in March 1974, Billy—now an established manager about to begin his miracle turnaround of the Rangers—told *The New York Times*, "I'm going to do a job for this guy [team owner Bob Short] . . . I'm going to win this year. Nobody believes me, but I'm going to do it."[17] Tom Grieve remembers when Billy took the reigns of the Rangers.

▶ **Tom Grieve:** *The interesting thing about Billy was he took over the team and he had a clubhouse meeting. He said he didn't come to manage the Rangers to try to get them to be a .500 team. That would be a miracle in a lot of people's minds, just to see this team play .500 baseball, but that's not why he came here. He came here because the Rangers were going to win, and they were going to win a division title, they were going* *to win a pennant. And I can remember the reaction of the players was, "This guy has done things like this before, and I'm sure he's a great manager and he's got a lot of confidence, but he obviously hasn't seen us play if he thinks he's going to do this with us." So he had the confidence and he obviously believed it, but it took a lot longer than just that one meeting for the players to believe it, that's for sure.*

▶ **Frank Lucchesi:** *I remember one of the meetings, he says, "Forget about it! Let's not live in the past. We've got a club here that we're going to challenge for this pennant!" And he made the ballplayers believe in him, in a sense. How did he do it? It's tough to answer that. Just being himself. I think the big thing is that a lot of managers at times put you on a little bit, but he was very honest. He said it the way it was. Period. And that's one of the reasons the ballplayers believed in him. He wasn't trying to con 'em. He was positive with the players. His philosophy was, when he walked in the clubhouse, "You guys are going to win today. You hear what I said?"*

Martin did get his charges off to a fast start, and in May he told *New York Times* writer Murray Chass, "I told everyone in the spring we would have a good team and no one believed me, and when I say now that we're going to win it, no one believes me. But we are going to win it."[18] As Rangers beat reporter Randy Galloway put it, "While [Billy] couldn't get any buyers from the media, he apparently sold it to his players."[19]

▶ **Toby Harrah:** *In spring training, we were young and cocky, and Billy got the focus in the right direction, as far as winning now, and we were excited about that. I mean, here's a guy that's come in, a former Yankee, and a great reputation for winning. I mean, you literally took everything this guy said as the gospel. And it started in spring training, so by the end of the season, we were converted. He didn't have to do anything. He didn't have to do a doggone thing with us to motivate.*

Martin's willingness to talk a big game was very much like General Patton. As a young man, Patton read a little-known book by Gustave

LeBon called *The Crowd: A Study of the Popular Mind*, which suggested that individuals can be given feelings of invincible power, can drop their inhibitions, and can absorb the contagion of a collective will when hearing powerful messages from hypnotic leaders. Patton responded by noting in his copy of the book, "The will to Victory thus affects soldiers. It must be inculcated."[20]

Many of Patton's eccentricities appear to have been preconceived, planned, and based upon his subscription to LeBon's ideas. And so it was with Billy, who could inculcate with the best of them.

▶ **Willie Horton:** *I remember a couple of times, he actually set up two plays. When I was coaching first for the Yankees, I had to get him out there so he could get kicked out of the game to fire up the team! I mean, this man did so much stuff. He could pick up things when the team was getting flat, so before it gets flat, he's got to create things to get things going. I remember one time, he told me, "In the third inning, when you come in that dugout, I'm going to get on your behind. I'm going to chew your ass all the way to the back of the tunnel." I said, "What?" He said, "The team's flat. We got to get them going." And then in the fifth inning, he said, "You've got to get me to that umpire out there." So I did, and he lit in to him. That's how smart he was. That was his commitment.*

Playing Tough

Billy seemed to believe he had to be tough to lead, and he was tough. He kept that "Billy the Kid" image out front and kept his gentler acts in the background to maintain the hard-charging aura, that while true was only a part of the actual man.

▶ **Charlie Silvera:** *One time when he was the manager, Muhammad Ali was coming in; he wants to visit. And we'd just lost a tough one. Billy said, "Tell him to stay out or I'll knock him on his ass." You know, he'd fight him; he didn't care. Same thing in Minnesota with Hubert Humphrey. Billy campaigned for him, but we lost a tough game in Minnesota, and Hubert came in there with his entourage, and he told Hubert, "Get your ass out of here! This isn't the time to come in here." Hubert* *left. And I was in charge of the door, and he [Billy] told me, "Don't let anybody in here till I tell you to let somebody in here!"*

▶ **Willie Horton:** *He wanted that tough image so he could get the best out of people, and I don't think people ever really knew that. But Billy was soft. He was a caring person. I hear so many things said about him off the field. It hurts me, because I don't think the world ever really knew this man. I feel he gave so much, not only to me, but nothing's never been said. I used to watch and say, "Why don't they ever say any good things about him?" And I think he could have helped that, but I think he had a commitment that I'll say myself was through his closeness to God, that he had to build up this kind of "Billy the Kid" character to get the best out of people. I think, to me, you could go to 100 percent of ballplayers, and if they will search their heart and soul, they'll see that Billy brought something out of them. I think things like this should be told.*

All of it was part of the attraction and the energy around Billy the Kid—someone who would ride into town having taken over a team that had lost more than 100 games, yet still talk championship. He was outrageous and he kept the rest of the league off balance with his antics.

▶ **Lenny Randle:** *I remember one time he got kicked out of the game. And the next day he's got a walkie-talkie and he says, "You carry this, 'cause I gotta know why this guy took me out last night." So he wanted him to say it—like Watergate. So he says, "I'm going to tape everything. I need you. You're my witness." And I said, "Yeah, well, OK." The catcher's there, the umpire's there, all three of the other umpires are there. And Billy says, "Why did you throw me out?" The ump says, "Billy, I don't want to hear it. Last night, I think you used too many adjectives that I didn't like." And he says, "What did I say to offend you?" And the ump said, "Billy, I just don't f—ing like you. OK? I just don't like you when you come out, you cuss, start up all this crap. I wasn't in the mood to hear it. So you're gone yesterday, and you're gone right now!" And he says, "You can't just throw me!" "Yes, I can. I don't need this. Guys, do we need this today?" Billy was gone. So Billy says, "You don't know this,*

*but you have no right to do this. I'm taking you to the commissioner.
I'm going to send him the tape." And the guy says, "What tape? What
are you talking about?" "You just said you had no reason to throw me
out of the game, right? You just said you just don't wanna be around
me. You just think my presence pisses you off. All I'm trying to do is tell
you that I'm protecting my players. I have to show my players that I
care about them enough to try to win these games. And if you guys are
taking your personal vendettas out on me, take 'em out on me at the
hotel—off the field. Send me a letter. Call an attorney. But don't take it
out on my players, that ain't right." So I have it on tape, and they just
about had diarrhea. The rest of the season, they were checking to see if
he was wired!*

Billy could be wild, but his excesses were calculated, because he
knew he was capable of getting the job done. When Billy stood at the
top of the dugout, he was much like Patton riding in his jeep—standing
up, sirens blaring, the stars boldly plastered on his license plate. The
image is strong and definite: Here comes someone tough who knows
what he's doing! George Steinbrenner, who has been a student of Patton his entire life, certainly appreciated that aspect of Billy, and it seems
to have influenced his original hiring of him.

▶ **Phil Pepe:** *I remember George Steinbrenner telling me things like, "I
don't want to see a manager take that slow walk to the mound and
look like he's got the weight of the world on his shoulder. Should he
make a change? Should he bring in a new pitcher? I want the kind of
a manager who goes out there, bounds out of the dugout, charges
onto the mound, and is very decisive and points to the bullpen and
brings in the new pitcher like he knows the problem, and he has the
solution. That creates that impression in fans that this guy has a handle on things." I'm not that smart, but it suddenly popped into my
head, "My God, he's talking about Billy Martin! That's exactly Billy's
style. I'll bet he's going to try to hire Billy Martin." And sure enough,
that was what he did.*

The players also appreciated that presence.

▶ **Tom Grieve:** *You felt good in a Ranger uniform those years when he was the manager, because you felt like you had an extra edge with him as your manager. You had a better chance to win with him as your manager than if anyone else was your manager. You felt that not just the players were going to determine the outcome of the game, but that your manager was going to help do things to win games: "What the hell's he doing? Wow!" It was the kind of thing that built confidence in his own players, because you knew you had to be on your toes, you knew he was liable to try anything.*

▶ **Mike Pagliarulo:** *There are some managers in the game, that when their team is doing good, they're on the top step. And when their team's doing bad—and man, I can name a bunch of them—they'd be sitting way back in the dugout, sitting on the bench, or trying to hide up the runway. Billy was always around, and if things were going bad, then he was up there, he was wanting to get a piece of somebody. And he didn't like losing. If things were going good, it was almost like the opposite, he just kind of quieted down. But he was there. You always knew where Billy was.*

Paul Stoltz holds that Billy's tough image, and his ability to use it to motivate his followers, grew naturally out of his high Adversity Quotient. As Stoltz says, "Higher AQ leaders attract and grow higher AQ teams. We are naturally drawn to high AQ people and make them leaders. Their passion [anger and feistiness], relentlessness, optimism, and drive are a magnetic force. A positive attitude is meaningless unless tested by adversity. That is why AQ far outweighs attitude. We just never knew what to call it. I'm an old Twins fan, and I remember the no-whiners mentality Billy instilled in the team. It was when they faced defeat that his AQ was particularly vital. He was the spark plug. He never caved. It drove some players nuts . . ."

Rallying around a Common Enemy

To stir up energy around the club in Oakland, and to help motivate his players, Billy even "created" a rivalry with the California Angels, who had been the 1979 AL West champions and were Oakland's neighbors in California. His many years associated with the wildly exciting Yan-kees–Red Sox rivalry seemed to inspire in him the desire to create a similar rivalry for his new charges. Unlike with the Yankees, however, Billy took advantage of a natural "David and Goliath" aspect to the two California clubs at the time. Billy enjoyed the David role and played it to the hilt. The two teams had several memorable brawls over the years, and according to Matt Keough, "We fought four times in one game. In the last two, we fought in our shower shoes behind the backstop."

▶ **Mickey Morabito:** *He always thought that there should be a rivalry, com-ing from managing in New York, where you'd go into Boston and God, it was unbelievable. Now, we'd play these teams and there was never any fuel for it or anything. So in spring training he said, "You know, we're going to get something going with the Angels this year." Basically because of location, and we had a few instances in some spring training games with them that I think made it a little easier for him to want to do it against the Angels. But he just felt that that should be a natural rival for us.*

It wasn't long before the plot thickened.

▶ **Mickey Klutts:** *Brian Kingman came to Billy one day in the outfield and said, "I have a friend in LA who runs a wood-lading place. He has a bunch of bats by the Angels, and he's corking them. They're paying him to cork these bats." And it was Dan Ford, [Doug] DeCinces, [Brian] Downing—big hitters. These guys, they don't need no cork! And so we just kept it real quiet and told Brian's friend, "Do your job and send them back." So one day Matt Keough was throwing in the eighth inning, and I was at third base. And Dan Ford hit a pitch—honest to God, it was about an inch off the ground in the dirt—he hit it just out in straight center field. And while he's running around the bases, I'm run-ning up to the plate, and Matt Keough's running up to the plate, to get the bat. And the bat boy comes out, and they're playing tug of war with the bat! And I'm right in the middle and all of a sudden, here comes their bench, and everybody's coming at us! We all fight over this bat.*

So we ended up nailing 'em on it. They caught three of the Angels that year with corked bats! They were at that time veterans, and we were the young hot shots.

▶ **Mike Heath:** *Well, the Angels, they had a couple more veteran guys. For some reason, they always felt that they were better than us, and when we started blossoming, I don't think they liked that too much. And a lot of those guys were using corked bats anyhow. They were starting to get spanked by a team that the year before, they were spanking royally. Now we come out and start spanking them, and they just didn't like it, and that's the way it went. We had to stick up for ourselves! Players will handle their own problems. See, we had to stick up for ourselves for things that had happened in the past.*

By getting the young A's to rally around a common enemy, Billy got them to believe in themselves and their ability and to perform at their best.

Getting the Public on Your Side

Of course, all of the excitement Billy generated was not lost on the fans. His aggressiveness, his winning, and his outrageousness all excited the fans, and teams always sold more tickets when Billy was at the helm. Very few managers contribute to ticket sales. Billy always did, both at home and on the road.

▶ **Jackie Moore:** *He could walk on the field and get a reaction out of the fans. He was the little guy's favorite, the guy that puts in ten hours a day at the factory and brings his kid out the ballgame to see Billy's type of baseball: "Son, that's how I want you to play!" He just carried that presence about him that people liked to be associated to. And those people in Oakland, I mean it was a happening for them. It carried the team and the fans. There was electricity there, you could just feel it.*

▶ **Mike Pagliarulo:** *Let me tell you what, most New York fans loved Billy Martin, and it's because of the way that he loved the game, the way that* *he loved New York, and I believe he loved his players. You can't get better than that. You can't beat that in any way! That'll win every time.*

▶ **Mickey Klutts:** *America—without being dramatic—likes the little guy. I see guys all the time, or people I've just met, and they say, "Aw, you played for Billy?" It's not Billy Martin most of the time, it's "Billy." And there's a personalization about him because people identified with him. My God, America likes the little guy, they like a fighter. He appealed to a lot of people that maybe didn't even like baseball, but they liked to see him out there on the field. I mean, he's such a weasel-looking little guy. And I think the A's was his biggest accomplishment.*

▶ **Marty Appel:** *He was a street fighter in a street fighter kind of town. And even those who wouldn't call themselves street fighters sort of had an admiration for the scrappiness of this guy who might have been the runt of the litter physically, but through the force of his personality—and occasionally through his fists—achieved respect and leadership and success. Certainly the "Man on the Street" New Yorker could relate to a guy who would be the hero and take on the boss. And even the bosses, I think, said, "Here's an interesting character, this guy. Why couldn't I have been more like that when I was working my way up?"*

▶ **Charlie Silvera:** *The people loved him, because there they were, they were out there in that #1 uniform themselves, fighting City Hall. Because he was fighting management, and you don't fight management. I used to tell him, "Billy, you can't fight millionaires." But you know, he'd fight 'em anyway. That was the reason he just didn't survive. But the fans loved him because he was a blue-collar guy—simple as that. That was part of his makeup, and he went after it.*

But it wasn't just the tough guys or the tough guy wannabes who took to Billy.

▶ **Sam Mele:** *In Minnesota he invited 50 nuns to a lot of the games. He would grab me, and we would go out in the stands. They let the nuns in early, and we would go up the right field stands—they sat way in the* back. We'd just stand there and talk baseball to them, and they were fabulous people. Now for Billy to do something with 50 nuns, you know he had to be a saint in a way.

▶ **Bill Reedy:** *There was five nuns, sisters, that were sisters—Sullivans—here in Detroit, and I knew their brother, Cliff Sullivan, who said, "The Yankees are coming, can I get five tickets?" I said, "Well, let me talk to Billy." . . . I told Billy, "Lookit, I got five sisters that are nuns." He said, "Look, if you've got five women that you want to get into the ballpark, just tell me." I said, "If I did, I would." So Sunday comes, and then they show up at my place, which was a block away, and I had my brother walk them over to the park, and I was with them. I asked for him in the dugout. Well, he comes up out of the dugout, and here's these five nuns standing there, and he says, "Oh, man, take 'em back to the clubhouse door, I'll be right there." So I walk 'em back there . . . And here he comes. He's got a glove on, and he's got five baseballs in the glove, and he had signed all five of 'em. So he gives each one of 'em a baseball. And he showed 'em his hat, where he had the crucifix on, and talked about them doing the Lord's work. I mean, he pumped these five nuns up like you wouldn't believe, "God bless 'em," and all that. And that was Billy.*

▶ **Bobby Richardson:** *I remember that when some of my friends, or maybe their children, would come up, I would not be afraid to say, "Hey, Billy, can I introduce you to these friends?" And he'd come over and just make them feel like they were special guests at Yankee Stadium. He had a unique ability. He wouldn't just come over and speak. Some personalities will do that and then just walk away, but he would make them feel just very special.*

He had the power and personality of all notable leaders to make others feel important too.

Notes

1. Billy Martin and Phil Pepe, *Billyball* (Garden City, N.Y.: Doubleday & Company, 1987), p. 249.

2. Leonard Koppett, *The Man in the Dugout* (New York: Crown Publishers, 1993), p. 293.

3. Murray Chass, "Can the Yankees Survive a Steinbrenner-Martin Battle?" *New York Times*, April 17, 1977.

4. Dave Anderson, "The Yankees' 'Messed-Up' Heads," *New York Times*, October 16, 1977.

5. Graig Nettles and Peter Golenbock, *Balls* (New York: Pocket Books, 1985), pp. 8, 14.

6. Roger Nye, *The Patton Mind* (Garden City Park, N.Y.: Avery Publishing Group, 1993), p. 54.

7. Martin and Pepe, p. 97.

8. Nettles and Golenbock, pp. 137–138.

9. Lou Piniella and Maury Allen, *Sweet Lou* (New York: G.P. Putnam's Sons, 1986), p. 163.

10. Martin and Pepe, p. 215.

11. Leonard Koppett, "Jackson Surprised at Benching, but Excuses Martin," *New York Times*, October 10, 1977.

12. Piniella and Allen, p. 177.

13. Phil Pepe, ". . . And Martin? His Model and Idol is Stengel," *Sporting News*, October 29, 1977.

14. Norman Lewis Smith, *The Return of Billy the Kid* (New York: Coward, McCann & Geoghegan, 1977), p. 97.

15. Martin and Pepe, p. 108.

16. Max Nichols, "Twins Column," *Sporting News*, October 9, 1965.

17. Murray Chass, *New York Times*, May 8, 1974.

18. Ibid.

19. Randy Galloway, "Rangers Column," *Sporting News*, May 18, 1974.

20. Nye, pp. 35–36.

Managing the Campaign

As intense as Martin was, he still realized that a 162-game season was an awfully long campaign. He was careful to remain a believer throughout, especially outwardly to his players. In fact, to Gabe Paul, the man who served as mediator for Billy and George Steinbrenner from 1975 through 1977, Billy's greatest strength was his positive thinking. In early 1978, after moving on to the Indians, Paul said of Billy, "He's always positive. And in a slump, he's effervescent. He never has a defeatist thought."[1]

On another occasion, when Billy went to manage Oakland, Paul said, "He may get very mad, but he'll never get down. He won't let his players get depressed either. He'll pump those kids up and they'll play over their heads."[2] That positive attitude was critical in managing a long campaign.

▶ **Mike Heath:** *Billy was real positive of number one, in himself, in being able to build a team like the A's. I think a lot of that rubbed off on the guys, too. We saw how positive he was with himself and how he went about his business. I think it had to spread to the other guys. There's not a lot of guys that carried themselves like Billy did, that's for sure.*

Billy's belief in himself, in his baseball knowledge, and in the Yankee way was crucial to his success as a man and manager. It rubbed off. As a player and manager, he had won, so if he looked confident to his players and told them they were going to win, why wouldn't they believe him? If he didn't give up, how could they?

▶ **Phil Pepe:** *He believed that he could teach people how to win, and he believed that he was better than the guy in the other dugout. He had a tremendous ego. I think that was probably an outgrowth of having been on a team that was always so successful. He prized that Yankee tradition, and remembered the days when he was there, and they always won when he was there. So you get to a point where you almost believe you are blessed, that if you stay with it, sooner or later, something good will happen, and you'll find a way to turn things around. He always believed he was going to turn things around. He never was willing to concede, even when the odds were tremendously against him. He had his own belief in himself. He believed that he was going to find a way, and do something, because he was smarter than everybody else.*

Being positive has nothing to do with ignoring reality. Being positive means learning from troubles and having enough belief in yourself and your goals to turn any situation around until you get the job done. Billy radiated confidence, no matter how great the odds might appear against his team.

▶ **Mickey Klutts:** *When we went from Oakland to New York for the American League Championship Series, we were all on the back of the plane, all the players. About an hour into the flight, we're back there just talking, sitting right on the tail by the bathroom. All of a sudden, we see him weaving his way up, bumping into all the seats and talking to guys along the way. When he got back there we had like a three-hour heart-to-heart. And he was sitting down on the floor, and you had Steve McCatty, and Keough, and myself, maybe [Rickey] Henderson or [Dwayne] Murphy. We just talked for the whole flight, just having a cold one. About baseball, and about being positive. How we're going to go back there and get 'em . . . But just sitting there and listening, I knew I wouldn't be able to absorb all of it in my whole lifetime, but I was just listening to his positive thinking.*

Never Let Your Followers See You Sweat

If a leader is worried, he or she should never let his or her followers see it. As Billy explained, "I don't want anybody to know my feelings, especially the players. You don't want them to get down, and start dragging their heads. You have to keep going, keep pushing, especially when you're losing, because they look at you and see how you're handling the situation, and even if you feel deep inside that you have no chance of winning, you have to act like you still can. And sometimes, even when you're losing by five runs, the team can come back and surprise you."[3]

▶ **Mike Pagliarulo:** *From hearing about the type of player he was—a scrappy, never-give-up kind of guy—that's certainly what kind of manager he was, too. Fighting, and all this other stuff. I mean, we could be getting our ass kicked, I never saw him sit back on the bench and say, "Ah, we'll get 'em tomorrow." I never, ever saw that. When we were getting our ass kicked, you better make sure you got heads-up on the bench, because he's looking down that bench. That's the time when you can't give up, because now his ears are wide open, his eyes are wide open, and he's listening. You gotta make sure that you don't quit on him, because he ain't quitting, and if you quit, that's it, he'll get you.*

Billy was careful of what he said in the press, and no matter how dire the situation with the Yankees in 1977 or 1978, he always talked pennant. Billy once said, "Don't forget, the players read . . . and how do you think it affects them? . . . If the general says we've lost the battle, how do you expect the troops to keep on fighting?"[4]

Your followers have enough problems performing their own responsibilities. If you are focusing on the big picture for them, they can concentrate on their own roles. Players need to focus and believe, and any little factor that can undermine their confidence should be avoided. It is certainly not going to help a team if they see their leader hanging it up. If you are a leader, your followers look to you for guidance, and no matter what you may be feeling, you must display confidence and a willingness to find solutions to problems. Otherwise, how can you expect your followers to do the same?

▶ **Mike Pagliarulo:** *I never saw—winning and losing—any difference in him. As passionate as he was, you feel that he'd get all excited from all that stuff, but he was pretty levelheaded when he'd come up that runway to the locker room, whether we won or lost. When we played stupid, watch out. He don't like mental errors, and when you played dumb, he'd get right in your face. But if we lost a good battle, he understood what a good battle was.*

Know Your Campaign

Billy's bottom line was that "Pennant races are all alike: Damned hard."[5] Indeed, anything worthwhile is damned hard to achieve. But Billy had learned how to win a pennant race as a player in 1950, 1951, 1952, 1953, 1955, and 1956, and he had managed teams to first-place finishes in 1969, 1972, 1976, and eventually 1977 and 1981. So when he was preaching patience and optimism, pushing his team, or laying off, he had his reasons. Many of Billy's fights with George Steinbrenner were rooted in a difference of opinion as to how a pennant race should be conducted.

Before purchasing the Yankees, Steinbrenner had been tremendously successful in the business world, and he had a background in both playing and coaching college football. Steinbrenner demanded perfection, wanted to win as badly as Billy, and believed that stiff discipline and focus were the keys. Yet in baseball, championship teams lose 40 percent of the time, and learning to persevere through the inevitable slumps without breaking down is critical to success. For Steinbrenner, especially in his first years in baseball, slumps were intolerable, and he regarded many games and series as "must win" situations. Billy did not see baseball in the same way, and he stood up for himself. In the early days of George and Billy's relationship in the late 1970s, their battles seemed to have a positive, motivating effect on the team, as Billy leveraged George's frustrations to push the team.

▶ **Paul Blair:** *You know, back then, that '77 team, George motivated us. When he would throw something in the paper talking about us as play-*

ers or as a team, that would kind of charge us up. And Billy led that charge. "Let's show him. Let's show him what we can do out here." George was really our motivating factor, and Billy kind of had us together in that charge. It wasn't anything vindictive or anything like that, it was just like, "Hey, he's the owner, and he doesn't have the confidence in you guys that I have. Let's just show him what we can do." And I think that helped us tremendously down the stretch.

▶ **Mickey Rivers:** *Billy, he knew how to communicate with the guys. Billy was a manager that goes out and works for his players. He didn't care what the front office say. That's why he got in trouble with the front office. But the guys, that's why the guys stick behind him. That made the guys a little closer to each guy. He'd go to bat for you. He'd do this for you.*

Billy once said, "I would have to say that the thing about George that bugs me most is his impatience. George has never learned to understand the 162-game schedule. He tries to run his baseball team like a football team, but football teams don't play every day . . . By its nature, and the long, daily grind, baseball is not an emotional game . . . You get mentally fatigued . . . You have to go through it to understand that."[6] Billy passed away before the Yankee renaissance began under Buck Showalter and Stick Michael and flourished under Joe Torre. During that time, Steinbrenner seems to have come to grips with the grinding nature of baseball. He still wants to win just as badly, and he still puts pressure on his employees and his players, but he seems to relate more to the nature of baseball than he did in the 1970s and 1980s when the club lacked much stability.

In the long 1977 season, Billy always believed that the team would come together and win, even amid all of the controversy among Steinbrenner, Reggie Jackson, Thurman Munson, and himself. Why? Because he believed that he had the best team, and he believed that a 162-game baseball season was long enough to enable the cream to rise to the top. Billy always tried to keep that perspective, especially in his dealings with the media. He did not want players to pick up a paper and read that their manager was panicking.

▶ **Buck Showalter:** *It's such a grind, the long season. You gotta look at the big picture. When you have someone in your organization looking at a day-to-day mentality—and there certainly comes a time when you have to—it creates a bad atmosphere for your players. Not that you want to make them just kind of cruise along, and say, "Oh, it'll take care of itself." Certainly there's a time to take the whip out. I, like Billy I'm sure, have had many times privately behind closed doors, where a loss eats at you, tears you up, one game. The beauty of our game is you get to go back out the next day and take that feeling away. But once you open that door and go out there, the players are looking at you. They're constantly looking to see how you're going to react, and they're going to follow your lead.*

After the horrid "Boston Massacre" weekend of June 1977 at Fenway Park—which featured a Friday night hammering of Catfish Hunter, the Saturday dugout confrontation with Reggie (see Chapter 5), and an 11–1 Sunday drubbing—Billy said to the press, "What's the difference? Next Sunday we'll be in first place. This is June, not September. We've got a better ballclub than they do, but they're hot right now."[7] The next weekend, with his job on the line, Billy led the Yanks to three straight wins over the Red Sox, pulling the team back to within two games of first place.

Still, the Yankees could not quite put all of their problems behind them, and as July continued and rumors that Billy would be fired mounted, Billy said, "I don't enjoy this. I mean taking the play away from the players. This 'who's going to manage' stuff can hurt their game and concentration. But I'm going to continue to manage my way, no matter what happens. I'll live or die on my own convictions. My mother didn't raise me to be scared. I'm just going to be Billy Martin and let the chips fall where they may."[8]

After a while, as we saw in Chapter 5, the players adjusted to Reggie and the media circus and began to win again. After one victory against first-place Baltimore, Billy finally saw a team emerging. "The way the players were pushing each other," Martin said, "when I see harmony like that on a club, players pulling for each other, that means more to me than anything else in the world. That means the team is clicking."[9] The 1977 Yankees had to adjust before they could regain that chemistry, and it was a hard process, but all along there was a confidence that they would win it all.

Finally, as the Yankees reassumed first place for good, pitcher Dick Tidrow said, "The guys finally realized the season was getting away from them. Everything that happened was behind us, and we had to play baseball the way we're capable of playing."[10] That same night, Billy flew in 12 dozen crabs from Baltimore for a postgame feast to show that he was proud of his team. Finally, Billy could say, "Patience. I've been telling people for weeks they just had to be patient. I was sure that sooner or later, we'd begin to play like we can."[11]

▶ **Ray Negron:** *You know what? We won in '76, and that Yankee team was so f—ing good in '77 that you never really had a doubt that we were going to win that thing. If anything, we were going to beat ourselves, but no one was really going to come in and beat us. And you know what, as pissed off as Billy would be that year, and as pissed off as he would be at certain times with Reggie's stuff, he always pressed the right buttons. The players always had the confidence that Billy was going to do the right thing. And you know what? He always did, right down to the point of bringing in Roy White when you had to pinch hit in the big spot. Big home run here and there. He always did the right thing. And he had the tools. He had Paul Blair there. He just had total, total confidence in his ballclub and his pitching staff. All he had to do was just guide. And he guided. And we got into September, and watching Billy manage from September 1 on was like no manager has ever managed before in their life, because he always did the right thing.*

▶ **Mickey Rivers:** *You can look at the different teams that are winning, and see the manager plays an important part on the team. The manager is the strategy maker on the team. Watch the different moves. And see, look, all our moves fell right in—perfect, perfect, perfect. And then you see him move his strategy when he moved his pitchers. That was Billy. That's all it was. It wasn't us. We was already set in the lineup, so it wasn't us. One day he said, "OK, take Chris [Chambliss] out, put Cliff [Johnson] at first." I said, "Oh man, he's makin' a mistake." He gave him*

[Chambliss] a rest day. The next day he put him back in, he hit. Boom, boom! He ain't stopped hittin' since then. And that helps. That helps. And it helps his players. That's how he was in the dugout. He knew what we could do. He said, "I know what I got over here." He don't scout it. He don't have surveys. He knew what it was, so he knew what to do.

The Difficult Campaign of 1978

The next season, 1978, was equally difficult, and a year that Billy ultimately did not survive as manager. Early on, the Yankees suffered from numerous injuries, while at the same time, the Red Sox set a blistering pace at the top of the division. Out for significant periods of time early in the season were Yankee hurlers Don Gullett, Catfish Hunter, Dick Tidrow, Ken Holtzman, and Ken Clay as well as the middle defense, namely Bucky Dent, Willie Randolph, and Mickey Rivers. But because the team was deep, they hung tight. For instance, with Dent out, the Yankees could call on a veteran like Fred Stanley off the bench to fill in.

As of June 19, 1978, the team was only seven games back, with the third best record in baseball behind the Red Sox and the Giants, but still, the pressure was mounting on Billy. By mid-July, the Yankees trailed Boston by what is now the legendary figure of 14½ games. Still, the team was not ready to give up. By this time, the team had been together for three years and was a deep unit, just hanging tough until all the starters returned.

Billy and George eventually had five go-rounds together as Yankee manager and owner; the rounds even came to be called Billy I, II, III, IV, and V. Thus, it can be difficult to step back in time to the summer of 1978, when there was no such thing yet as Billy I, II, III, IV, or V. In 1978, Billy was just the Yankee manager, and George was an owner who had earned his early success (though in retrospect, he was maybe a little spoiled by it). Up to that point, Steinbrenner had threatened to fire Martin many times, but there had been no actual firing. After all, there had also been two straight trips to the World Series. Both the threats and the World Series visits stirred up great fan excitement and interest in the Yankees. Steinbrenner believed in, and up through 1978 succeeded with, an approach that kept everyone on edge, especially Billy.

▶ **Fred Stanley:** *What'd George used to say, "A ship on a calm sea is not always the best situation"? He wants to create a controversy; that's George Steinbrenner's attitude.*

It motivated the players to perform, both to "protect" Billy and to defend their own honor against a very critical owner.

Even though the Yankees were playing .550 ball, they were falling further and further behind in the race, and Billy was being hung out to dry for it. Every day, the papers ran stories about Billy's status as club manager along with photographs depicting a visibly exhausted Martin.

▶ **Mickey Rivers:** *George roughed him up on account of a lot of things happened. It wasn't called for, because you know what? We was going to win no matter what. We had three or four different guys coming back in a hurry. It didn't make no difference.*

▶ **Phil Pepe:** *I will go to my grave believing they would have won with Billy that year. They did win five in a row before he got fired. They were beginning to win. The reason the Red Sox were so far in front, and the Yankees were so far behind, was that the Red Sox had no injuries the first half of the season, and the Yankees had all their people hurt. And then it was just like two completely different seasons. The second half of the season, all the injured Yankees came back, and the Red Sox began to break down. And so it was inevitable, I think, that they would catch up. And I think it would have happened even with Billy.*

Meanwhile, however, the turmoil with Reggie Jackson had not entirely subsided. In the ninth inning of a July 17 tie game against the Royals, a slumping Jackson was given the bunt sign on the first pitch. Jackson squared to bunt but took the pitch. Jackson was then given the sign to swing away. Angry that he would be asked to bunt, and dealing with frustrations with both Billy and Steinbrenner that went beyond the scope of the particular ballgame, Jackson decided to continue bunting. With two strikes, he fouled off a bunt attempt and was out. His defiance resulted in a five-game suspension, but ultimately led to Billy's undoing as manager. Just after Reggie's return from suspension, Billy self-destructed when all of the pressures he was feeling caught up to him. Speaking to reporters at Chicago's O'Hare Airport, Billy—referring to Jackson and Steinbrenner—let slip the statement that "one's a born liar, the other's convicted." Within a day, Billy had resigned under fire, and Bob Lemon took over to complete the Yankees' miracle comeback.

▶ **Phil Pepe:** *He had only himself to blame. I don't think Steinbrenner was even contemplating firing him because they weren't winning. Steinbrenner knew why they weren't winning. Steinbrenner understood all the injuries and hadn't given up hope. I think he was going to stay with Billy. The plane was delayed, they went to the bar, they started drinking, and Billy started jumping on Steinbrenner and Jackson. And all his frustrations surfaced, and he made that comment. How could Steinbrenner not fire him? That was the most insubordinate Billy ever has been, to make a statement like that.*

▶ **Mickey Rivers:** *I didn't like it. I know the situation they tried to put Billy in—say this and say that. That's what made me want to leave. That made a lot of guys see different. But the guys didn't want to stop playing ball, because they knew the situation. But the guys didn't like it, especially the big guys.*

Had Billy been wrong in making the statement? Certainly. A leader has to be responsible to all constituents—which includes owners and shareholders as well as staff members. At this point in 1978, Billy had clearly let his emotions get in the way of his responsibilities. In this case, feeling wronged and under a great deal of stress, Billy lashed out, costing him the job he so cherished. However, his players, now firmly cast in his image, finished the job, capturing a second straight World Championship that October.

Knowing When to Push and When to Back Off

People remember Billy Martin as a little tough guy, and he certainly could be tough. But he had many dimensions to his personality that were reflected in his managerial approach. Only a foolish leader handles his troops exactly the same way under different circumstances and during different campaigns. Billy rolled with the ups and downs of his teams and the long summers and tried to manage accordingly.

▶ **Jackie Moore:** *He had a sense about individuals and also his club. I mean, he knew the heartbeat of the players, and when to really push and turn the pressure on and when to take it off. He just had a different sense about him of how to compete, how to be successful. Whether you are a professional baseball player or you're a car salesman, there's a way to do it and be successful with it. There's just a little different higher level that you can do these things, and be a little better than your competitors.*

There are four aspects of handling his team at different times that Billy adhered to: (1) push hard during the good times, (2) pull back during a slump, (3) appeal to pride with a fatigued team, and (4) discipline a complacent team. Let's look at each in turn.

Push Hard during the Good Times

We have already seen how Billy Martin took over a hapless bunch of Oakland "Pathetics" and whipped them into winners overnight. Because they were hungry to learn, and because they were in awe of him, he had free reign to push the A's to their absolute physical and mental limits. When Billy took over, the players believed it could be different. It was new. They felt good. This gave Billy the opportunity to push them hard.

▶ **Mickey Klutts:** *You had to respect where he came from and his record. Remember, we're a bunch of young guys, we lost so much, we can't tell anything to anybody. We lost 108 games—we can't say nothing. But we wanted to win. We all came from winning programs—winning organizations in the minors. All of us had won something or played in a title game. We were all leaders of our teams. We're like, "All right, we're ready to go."*

▶ **Mike Heath:** *He didn't have many guys question what he was doing. It was like, "He put this play on, let's do it. Now's the time to do it." If the*

play was on, you executed, that's all there was to it. And if you were out,
if he put it on, then it was his fault.

Part of Billy's approach was getting the players to feel good about themselves, to feel they could win. General George Patton believed, ". . . a coward dressed as a brave man will change from his cowardice and, in nine cases out of ten, will on the next occasion demonstrate the qualities fortuitously emblazoned on his chest . . . We must have more decorations and give them with no niggard hand."[12] Billy's presence helped to "dress" his A's as winners, and in those early days when they felt good, he worked them hard.

When an individual's self-confidence and image is strong, criticism can be absorbed without damage to the psyche. The "big picture" is so positive that a little yelling or prodding brings additional benefit without breaking down relationships.

▶ **Jackie Moore:** *If this guy's going good, Billy'd want to push him to a different level. I thought that was real unique, and I learned something there. He's right. It's that human element. If you're on a roll, let's just see how far you can take it, and just run the streak as long as you can.*

Clete Boyer, Billy's third base coach in Oakland and a man with his own Yankee past as a third baseman in the 1960s, remembers, ". . . he took those young kids and taught everyone how to play . . . and they listened to him. And the kids now are on a roll and now they listen to him more . . . Now whatever he says, it'll work . . . Billy took young kids and made them win. Forced 'em to win. Scared 'em to win . . . And he gave them pride in themselves and playing."[13]

As Martin pushed and pushed, his A's learned to win and began to win. The 1980 and 1981 seasons were very successful, and Martin kept pushing when he could. For example, in 1981, the A's broke out to an 11–0 start and won 17 of their first 18 games.

▶ **Mike Heath:** *You always have that confidence coming out of spring training. We ripped off 11 in a row. We were pretty high on ourselves, and we thought things were going to happen. But guys always say, "It's* *still early. It's still early. Let's keep going." We were beating some pretty good teams. We felt pretty good about ourselves. It just kept going, a snowball effect.*

During this time, Martin pushed his A's as hard as possible, harping on every little thing that would go wrong.

▶ **Jackie Moore:** *Billy was tougher to coach for and play for whenever you were winning, and I asked him once, "Billy, why are you so mad? We won five or six in a row." And he said, "Partner, let me tell you, in the game of baseball, you're gonna have your winning streaks and you're gonna have your losing streaks. The clubs that are going to be successful are the clubs that take those winning streaks and continue 'em farther than you're supposed to." He said, "When things are going good, you can push your players a heck of a lot further than you can when things are going bad." He said, "Now, if we win ten in a row, let's don't be satisfied with winning ten in a row. Let's push 'em to win 15 in a row. And that's the difference when the dust settles at the end of the season, that's the difference if you're successful or if you go home early."*

▶ **Fred Stanley:** *He was harder on our club, in the clubhouse, when we were winning than if we happened to lose a few. Because he said, "When you win, you start taking things for granted, and you start making mental mistakes." So when we were winning, and somebody would screw up, he'd be on your butt big time, which was a little easier to take when you're winning because the pressure's not on you. Your confidence is good, you come back in, now he's jumping on your butt, you're feeling bad for a minute, but you realize, "Yeah, he's right." We'd lose two or three in a row, but as long as we stayed focused, he didn't say much. It's when we were winning that he'd get upset if we didn't play well.*

Martin's philosophy came directly from Casey Stengel.

▶ **Gil McDougald:** *Casey's philosophy was the same. It's rather simple. If things are going great, that's the time to get on somebody, because they more or less just let it ride over their head. Because we're winning, you*

*say, "What the hell is the deal? We won, we won." But the point is, if he
really gets on ya, you also are going to think, "Well, what the hell, is he
right? Did I do this? Or did I do that?" But you get on a player in a losing streak, and you can destroy a guy.*

Pull Back during a Slump

When Billy's 1981 A's slumped on an East Coast swing, Billy instantly
adapted a more grandfatherly style. Noted one writer covering the
team, "He became tolerant, forgiving. After the A's had been swept in
Milwaukee, he took them all out to dinner."[14] When people are losing
and that self-confidence is waning, the manager can't deliver a blow
that could turn a slump into an inexorable downward spiral. That's
when he needs to pick his guys up again.

The 1982 A's season unraveled from injuries almost before it had
even started, giving Billy no opportunity to push his squad at all. By
July 1982, the A's were in next to last place, and Billy—who had been
hoping to win the World Series—was so outwardly calm that reporters
wondered if finally, at age 54, he had mellowed. "Mellowed? No," he
said. "When you're winning, you push hard, so guys don't get too fat
with themselves. But when you're losing—and guys are giving good
effort and getting bad breaks—then you try not to get on their backs.
You compound things. It's a hard pill to swallow, but you have to.
Casey Stengel taught me that."[15]

Billy not only stayed off their backs, he actually tried to cheer them
up with some humor and support.

▶ **Mickey Klutts:** *After we lost a game to Texas, Billy came in and blew off
a whole bunch of firecrackers. Then he said, "I thought Texas was still
hitting!" . . . He lit off like a whole block. And the next night, we went out
and won, and he had a bunch of lobster flown in from the Houston area.
The clubhouse in Texas was known for the worst food, but it had the
coldest beer on tap!*

As long as the effort was there, Billy would not act to further break
down the team's confidence. Instead, he stayed outwardly optimistic to

help buoy the players. Sometimes, things go so poorly for a while that there is just nothing you can do but sit back and wait for a break to come.

Appeal to Pride with a Fatigued Team

Contrast Billy's 1982 A's with his 1977 and 1978 Yankees, who came out of the gate very slowly, largely because nonbaseball matters were disrupting the focus on the field. In 1977, with all of the monetary gripes and the Reggie Jackson situation on everybody's mind, baseball was often almost an afterthought. Even as Billy himself was embroiled in much of the controversy, it was still his job to refocus the team. In 1977, he did it by appealing to their Yankee pride.

After one tough July loss to the Brewers, Martin held a team meeting to clear the air. Lou Piniella credited the meeting with refocusing the players on their individual responsibilities to play good ball. Said Piniella, "He said the Yankees are the defending American League champions and we haven't played nearly up to our capabilities. If we're going to lose, let's do it like champions . . . He said he was very, very proud of the Yankee uniform. He brought out the theme of let's have more pride in ourselves, play like we're capable of playing. If we can't win it, at least let's give it our best shot. I think it sank in. After that, everyone started hustling."[16]

If Billy could appeal to the history and tradition that they were part of simply by wearing the pinstripes, perhaps they could dig in and find a little spark. It seemed to work in 1977. As Patton would say, "Romance is the emotion which sways the populace to war,"[17] and perhaps no athlete ever could appeal to the romance of the team—and in particular, the pinstripes—than Billy Martin.

Discipline a Complacent Team

In 1968, the Detroit Tigers won the World Series against the St. Louis Cardinals and the legendary Bob Gibson. But in 1969, the team slipped to 90 wins and a second place finish in the new divisional format, and by 1970, the team came in an uninspired 79–83. General Manager Jim Campbell, looking to coax a few more good seasons out of the popular Tiger veterans, hired Billy Martin for a "quick fix."

In Detroit, Billy didn't have to teach the game the way he did in

Texas or Oakland. He had essentially the same club that had won a World Championship only three seasons earlier. But what Billy did need to do in Detroit was to take a team of players who had enjoyed the pinnacle of baseball success and either convince or force them to want to reach that same level again. He succeeded. In 1971, the club went 91–71 and ended the season in second place, and in 1972, the team won the American League East, temporarily ending Baltimore's reign at the top of the pack.

▶ **Charlie Silvera:** *Now, here was a country club atmosphere, because they had won it all in 1968. In '69 and '70, they had the older guys, good players, but they had lost desire it looked like, and they needed someone to come in and put some fire under 'em. And we won, but it was tough. They went around and they did what they wanted to do. There was no discipline. But he established some discipline there.*

▶ **Willie Horton:** *Billy would come around, and in conversation, it might be having a beer or just walking in the street, or riding on the bus, or whatever, where he would ask you a question. I guarantee he would ask you something where you think you should have knowledge of that yourself. He'd ask you something that would help you to improve yourself. And it upset him if you're helping a person, and he's not helping himself.*

Taking control of and imposing discipline on the team, and establishing himself as the leader over the players, played a big role in the Tiger turnaround.

▶ **Willie Horton:** *That year, we had a team where half the team had operations—myself, Frank Howard, everybody on the team. Bill Freehan. He took a hospital team all the way to the final game of the playoffs. And let me tell you, he got the best out of us. He'd tell you, "If you don't believe in it, there's the door!" Oh, man, he put that fire in you. I had that fire back in me. Without Billy, I don't think we would have got that far. I just don't believe it. Maybe I will have to argue the rest of them, but I don't think we would.*

▶ **Charlie Silvera:** *Some of the guys didn't like how he would turn them around. Detroit was an atmosphere where they could draw fans and they're making good money, so more or less, don't shake up the damned boat. That was what I understood. There were guys in Detroit that went up to [Jim] Campbell's office. See, this was some of the interference with guys that didn't like the way he did things. One of 'em, Billy challenged him to his face, he closed the whole damned clubhouse. He said, "Any of you guys, if you want to fight, we'll fight." And the doors were locked. And there was Frank Howard there and Willie Horton. They're big guys. Course, they were on Billy's side at that time, but he more or less challenged the whole club, saying, "I'm the boss, not you guys."*

Silvera, who was with Billy in his first three cities as a coach, considered the Detroit success to be Billy's biggest as a manager because of the difficult clubhouse atmosphere that he had to overcome through his personality, will, and leadership.

▶ **Willie Horton:** *He refocused us. When he first came, it was something different. He's the type of person who would take all the criticism on himself to make you shine. I know that he's the type of person that whatever it takes to bring your best out in you, he's willing to sacrifice himself for that. And I know in so many ways I think he did that for me. He thought about the players and the team. Just watching him, his knowledge of the game, and his strategy—Billy's like three or four steps ahead of everybody. And he made you think that way. He made you think, and he was the type of guy that taught that you've got to do this job if he ain't around, you've still got to play Billyball. He made you always keep your mind in the game.*

When Martin was really exasperated with his clubs, and felt like the players' minds weren't in the game, he would light into people and threaten to trade people. A lot of it may just have been his emotions running high, but he could be his most ornery when he felt the team didn't give its all.

▶ **Lenny Randle:** *You know, you stayed away from him when he was like that 'cause he would need ten to 15 minutes to regroup. He'd say, "What am I going to tell these f—ing writers? I gotta deal with that bullshit to protect you guys, damn it. That's the thing about this game—I can't defend all of you. They're gonna ask me, all I can do is talk about why I did what I did. I gotta be diplomatic." Sometimes we'd have a meeting before we let 'em in, I mean right there on the spot. And I was like, "Oh, God. Who's he gonna jack up?" Because sometimes he'd say, "Any of you f—ing guys don't like the way I'm doing stuff? I hear the mumbling going on down in the corner. Come in my office, close the door, and we'll see who comes out. If you want out of here, I'll send you. If you want to go, just pick a team—if they want you. Because if I got ya, I could be your last hope. That's reality. So if you think you're greater than the game itself, fine, it's good to have that kind of confidence. If you don't want to do it here, we'll send you to where you want to go. You want to go to Cleveland?" That was his kind of joke, man. "I know you don't want to go to Minnesota." He would just sarcastically say stuff like that. At that time, we would joke about teams and where the worst places were to play. And it was his way of saying, "Heads will roll!" And that kept you on your toes without being a threat to you personally.*

▶ **Charlie Manuel:** *When we'd start going bad, he'd close the door and really get on you. One of the things that I really admired a lot about Billy was that when you'd look there and you'd see stars like Harmon Killebrew and [Rod] Carew and [Tony] Oliva and those guys, he'd get on those guys just as much as he'd get on [Graig] Nettles and I. If those guys would do something he didn't like, he would address that. If something happened on the team he didn't like, he'd close the doors, and he would definitely tell you. He held nothing back.*

Be Persistent and Do Not Quit

To be fired as many times as Billy Martin was, you also have to be hired a lot. Billy Martin was a survivor. He always came back. At the time of his death, even after nine firings, Billy wanted to come back as a manager again.

Billy has said, "I'm a firm believer in the Peter Principle, the idea that people will tend to sink or rise to their level . . ." Because Billy believed in himself, he always knew that in the end, he would rise to his level, which he saw as "Number 1." In 1987 he wrote, "Would I manage again? . . . To be honest, I'd have to say, 'Yes, I would.' I'd like to show somebody just one more time that I can do it, that I can win." By the time Billy wrote these lines, he had achieved just about everything possible in the game of baseball. Still, he was ready to go one more time.

▶ **Frank Lucchesi:** *One last thing—1989, they had the baseball meetings in Nashville. We were in the lounge. He saw me. He said, "Hey, come and have a drink with me." He bought me a drink, and the old Italian, he said, "Salud." And then he looked around, and he kind of whispered, he said, ". . . "Dago, I'll be back, and I want you with me." He says, "I'll be back, and I want you with me." I'll never forget that.*

Martin was a competitor, and competitors come back. According to British statesman Winston Churchill, "Success is going from failure to failure without loss of enthusiasm." By Churchill's standard, Billy was a great success.

Martin's capacity to come back was reflected in the teams he managed, especially his 1977 and 1978 Yankees, teams famous for both their sniping and their ability to win in crunch time. In 1977, when the Yanks finally won it all on the strength of Reggie Jackson's amazing three successive homers in Game Six of the World Series, all of the controversy and pain of a long, tough season was forgotten—at least temporarily. They had accomplished their goal. The Yankees were World Champions for the first time since 1962.

▶ **Ray Negron:** *I laugh, because at that moment, everybody loved everybody. Thurman loved Reggie. Reggie loved Thurman. Billy loved Reggie. Reggie loved Billy. Billy loved George. George loved Billy. That's what it represented. I was really exhausted at the end of that season, because I knew I had to help Billy a lot that year with Reggie, and I was exhausted after the third out. I'll never forget Reggie sitting in the man-*

ager's office with Billy, and they had their arms around each other. And I was standing at the doorway looking in, and looking at them, because I wanted to hold on to that moment, because I knew I would never see it again.

▶ **Phil Pepe:** *Well, the one thing that stands out in my mind so vividly is the scene in the clubhouse after, the scene between him and Reggie Jackson, which to me was these guys burying the hatchet, these guys swearing fidelity, and promising next year was going to be better. I just thought that was remarkable. Winning—it was such euphoria that everything that went on in the past, the problem in the dugout in Boston, the problems in spring training, all of it was forgotten. Winning justified everything. He was so excited and so happy that he could even embrace Reggie Jackson. And Reggie sitting in Billy's office, hours after the game was over, just talking about how great the season was—of course, Reggie was the star, he hit the three home runs, he was basking in the glory of that. That's why winning a World Series was so important, and doing it in New York too. Doing it for the Yankees in New York. It just couldn't possibly get any better than that.*

Billy and his team had been persistent. They had not quit, and they had won. This could well summarize Billy's entire career as well as that Yankee season. There is a tendency today to belittle Martin for the many firings he endured. Why? Should he have just gone home with his tail between his legs, written off his methods for managing, and found another pursuit? Billy was no quitter, and Billy liked managing. He once said, "I don't think there is such a thing as a good loser. There's being a loser who won't truly accept the loss but bounce back and be a competitor. But to be a good loser—'Well, the hell with it'— to me that's a stone loser! And the world's full of quitters . . . They packed it in. They tried to find an easy way out . . . I don't want my players ever to think that way."[18]

And Billy never let them think that way. Sam Mele recalled advice Billy had given him, back when Billy was just a coach with the Twins in the 1960s.

▶ **Sam Mele:** *In '65 we won the pennant. '66 we're tied with somebody, and we need to win to finish second, because Baltimore had it locked up. And I'm making the lineup out, and I've got some guys in there that you don't know if you're going to win the game or not. And he sat down and he said, "What the hell are you doing? Why don't you put the regulars in there, damn it? Let's finish second." I said, "Billy, it's the end of the year." "So what? Damn it, let's go all the way. Second's better than third." I said, "You're right, Billy." He pushed me into it, to finish second. So I put the regular lineup in. Instead of using the pitcher I was going to use, I used a better one. And I got my best reliever in toward the end, and we finished second rather than third, which is the way it should be. But that's the way he was, he wanted to finish as high as he could at the end, and it brings over to the next spring, that you finished second.*

This unwillingness to quit applied to Martin the manager, and Martin the person. Even after his nine firings, he hadn't quit. He expected to manage again.

▶ **Phil Pepe:** *I think he believed that he was going to manage the Yankees again. Till the day he died, I think he believed that George would turn to him one more time. And this time it was going to be right. It was always going to be right this time. He never thought of himself as too old, or passe, or from the old school. He always thought that he was modern and up to date and could adjust. People on the outside might not have seen it, but he believed it. He was a very young 60. He was so youthful, even at that age. That's not old anymore. It was when Stengel was 60. He was still vital. He was still vibrant. I think that he was probably going to get another chance to manage, if not with the Yankees, with somebody who was looking for a quick fix. Some owner was going to say, "That's the guy we need, even if it's for a year or two. He'll straighten things out." And he was looking forward to that.*

Billy wanted one last campaign.

Notes

1. Dave Anderson, "Gabe Paul Speaks," *New York Times*, March 5, 1978.

2. "Martin," news clip from the National Baseball Hall of Fame Library archives, circa Spring 1980.

3. Billy Martin and Peter Golenbock, *Number 1* (New York: Delacorte Press, 1980), p. 22.

4. Billy Martin and Phil Pepe, *Billyball* (Garden City, N.Y.: Doubleday & Company, 1987), p. 226.

5. Joseph Durso, "Billy's Battles Go On," *New York Times*, September 23, 1977.

6. Martin and Pepe, p. 207.

7. Paul L. Montgomery, "Yankees, Quiet in Dugout, Are Routed, 11–1," *New York Times*, June 20, 1977.

8. Parton Keese, "Yanks Beat Royals, 3–1, as Gullett Takes 9th," *New York Times,* July 25, 1977.

9. Murray Chass, "Yankees Win in 10th on Jackson Homer," *New York Times*, July 27, 1977.

10. Murray Chass, "Yankees Subdue Twins, 6 to 4, As Rivers Again Leads Attack," *New York Times*, August 2, 1977.

11. Phil Pepe, *New York Daily News,* August 29, 1977.

12. Roger Nye, *The Patton Mind* (Garden City Park, N.Y.: Avery Publishing Group, 1993), p. 79.

13. *Billy Martin: The Man, The Myth, The Manager,* videotape (Cabinfever Entertainment, 1990).

14. "Billy Martin," A's Program, 1982.

15. Ira Berkow, "Martin is Unshaken Despite Adversity," *New York Times,* July 15, 1982.

16. "Yanks Romp, 9–3; Gullett Is Ailing," *New York Times*, July 31, 1977.

17. Nye, p. 75.

18. Ben Fong-Torres, "Billyball," *Parade,* April 19, 1981.

In the Dugout

Billy Martin ran a baseball game the way George Patton ran a war: aggressively and to win. The vision of Billy Martin in the dugout is very memorable for most fans. The dugout is where Billy Martin was truly alive and at his best.

Martin's face often looked almost pained with focus, his intense eyes darting around the field, searching for an advantage—any advantage—to exploit. Marty Appel, who for many years produced Yankee television broadcasts, recalled, "The veins in his neck and the fire in his eyes, they were important dramatically to building the telecast. The . . . cameras would show that." And Buck Showalter recalls "the steely look of him in competition times, and how much he loved being in that environment."

Looking for Opportunities

"Just give me a little room," Billy once said. "I'm going to take advantage of it. What the hell. When you're a leader, you have to lead. That's when you stick your neck out. Leaders are not followers. They are innovators. They are gamblers. They're not afraid to take a chance, not afraid to fail." He continued, "Billyball is nothing more than just aggressive, old-fashioned baseball where you're not afraid to make a mistake . . . forcing the opposition to make mental and physical mistakes. Going against the grain. Going after them all the time . . . Force the other team to execute perfectly . . . Always looking for an opportunity out there to create something. But get it quick. Right now. Not two innings from now."[1]

▶ **Rod Carew:** *He just knew the game and what he wanted to be done. Aggressiveness. He wanted an aggressive ballclub. We never stopped at second base. Make them make mistakes. Force them to make mistakes.*

▶ **Jackie Moore:** *Billy was a street fighter. He wasn't scared to do the unexpected. It was never a matter of "Should I do this? And if it doesn't work, then I have to explain it or be questioned about it." If he thought it was something to win a ballgame, whether it was a suicide squeeze at an unexpected time, he would try it. Billy was the first manager that I ever saw where the opposing manager would make a change—he'd bring in a relief pitcher after a guy hit a triple or a guy got to third base, and first pitch—boom—he'd put the squeeze play on. That's the last thing in the world that the opposing manager or player should be thinking about, because the manager just made a pitching change, and the reliever, first thing that he wants to do is throw a strike, 'cause he just come into the ballgame. And so that would put your club in a situation to squeeze a lot easier, and it worked time and time after. He wasn't afraid to do it. He just thought, "I have a chance to win a game here, and I'm going to use all my bullets to win this ballgame."*

Again, tremendous parallels between Billy and George Patton exist as it applies to aggressiveness. Says biographer Roger Nye of Patton, "Perhaps the greatest legacy that Patton derived from his two decades of reading history, theory, and practice of cavalry operations was his conviction that battles are won by those who take risks . . ."[2] Billy practiced the same theory. You can almost hear Billy telling his players, "Use the means at hand to inflict the maximum amount of wounds, death, and destruction on the enemy in the minimum time . . . IN CASE OF DOUBT, ATTACK!"[3] But that was said not by Martin but by Patton.

▶ **Tom Grieve:** *He didn't manage by the book. He didn't care what the owner thought, and he didn't care what the sportswriters thought. Today,*

*a lot of managers manage by the book. I mean, there's very little sur-
prise in a big league game. Billy, if you were behind by a run in the ninth
inning, men on first and second and two outs, you're just hoping to get
the guy from second home to tie the game. Three or four times that year,
usually with Cesar Tovar at second base, he'd double steal. Not only to
score the tying run, but because he wanted to win the game so that the
guy at first would be at second and score on a hit. I know it worked.
Managers today would never do it. I mean, I've never seen anybody do
that, because it's looked at as a risk-to-reward ratio that isn't worth it.
And if a guy gets thrown out and the game's over, the manager gets second-guessed and grilled by the sportswriters, and then the owner gets
upset and doesn't think he knows how to manage. As players, you just
watched Billy do this, and it was obvious that the other manager was
surprised a lot. Billy never did things by the book, and I don't think the
other manager ever matched up very well against Billy as far as playing
that game.*

Risk was part of Billy's game, as directed from the dugout. Taking
bold risks was part of Patton's agenda as well. In 1918, some 25 years
before his great World War II exploits, Patton wrote, ". . . boldness is
the key to victory. The tank must be used very boldly. It is new and
always has the element of surprise. It is also very terrifying to look at as
the infantry soldier is helpless before it."[4] Boldness was the key to Billy
Martin's warfare, too.

The Case of Rod Carew

In the spring of 1969, Billy approached young Rod Carew with an
exciting idea that would come to symbolize the Twins team of that season, and in a way, would come to symbolize Billy's entire managerial
career: stealing home.

▶ **Rod Carew:** *He came to me one day in spring training and said, "What
do you think about stealing home?" I said, "I don't know how." He says,
"Would you like to learn?" I said, "Sure." So he took me down the third
base line and started talking to me about getting walking leads, what
kind of leads I should get. And talked to me about studying pitchers,*

their windups, their timing. Slow windups, quick windups. We spent a lot of time going over this stuff. Then he would take me out some days with the pitchers and we'd go through different windups so that I could get the timing down as far as getting the walking lead slowly towards the plate. We worked at giving the hitter the sign so that he knew that I was coming, just all the things that you needed to know. And not having any fear at all about doing it. I said, "If I learn how to do it, if you teach me how to do it, I won't be afraid, as long as the guys don't swing!"

When Billy and Rod launched their home-stealing attack, a clever scribe couldn't resist putting the worst possible scenario into verse with the line: "There goes Rod Carew, lined to left by Killebrew." But the play invigorated the Twins, energized the fans, and demoralized the opponents. Carew would tie an age-old record of steals of home that year with seven, and he would have set a new record with eight if he had not been robbed of a steal in a game against the Seattle Pilots.

▶ **Rod Carew:** *The reason that he wanted me to do that is he felt that at times if the ballclub wasn't hitting, and I was on base, if we could steal a run, why not? That's how it all started, and I just kept doing it, under his tutelage. It was exciting. It was just an exciting thing to do, because no one was doing it. It created some mayhem. He told me, "I don't want you to do it just for the heck of it. I want you to pick your spots. If the game is tied, if we're down by one run, if we need it to go up by one run, those are the situations that I want you to do it in." They were the only times that I really tried to do it. I mean, I could have done it a lot more times that year. But there was a lot of adrenaline. I think after the first time I did it, or after the second time, every time I got on third, people started yelling, "Go! Go! Go!" It just became a big thing that year.*

Taking the Offensive

Whether you were playing for Billy or against him, you realized that he was capable of calling for any play at any time if he thought it might help the club win a game.

▶ **Ron Hassey:** *You knew when you went into the game with Billy he was going to do something. I mean, if it was a squeeze, you gotta be ready for a squeeze. He could be doing a double steal. He could be doing a first and third steal. You really had to be on top of your game, and as a catcher, you always were looking for something.*

▶ **Lenny Randle:** *He had games he had me bunting four times. Squeezes! I could have been killed. But I didn't care, 'cause I knew I would either get hit by the ball or I'm going to lay down the bunt. I know I'm going to get the man in. How could he 3–2, 3–1 squeeze? Not too many guys will do that.*

▶ **Willie Horton:** *You don't have to have home runs to win the game. You don't have to have all base hits. Walks, anything. He always tried to force the other side into making mistakes, and we'd take advantage of it. That's what winning is. Because his theory was, we're all athletes, we're all trained, but we've got to force them to make that mistake and take advantage of it.*

Taking the offensive is empowering. It gives you a feeling of control over your destiny. We want to act upon our world—not be acted upon by it. We want to be proactive, not reactive. When we take the offensive, we feel that we are doing the acting. Billy had the mentality of having to push really hard for everything he earned in life. His life was spent on the offensive, and this filtered into his strategies on the diamond.

▶ **Mickey Klutts:** *His size, his demeanor, he was always being picked on until probably the day he passed. His size led people to kind of look at him a little different and challenge him in a lot of ways. His whole attitude was that he's a fighter. He wasn't a thinker, a self-proclaimed genius, or anything like that. He used a lot of common sense. He was just a player's manager, someone who was constantly adjusting to everything in all situations at all times. He would just adjust to it; he wouldn't panic or anything.*

His focus and intensity in the dugout—and the constant adjustments he made—symbolized Billy's baseball success. You go and get knocked off track. You adjust, go a little more, and get knocked off again. Each whack you take, you get a little tougher, and you stay focused. Eventually, you go out and you win.

With this frame of mind, Billy elevated the emotional intensity of his players like Patton did with his soldiers. In a letter to his wife, the World War II hero wrote, "We shall attack and attack and attack until we are exhausted, and then we shall attack again."[5] Attacking was a fundamental part of Billy's baseball strategy. He could manage any type of ballplayer, but he loved the player who could attack. Billy loved the speedsters. In the spring of 1976, he was excited because on his team he had speedsters in Mickey Rivers, Willie Randolph, and Roy White. Said Billy, "I think we've got an excellent club, a club that can create a lot of things. When you have jackrabbits, guys who can run, you can force the pitcher to throw a lot of fastballs, you can force the other team into mistakes."[6] Billy's choice of verbs tell the story of the man: *create* and *force*. These are the words of a man looking to exert his own will over the game rather than wait for opportunities that may never come.

▶ **Mickey Rivers:** *He knew that "Mick going to get on base." He said, "I want you hittin' here." I said, "Well, you know, I can't hit no home runs." He said, "I know that. That's why I got you here." He said, "I want to set it up like this: You, Willie, or you, Roy. [Thurman] Munson, then [Graig] Nettles or Chris [Chambliss]." I said, "Well, shoot, I guess so. If that's what you want." We had me leading off. I said, "Aw, I want to get some ribbies, man. Put Willie up there." He said, "No, no, no, no, no." And we talked. I said, "No, I want to get some ribbies. I want to see somebody on." See, but it worked out the best, and he got the best out of the guys. Every day you see nine guys producing.*

Billy brought that extra dimension of intensity and aggression to these good established ballplayers, keeping the other team off balance, and enabling the 1976 Yankees to run away with the AL East Division Title.

▶ **Marty Appel:** *My best recollection of '76 was that after 12 years without a pennant, this one came so easily, it was almost lacking in excitement. They just ran away with it and it wasn't even a surprise.*

Billy knew that succeeding meant getting on the offensive. Don't sit back passively in your own dugout, waiting for something to happen. Make it happen. If you take responsibility for finding your own "edges"—whether through reading trade journals in the evening, spending time on the phone with contacts, or learning new skills—eventually, you will see your way through to a victory.

Getting Your Players to Be Like You

To win with his method, Billy needed players who were reflections of their leader: aggressive, attentive students of the game. Billy then served as their orchestrator, staying two or three steps ahead of the other team and its manager at all times.

When Billy became manager of the Yankees in 1975, he had a good veteran team, with on-field leaders like Munson, Chambliss, Nettles, Lou Piniella, Catfish Hunter, and Sparky Lyle. The added direction and fire from Billy put them over the top.

▶ **Fred Stanley:** *We knew we had a fairly decent ballclub, but we weren't expected to win. The Yankees, for ten years, had not played well. So we just went into spring training with this new guy, and you could see it start as we played. You could kind of see that we were going to be competitive. It is a team sport, but everybody's doin' their thing individually. I mean, Graig was a great player, Thurman was a great player, Chris Chambliss was a very steady and very solid player. Willie Randolph, he was a rookie. But I think they were looking for direction.*

Billy's managerial style was very different from the CEO-as-coach style perfected by NBA leaders like Pat Riley and Rick Pitino.

▶ **Fred Stanley:** *In basketball, with those big guys, they don't brawl. You don't see the coach going out there. You don't see the coach leading the* *charge. You don't see the coach screaming at opposing players and doing those things. They just don't do that. Billy did that. This little fiery guy, uniform baggy on him, just coming out there, just screaming, and just trying to intimidate the hell out of everybody. He'd just come out there and try to chew up everybody.*

Billy's was a raw, animal-instinct type of leadership. Billy got up for the game. He underwent a virtual psychological reaction, and his focus became intense. No matter what his personal problems, when he was in the dugout, his adrenaline was going and his energies were focused on the one thing he was a master at: managing his club. As Dave Righetti says, "Once the game started, that was his fix."

▶ **Phil Pepe:** *He once told me, "I don't know what it is, but I become a different person when I cross the lines. I drive up to the Stadium, I park my car in the parking lot, I'm one person. I get out of the car, I'm still that person. As soon as I go inside and put on my uniform, I change, and I'm a completely different person. And I don't know why it is. I don't like it, but I can't help it." So he understood that something happens to him when he puts the uniform on. He becomes competitive. He becomes belligerent, a guy with a chip on his shoulder.*

So the Yankees had a new fiery leader, and when he first arrived in 1975 and 1976, the attitude was infectious. The whole club became belligerent. The 1976 club came out of the blocks strong, capping its rebirth with a famous May brawl with the Red Sox. The fight—fueled by a collision at home plate between Piniella and Carlton Fisk, and remembered for a brawl on the mound starring Bill Lee, Nettles, and Rivers—heralded the reopening of the long-standing Yankees–Red Sox rivalry that would continue over the next few seasons, culminating in the famous 1978 one-game playoff to determine the AL East Champion, featuring Bucky Dent's dramatic home run.

▶ **Fred Stanley:** *When we got in that scuffle with Boston, it was as though "We are back." The Yankees are back, it's time that they have to start taking notice, because we have a pretty good ballclub.*

▶ **Mickey Rivers:** *I think Nettles and the Spaceman, Bill Lee, wasn't a big incident, because the rivalry's already started. They just broke out the rivalry, and that made us play better. They couldn't beat us after that, and I thought they had a better team. They had a good, champion team. [Manager] Don Zimmer was there. They knew they could beat us. But we used strategy. With Billy, it was our strategy. He could see all the changes.*

The cockiness was reflected in the entire team running. Not just Rivers, Randolph, and White, but everybody! The team adopted a "Come and stop us!" attitude. In 1976, catcher Thurman Munson— not a speedy man—stole 14 bases in 25 attempts. For his 11-year career, Munson stole only 48 bases in 98 attempts. That same year, Graig Nettles stole 11 bases in 17 attempts. For his 22-year career, Nettles was 32 for 68 in steal attempts. You never knew what Billy was going to do.

▶ **Marty Appel:** *Well, one thing he did was to start the team running. Even Graig Nettles—he had him running almost every steal opportunity. If there was one turnaround from [previous manager Bill] Virdon to Martin, it was the very aggressive base running. And those guys could not run, and yet he had them stealing—doing things they hadn't felt they were capable of, that weren't part of their "kit." It was quite an accomplishment.*

The style of play, pure in-your-face Billyball, brought out big crowds.

▶ **Fred Stanley:** *We had this tenacious attitude that we were going to come out there, and we were going to beat you. And you know what, we may embarrass you. It was one of those deals. So if you don't play real well, you're liable to get thumped real good.*

▶ **Mickey Rivers:** *Any time we go to these different parks, the guys were scared, the people were scared. "Oh, man, here come the Yankees. Oh, here come the Yankees." Everybody said, "We want to come see the Yankees lose." At that time, we packed all the parks. They were going to come see the Yankees lose.*

Especially in Boston. Center fielder Rivers, a big part of the fight in New York that had clipped Boston southpaw "Spaceman" Lee, was a target to the Beantown faithful, and on the first trip into Fenway in 1976, he suffered a steady stream of projectiles from the bleachers, including batteries, while he played defense. Rivers just grabbed a batting helmet and kept on playing.

▶ **Mickey Rivers:** *I still had to play. And I didn't want to stop playing for Billy, because Billy did a lot for me. And I said, "Look, if I have to go out there, just give me a helmet, I can go out there. But I'm going to play." And see, I didn't try to miss too many games in Boston, because I could hit good there. I played if I wanted too, but I always hit good there.*

Mickey Klutts was a young utility player on the great Yankee teams of the late 1970s, and he learned something watching his veteran teammates.

▶ **Mickey Klutts:** *When we walked out there, we were going to beat you. You were going to go down. That was it. They talked. Carlos May was hittin' off the bench. He would come into the dugout and just start yappin' at the other team. Just, "You guys are going down! That's it! That's it! Going down!" They would hear him, believe me.*

The attitude all started with Billy. Consider the 1985 Yankees, a 6–10 squad that Billy took over from Yogi Berra early in the season and brought home with a 97–64 mark, finishing only two games off the Blue Jays' pace. The startling turnaround was classic Billy. Said Lou Piniella on May 20, not long after Billy's return to the club, "Managers who expect more, generally get more from their players and Billy Martin is a great example of that . . . Billy expects a lot. He is an aggressive motivator who is going to piss some players off, but more often than not get the players to work harder and play better. Some guys are self-motivated. Most guys aren't. Everyone loved Yogi. Yogi is a good manager and knows the game. But the guys weren't playing hard enough."[7]

Don Baylor, a huge fan of Yogi's, put it another way: "Yogi just expected us to play aggressively and like professionals without having to rant and bark at us. And we didn't. Isn't that a sad commentary on us, as players?"[8] Billy did indeed exert a change on the team.

▶ **Ron Hassey:** *Unbelievable—the change when Yogi left and Billy came in. We had a good team that year, and I like Yogi a lot, and I don't think they gave him that long of an opportunity to turn things around, but we started off pretty slow. The veterans and really nobody was doing anything for the first 16 ballgames. First of all, I'm scared to death, because I'm going into New York, where I've only played in Cleveland. But now, I'm not really playing that much, and I'm able to sit back and watch everybody for those first 16 games, and I'm thinking, "Oh, man, it just doesn't seem right." Guys just seemed to me to be going through the motions. As soon as Billy Martin took over it was a completely different ballclub, the way guys were moving and hustling. It was unbelievable. I saw an unbelievable change. I could not believe the pace. When Billy took over, man, I thought, "God dang." And I mean, he turned it around, and we started playing, and we started winning.*

▶ **Dave Righetti:** *Whenever he was around, we were winning. And I knew a career only lasts so long. I liked to be around these kind of guys. We weren't going to win without somebody kicking us in the ass sometimes. And it wasn't so much he kicked us in the ass, it was the way we played. We went out there to kick guys' butts.*

▶ **Mike Pagliarulo:** *I have a lot of respect for Yogi. I mean, I felt bad. In '85, I was real young, but I know that I certainly felt that there was a sense of something different in that locker room, even though it was only 16 days. Guys were looking over their shoulder—no more easy time. Not that Yogi was easy, because Yogi's really intelligent and he would get on you too, in a different way. He would come up on you kind of quiet, and tell you things. Billy was more up front, yelling and screaming. They were both old school, they both had a different approach, but they both approached you at the right time. But Billy, it seemed like more guys were afraid of that situation, as a team, for some reason. It seemed like more guys were looking over their shoulders. Maybe I was too, I* *don't know. I played the same way, I believe. I think most guys did too, but they were just looking over their shoulders.*

Billy's psyche left him as someone who always had something to prove, no matter how many championships he already had won. Because of this component of his personality, he forced his players to feel that way too. Players knew that no matter what credentials they had already accumulated in the game, if they didn't have anything to prove any more, they were going to sit soon. For most players, that was enough to get the juices flowing, whether they liked Billy or not.

▶ **Bobby Meacham:** *As soon as he became manager again, immediately everybody played harder, everybody played more aggressively, everybody turned it up a notch. But the very same guys that turned it up a notch, most of 'em were veterans and didn't like him. We had a lotta guys who were unhappy, but it was weird. Baylor was unhappy, but he drove in like 95 runs. I mean, a lot of guys were not happy, but they still did their jobs and busted their tails for Billy. I wish I knew what the whole magic of it was, but guys just played harder when he was managing. Now that I'm in coaching and managing for a while, I've noticed that the team—each team that I've ever seen, wherever I've been—takes on the personality of its manager. I don't know if it's words that he says or just the way that he acts, but we had a swagger about us that other teams didn't when Billy was our manager. We automatically had an edge because Billy was our manager.*

By late June 1985, with Billy's magic continuing to work, Ron Guidry had this to say about the manager who always seemed to be around when he had his best seasons: "He's not the pitching coach, so you can't say he's helped me, but when Billy's here guys play harder and pitch harder. They know if they're not playing hard that they might not be in there the next day. So you wind up with eight guys behind you who want to play hard. You see guys diving behind you for balls now and I don't think you can say you've seen that around here the last couple of years."[9]

Billy was a leader who put his values on the table and let the players fall in line. The 1985 Yankees understood that they had to hustle every single day or face being replaced by someone else who would. Financial security had nothing to do with their efforts: By this time the average ballplayer was making big money. Instead, the ballplayers were playing for something more. They were digging down deep, finding the qualities of pride, desire, self-sacrifice, and the will to win that their manager wore on his sleeve.

▶ **Ron Hassey:** *Just by watching him, just watching during a ballgame the way his body language is, the way he acts, the way he yells. You knew he was intense. You knew he wanted to win. And when you see that in a manager, you want to win, you want to give it all you got. When you see a manager as feisty as he is in the dugout, he was just right there. He had us in the race, I mean we went all the way down to the last week. He didn't give us any pep talks in the locker room by any means, not that I can remember. He just put that lineup up, and he expected you to give 100 percent every night. He was giving it, no question.*

With the veteran ballplayer, Martin appealed to Yankee pride, desire, self-sacrifice, and the will to win. Billy got his players to do the right thing instinctively. He got them to go all out all the time by playing the fellows who "wanted it" and sitting those who didn't. Just his own presence had that impact on players throughout his career. No matter how much Billy had achieved in his life, he always wanted to achieve more, whether as a player or as a manager.

▶ **Charlie Silvera:** *I very seldomly ever told this story. The year was '72 that we [Detroit] lost the final game [of the AL Championship Series] to Oakland to go to the World Series. So we went back there, and they had the champagne ready, so he says, "Well, let's drink some of it." So we drank it. He said, "Come on, I have to go up and see Campbell." Jim Campbell was the general manager, and his office was up there through the right field upper deck. So we went up there and on the way he stopped, and he started to cry on my shoulder. He said, "Charlie, I wanted this more than anything in the world to go the World Series." I said, "Aw, come on Billy. It's over now." And he did, he cried on my shoulder. He hated to lose.*

The Value of Intimidation

Billy Martin believed in the value of intimidation, of keeping the opponent guessing and maybe even a little scared—of doing anything to get the other team off guard. Billy's teams did things, and when you are active, at the least, you have your opponents' attention, and at best, you have them running scared about what you are going to do next.

▶ **Tony LaRussa:** *You prepare for a team, you don't prepare for a manager, so I didn't really prepare for Billy any differently. What was different about Billy was in the dugout. He was so active that you constantly had to be aware and on guard for what he was going to do. He was active offensively. He was active defensively. He was very aggressive, and it was nonstop with him. A lot of managers aren't like that.*

▶ **Ron Hassey:** *One thing about Billy—he wasn't right out of the book, that "text" everybody talks about that's etched in stone, "This is the way you're supposed to do it." He wasn't that way. He would figure out a different way. You thought maybe they were going to be bunting, they were hit and running. You had to be on your toes, and you had to be prepared. Your advance scout might have given you some information of what he was doing on the first and third steals. That wasn't done much at all, but he was doing it. He could squeeze at any time. Be prepared. You had to be ready! There wasn't nothing to say that, man on first and second with no outs, that he was going to bunt the ball. That's pretty standard, isn't it, if you're down in the game? They ain't saying that if you're playing against Billy. He might be hit-and-running instead of a bunt. Or he might just let the guy hit. He never set a pattern of how he was managing.*

▶ **Mickey Klutts:** *Billy represented a cocky attitude, and whatever team he managed had that swagger. We made the other team fear what we were going to do—double steals, moving guys over—and whenever you do that, you take their mind off a lot of other things in the game. We let the other teams beat themselves.*

▶ **Matt Keough:** *He would play games early in the game. He would get guys up in the bullpen he had no intention of using. Billy made every-*

*body on the other side so anxious, so perplexed about what was going
to happen, they stopped playing the game. They just worried about looking stupid. And that was all Billyball. A definition of Billyball would be:
What we did equaled making them worry. Talk about spitters and all that
stuff—the whole thing was to create anxiety. And when you create anxiety on the other side, you beat 'em. That's all it was. He generated a
tremendous amount of anxiety, because no one wanted to look stupid.*

Billy never wanted his players to allow the opposition to intimidate
them. He had battled his way to the big leagues on sheer guts and
determination, never letting bigger, stronger players push him around.
As a manager, this spirit oozed from Billy to all of his players and even
to the opposition. Consider a June 10, 1978 game with the Angels in
which Thurman Munson was knocked out with an injury and was
replaced by rookie Mike Heath, just up from the minor leagues. In the
ninth inning of the game, veteran Angel Bobby Grich barreled into
Heath at home, smacking him with a good elbow.

▶ **Mike Heath:** *What happened was there was a base hit to center field,
and Paul Blair made a great throw home. Bobby Grich stopped three-
quarters of the way to home plate, because he would have been out. I
come up to tag him, and he forearms me as hard as he could to try to
knock the ball loose. Well, I didn't think nothing of it at the time, but Billy
comes walking out to the mound to change the pitcher, and he is telling
me, "You can't let guys do that to ya if you're going to stay in the big
leagues. They're trying to intimidate you and run you out of the game.
You gotta stick up for yourself at home plate!" He says, "Next guy that
comes in to that plate and does that crap to you, you get up and whip his
ass. You gotta stand up for yourself, son."*

As if by design, on the next play, Carney Lansford came barreling in
with another message for the young backstop. This time, Heath had a
response, and the two brawled at home plate.

▶ **Mike Heath:** *Carney Lansford slides in, which was a clean play, a little
aggressive, but at the time I just said, "Man, I'm gettin' up fightin'. I gotta*

come up fightin', man!" After I got thrown out of the game and stuff, Billy put his arm around me and said, "Now that's what I'm talking about! You gotta stick up for yourself! Now these guys know you mean business!"

Heath had learned the value of intimidation and of not allowing himself to be intimidated.

Intimidating Other Managers

Billy understood Patton's notion that ". . . the fact that you are attacking induces the enemy to believe that you are stronger than he is . . ."[10] Through his attacks, Billy kept other managers on edge.

▶ **Lenny Randle:** *They were intimidated. The opposing manager: "Oh, he thinks he's so smart." Because I not only played for him, I played against him. The opposing managers say stuff like, "Oh, God, here we gotta go. Here he is, and he's coming out. Everybody's coming out to see him." And Billy had no idea that they thought that people were coming to see him. He's coming out to protect his players. He's coming out to strategically set his game plan or warfare strategy. Whereas the other manager is already defensive. They're already on the defensive, so he's already got one run on them. As far as I'm concerned, we're already one run behind because of Billy. So the other way around—playing for him—I always felt we were one run ahead.*

Billy's longtime coach Jackie Moore matched up against Billy when he himself became a manager—for the A's—in the mid-1980s, and Moore remembers it well.

▶ **Jackie Moore:** *It was an eerie feeling. It put pressure on you. You knew, "I've been in the same dugout with him. I know what he's capable of doing." And now, you're in the opposing dugout with a different uniform on, and you better be prepared, because it could be a long night if you're not. And you know, I think all managers felt this, talking to 'em over the years. The game is like a game of chess, really. And they knew that any time you played Billy, you better be prepared, because the wrong move at the wrong time, he's got ya. It was an eerie feeling, really.*

▶ **Fred Stanley:** *I would watch him play games with other managers, and the other managers were so intent at trying to outmanage Billy that they'd put their club in a bad situation, meaning they'd pitch out two balls and no strikes, thinking we were running, thinking we were squeezing. Now they gotta come in with a fastball. Whack! Gene Mauch, for example. Gene Mauch would love to try to outdo Billy. He would love to do stuff that would cause us to lose us a game, so he could say, "I outsmarted him." But it almost never happened. We had an awful lot of talent on our club, and if a guy made a mistake, usually it would lead to two or three runs. And that's where Billy was so good. We had good talent, and yeah, we played hard. We did things. But I think a lot of that intimidation also went to the other club with their manager trying to outsmart Billy.*

▶ **Bobby Meacham:** *One time I remember, he and I believe Gene Mauch. It was weird. I sat back in the dugout, and these two guys were just looking at each other across the diamond. And they're laughing, and you could see it was almost like they were playing the game without us. It was one of those things where I think a lot of what Billy did as a manager was he put fear in the other manager. I think a lot of the other managers were afraid to get embarrassed by Billy because he was so bright as a manager. We knew it as players, so they had to know it as the other managers and coaches. So they were always worried about what Billy was doing, trying to make sure he didn't outsmart them, and in the meantime, we're beating their brains out. So I think a lot of what I saw when I wasn't playing was a little cat and mouse game that always favored us. Because I mean Billy was always going to come out on top of that. He knew more than they did.*

The Case of Tony LaRussa

One manager who was just emerging as Billy's career peaked in the late 1970s and early 1980s was Tony LaRussa, who took over the Chicago White Sox in 1979 before gaining fame with the A's and Cardinals. LaRussa cut his managerial teeth against Billy's Yankees and A's clubs, and he made the most of the opportunity.

▶ **Mickey Morabito:** *Tony LaRussa, when he started managing us [the A's], said that he learned more as a manager from the other dugout by managing against Billy Martin and trying to match wits with him. He just watched the things that Billy did. He said he learned so much by managing against Billy, and that's a great testimony from probably one of the great managers in the game today.*

▶ **Tony LaRussa:** *Well, any time you go up against somebody who's better than you, you're going to get better. I think in New York, and everywhere he went, he proved he could win with good players. But in Oakland, where he didn't have the talent, he was really active, and for him to win was quite an accomplishment. I think with Billy, he just used his instincts and he wasn't afraid to make a move. And you learn just by watching that and having to go up against that.*

In one incident during LaRussa's stint with the White Sox, the young pilot trumped the master by not only stealing the Yankees' signs but also by managing to camouflage the source from which he was getting those signs throughout most of the series.

▶ **Tony LaRussa:** *We felt like we had the signs from [Yankees third-base coach] Zim [Don Zimmer], and so we decided we were going to try to use them for whatever advantage we could. We had [as one of our coaches] Eddie Brinkman, who played for Billy [years earlier], shadow him at all times so it looked like we were getting them from Billy. So we did this the first game of the series, and it worked, so we used them the second game of the series too. And by the third game, Billy was kind of hiding down in the runway. Finally, I don't know if he had changed the signs, or at least changed how the signs were going to Zim, but when he figured it out, he came up on the top step of the dugout and kind of laughed. I think because it was Eddie Brinkman, whom he loved so much, that he didn't get too mad.*

Billy liked LaRussa and went out of his way to congratulate Tony when he won his World Championship in 1989. To this day, LaRussa remembers many things about Billy, but most of all, he recalls Billy in the dugout doing what he did best.

▶ **Tony LaRussa:** *Most of all, there was the competitive side to him, in the dugout. When you cut through all of the b.s., that's why all of us do this. You don't do it for the money. You don't do it for the publicity. It's about the competition, and Billy loved competing. Whether it was for a game, a series, or an entire season, that's what it was all about for him.*

Intimidating Opposing Players

The Yankees met the Kansas City Royals in the AL playoffs in 1976, 1977, 1978, and 1980, with Billy managing the Yanks in 1976 and 1977. During that time, Kansas City had a pitcher, Larry Gura, whom Martin had not gotten along with when both were in Texas and New York. Both times, Billy had not used him regularly, and both times, he eventually traded him.

Gura, normally a soft-spoken gentleman, was always outspoken in his dislike for Martin. So he looked to the 1976 AL playoffs for personal retribution on the national stage. After pitching a four-hit shutout against defending champ Oakland to clinch a tie for the division, Gura told reporters that he wished he could pitch in every playoff game against Martin's Yankees. Billy loved the pitcher's response, believing that an emotionally charged Gura would not pitch the controlled type of ball he needed to win.

Knowing Gura's personality, Billy launched a psychological war in the press and from the dugout, trying everything possible to rattle the pitcher's concentration. After hearing of Gura's desire to pitch in every game, Martin shot back, "I wish he could pitch every game, too. If he could, I know we'd win. I got rid of him in Texas because he didn't get the ball over, and I got rid of him this year because he wasn't as good as any of my four starters. And if I had him now, I'd get rid of him again . . . He nibbles at the plate. In a big game, he'll get too fine and start walking guys." Gura retorted, "Pressure doesn't bother me. Pressure is when you're not sure you can do something . . . but in baseball I know what I can do."[11]

Yet the next day, in the first game of the playoffs, Gura loaded the bases with nobody out in the first inning, and the Yankees scored two runs. The Yanks went on to slug 12 hits against Gura and led the entire way to win the game, 4–1. Said Gura about Billy's bench jockeying, "He was calling me some names, typical low class. Nothing you can print. He was yelling, 'Get the change over, you ——.' That doesn't show me much at all. I wasn't paying much attention until I heard that word." Gura's use of the word "until" is interesting. Was he paying attention after he heard Billy's magic words? Did Billy get into his head? It appears as though he did, especially when after the game Gura did not go out to the formal interview area until his nemesis was gone, noting, "It's not that I don't want to face him, but I'd rather not go there if he's still there."[12] Billy's vulgar attack may not have shown Gura much, but it did seem to rattle him on the mound.

For his own part, after the damage was done, Billy became gentlemanly: "He pitched very well," was all the media could get from the Yankee skipper. He later confided to friends, "I just said that because I want them to pitch him . . . again."[13] The Royals did, and the Yanks chased him again, this time in the third inning.

A year later, the Yankees met the Royals again in the 1977 playoffs, and Billy renewed his verbal assault on Gura. This time, Gura was pitching with a two games to one lead over the Yankees, meaning that with a victory, he could send his team to the World Series. Martin told as many members of the press as he could find, "The only worry I have is that Gura doesn't get hurt on the way to the ballpark, I mean in an accident or anything."[14]

Billy and the Yankees won again, with Gura chased by the fourth inning, down 4–0. Frustrated Kansas City manager Whitey Herzog noted, "In the second inning, he was throwing nothing but fastballs and sliders, and he can't pitch that way. I don't know what he was thinking about, but he has to use his change and curve." The next day, lefty Gura entered the game again in the ninth inning, as managers Martin and Herzog played lefty-righty chess. Martin let lefty-hitting Mickey Rivers face Gura, and the pesky Rivers pulled a Gura pitch into right field on a hit-and-run play to tie the game.

The Royals met the Yankees again in the playoffs in 1978 and

1980, after Billy had left the Yankees. In these two series, Gura won two games against no losses and had an ERA of less than 3.00. Certainly, Gura had matured into a stronger pitcher over time, but no doubt the absence of his principal agitator left his mind a little bit clearer. And if you don't believe this, note that in the 1981 divisional playoffs between the Royals and the A's, with Billy managing Oakland, Gura got shelled, giving up four runs on seven hits and three walks in 3⅔ innings.

Clearly, Billy was a master of the art of intimidation. In most lines of work, heckling or belittling your competition isn't really appropriate or even an option. However, there may well be ways for you to apply the lessons of using intimidation, to force your competitors into making mistakes.

The Value of Being Unpredictable

Billy wanted not only to deflate his opponents but also to flat out humiliate them if possible. Martin's tactical daring and unpredictability could annoy and unnerve even veteran performers. A case in point came with Martin's pesky 1980 A's in an early-season game against the Tigers and its star battery, Jack Morris and Lance Parrish. Billy's A's stole home in the game twice, once with slow-footed Wayne Gross and once with speedy Dwayne Murphy. Most important, the A's won the game, 5–3.

▶ **Mike Norris:** *I mean, it's just mad! It's just unbelievable. It's the furthest thing away from the other team's mind. A lot of times, it caught our team by surprise! You go, "Whoa!" I think Wayne Gross stole home two or three times that year. It just was incredible. Lance Parrish, the catcher for the Detroit Tigers, one afternoon, Wayne Gross stole home on him, and he threw the ball all the way into center field. And anyway, we wound up scoring about five or six runs in that inning, and Parrish came in and took the water hydrant and just tore it apart. Flooded out their dugout—they couldn't even sit in their dugout. So it was adding misery to injury right there. Oh, God! That was the effect that we could have on a ballclub. It was incredible. Oh, it was the best! It was the best time I ever had playing baseball, no doubt.*

▶ **Matt Keough:** *When you see Jack Morris and Lance Parrish go completely apoplectic because we're stealing home base, now you know you have them! [Tigers pitching coach] Roger Craig goes to the mound and says, "I want you to go into the stretch, because they're stealing home." And Jack says, "I'm not going to go into the stretch." And we had second and third, and we had two outs. And sure enough, Wayne Gross steals home, and Mitchell Page almost steals home on the same pitch, because it gets away from Lance Parrish. Lance goes into the dugout and tears the water cooler out of the side of the wall and throws it onto the field!*

After the game, third base coach Clete Boyer, a man who had played for great Yankee managers like Casey Stengel and Ralph Houk, told the press that he had learned more baseball "in one month with Billy than I learned the rest of my career."[15] And this is a man who played in the World Series five times!

As we have already seen, in 1980, Billy's aggressiveness transformed the misfit A's completely, such that by mid-July, they had had a triple steal, six suicide squeezes, and five steals of home. The 1979 A's never attempted a suicide squeeze, and the A's team from 1968 to 1979 stole home only five times. Billyball certainly caught the attention of owner Charlie Finley, even though he had distanced himself from the club and was actively shopping it.

▶ **Phil Pepe:** *Charlie Finley was going through a divorce and his insurance business was in trouble, so he was staying back on his farm in Indiana, but he'd get reports on the game the next day. And he'd call Billy up and say, "What? You stole six bases yesterday? How did you do that?" "What? You stole home three times?" I mean, he was astounded and amazed at what Billy was accomplishing with all young guys.*

All of the A's were given Billy's tutorial in stealing home plate. If the runner could catch the pitcher focusing too much on the hitter, then a brief window opened with an opportunity to be exploited.

▶ **Mike Heath:** *It all depends on if the third baseman's not really playing close enough to you, and the pitcher's got a slow windup. That's basically* *all he taught us. Sometimes a pitcher wouldn't look you back. It was more of a fear factor—"Hey, watch him, they might steal home"—and all that. You gotta glance over there and look at him. So, that's what we looked for. If we find a guy getting a little complacent out on the mound, next thing you know, here we come! I think complacency is the main thing.*

▶ **Jackie Moore:** *He'd do it in a situation when he wasn't going to score anyway. Say it might be two outs—it'd take a base hit to score you— and you'd pick the right pitcher that took the long, slow windup. And it was the combination that they knew that they could be successful, that they could beat this particular pitcher. There's also an art of how to do it. It's a heck of an exciting play, not only for you as part of the club to watch this happen and be successful with it, but just the reaction of the fans in the stands.*

Billy once said, "You gotta push, push, push. Take nothing for granted. Make the other team wonder what you're gonna do next. That's managing."[16] Billy never sat back and waited for a break. He never became complacent on the field. When he saw complacency from the other team, he attacked it instantly, and he expected his players to be ready to attack it too. That's why he was successful. Billy Martin did not simply wait patiently for opportunity to present itself—he created opportunity, in part by having his players execute unpredictable plays.

▶ **Mickey Klutts:** *I tried to steal home against the Yankees. That's the way we played. He had me try it against Guidry. It was '80, the first time the Yankees had been to Oakland that year. There was two outs and [Tony] Armas was up. Clete Boyer gave me the sign from Billy and I could hear Billy in the dugout yelling at me, "Get more, more, more, more, more!" And I took off, and I thought I was gonna die because Armas was going to swing. I thought I got under [catcher Rick] Cerone's tag. And I remember him hitting me really hard on the shoulder, which meant my hand was through there. I mean, we were all expected to do that— Wayne Gross and myself, two of the slowest guys on the team. Well, that was Billyball.*

Notes

1. Billy Martin and Phil Pepe, *Billyball* (Garden City, N.Y.: Doubleday & Company, 1987), pp. 110, 111.

2. Roger Nye, *The Patton Mind* (Garden City Park, N.Y.: Avery Publishing Group, 1993), p. 138.

3. Ibid., p. 136.

4. Ibid., p. 45.

5. Ibid., p. 137.

6. Phil Pepe, "Yankees Column," *Sporting News*, February 21, 1976.

7. "Yankees," *San Diego Tribune*, May 20, 1985.

8. Ibid.

9. Mike McAlary, "Lighting Strikes Back!" *New York Post*, June 28, 1985.

10. Nye, p. 136.

11. Dave Anderson, "The Larry Gura–Billy Martin Feud," *New York Times*, October 9, 1976.

12. "Martin's Needle Pierces Gura and Brett on Field," *New York Times*, October 10, 1976.

13. Dave Anderson, "Steinbrenner and Martin: Yankee Psychology Professors," *New York Times*, October 9, 1977.

14. Ibid.

15. George Vecsey, "How Billy Martin is Winning the West," *New York Times*, May 5, 1980.

16. *Billy Martin: The Man, The Myth, The Manager*, videotape (Cabinfever Entertainment, 1990).

Chapter 8

Do Something You Believe in with Your Life

n looking at the sum of Billy Martin's life, from the dreams he pursued as a boy to the fire that still burned when he died, there is a lesson to be learned. Billy knew what he wanted to do with his life, and he went after his goals as energetically as he could despite humbling, extremely public setbacks. And in the end, he made an impact still very much felt in his game to this day.

Yankee Pride

Billy Martin was first and foremost a Yankee, throughout his entire life. The Yankee way was what he believed in and what he strived for. As a Yankee, Martin learned about pride, about teamwork, about self-sacrifice, and about the will to win. It was what he believed life was about. And so he went after it, time and again as a manager—even when critics and comics all had an opinion, even when everyday logic would dictate that he should go elsewhere, and even when he knew what he loved would ultimately bring him pain. The Yankees meant that much to him.

▶ **Marty Appel:** *I never saw anybody tied to a team in his spirit as Billy was. I make the comparison of a college fraternity. To think that he was* *"in exile" for 20 years was tragic for the man. He must have been so lonely and miserable for what he once had for those 20 long years in the desert till he came back. Coming to know him then, for all the success he had in Minnesota, and Detroit, and Texas, I can't imagine he was very happy. He always felt like he was still doing it in the wrong place.*

That association with something meaningful could sustain Martin through the tough times. All of us want to do something meaningful with our lives. When we do something that gives us pride in ourselves, we perform better and feel better about ourselves. Roger Nye noted this in General George Patton, saying, "Patton saw a linkage between pride in self and victory on the battlefield."[1]

Late in his life, Billy said, "I played for the New York Yankees and I managed the New York Yankees and that's like a baritone singing at La Scala or an artist having one of his paintings hanging in the Louvre . . . Being a player and a manager for the New York Yankees . . . has been a thrill and a privilege that I will never regret, even though it didn't always turn out the way I hoped it would . . . it's been a great life. Very few people get to work at a job they love, and I'm one of them."[2]

Billy loved managing, but more important, he loved managing the Yankees. Working with another team might be meaningful and satisfying, but for Billy, it wasn't what he really wanted to do with his life.

▶ **Bobby Meacham:** *One of the different things I remember about him was when he wasn't managing. He came to Old-Timers Day, and he had just gotten fired the year before, and I talked to him. I said, "How you doing?" and he said, "Not too good. I need to manage again. I need to manage this team. It's frustrating, but it's killing me not being able to manage this club."*

▶ **Jackie Moore:** *Oh, there's no doubt. Billy, he might have had an Oakland A's uniform on, and he was very loyal to that organization, but his deep roots was Yankees. And there was no question about his teammates or that Yankee pride, his close relation with Mantle and those guys. Mickey would come around a lot, and to listen to the stories and listen to the things they talked about, you never got tired of it. You could just feel the* *electricity again—them talking about the old days and them talking about the Yankees and the pride that they had.*

▶ **Mickey Morabito:** *You know what? He's a Yankee. I still think, because of the amount of time in New York, and the fact that also he played for the Yankees, and the whole thing as Casey [Stengel]'s boy, that he's a Yankee. He always talked about Casey. There was always that Yankee in him. As much as I cling to what we did out here in Oakland, I still see Billy as a Yankee. Even before it started to deteriorate [in Oakland] in '82, even in the good years—as good as we were going in '81 and as exciting as it was—there was still something inside of me that said, "This is not going to last and Billy's going to be a Yankee again." I don't think Billy and I really ever talked about that, but it's just something that you feel.*

Did Billy ever get tired of managing? Of course. But he never wanted to stop. After winning the 1977 World Series, Billy told Phil Pepe, "I'm very happy, but I'm very tired . . . I am the manager of the Yankees and sometimes I want to walk away from it all, it gets so tough. But it's the only job I ever really wanted."[3]

▶ **Mickey Klutts:** *Some days he didn't feel like managing . . . He had his days, too. I saw him some days down, and I don't know what it was from. Most of the times he loved the game, but sometimes I saw him real down, especially in his dealings with [George] Steinbrenner. And if something was in the* Post *in the morning, or something was going on, it got to him. He's a human being. You know, they were America's favorite couple there for a while. But Billy had a tremendous heart and I think it hurt him in a lot of ways, a lot of things that were said about him. I don't understand to this day why he took the job five times.*

Doing Something You Love

Billy took the job managing the Yankees five times because it was what he wanted and what he loved. When you believe in something, when you are dedicated to a cause that is greater than you are, nobody has to tell you to do it and to work hard. You aren't just punching a clock and putting in your hours. The effort comes easily. The effort is not draining. In fact, the effort is invigorating. When you do something you love, it doesn't feel like work. Billy loved the game, and it was all he wanted to do.

If you want something badly enough, you are willing to go out and work for it. You survive the bad breaks that lead your peers to quit. You learn from your mistakes and persevere. Billyball worked because Billy "wanted it" and he could spot ballplayers who "wanted it" too. Billyball also produced victories, and while it didn't always endear him to some of his players, many of the writers, and various critics, it—and Billy—gave many players pride in themselves and the job that they were doing for their team. He loved that part of his job.

▶ **Fred Stanley:** *It was his whole life—no question. You know, when you wake up, and you're so proud of what you've been able to accomplish, and what you think you're going to be able to accomplish, and you've got this drive that he had. It was something that he loved so much, and he felt that he was good at it. And he got praise for doin' it. And it wasn't work. It wasn't work. What he wanted as a legacy when he was finished was that Billy Martin was one of the best managers that ever managed the game. That was his goal.*

▶ **Mike Pagliarulo:** *He really loved doing it. He loved being there. He looked like that was what he was made to do. He had genuine love for his position in the game and New York. And when you have that passion or that love, it's normal to have a lot of pride in it, and to fight for it.*

▶ **Toby Harrah:** *He really tested what you were made out of inside. It wasn't like a job to Billy. It was like an extension of himself, his personality, and what he stood for.*

Judging Oneself

If we devote ourselves to a cause the way Billy did to managing players and to the Yankees, through both good times and bad, we can succeed, no matter what anyone else says. Ultimately, each individual determines for him or herself whether his or her life is a success. Billy knew that he could be the only judge of what he should do in his life.

Should Billy have gone back for four encore engagements as manager of the New York Yankees? Would Billy have been better off going to another ballclub where he might have had more stability and a free hand to run an entire organization his way, like he did in Oakland? He would have answered yes and no, respectively, to those questions, and to a large degree, only his answers matter. Billy's conditioning was in Yankee pride. Billy believed so strongly in being a Yankee that he was able to ignore the snide remarks of the reporters who made jokes of his second, third, fourth, and fifth returns to the New York dugout. Some of his associates can understand why he returned, time and again.

▶ **Buck Showalter:** *It's very addictive. There's nothing like the passion and the energy of the Yankee fans. And I understand that allurement to Billy, and he understood completely what he was getting into each time. That's the thing that I learned—you know the job description going in there, so nobody wants to hear you bitch and complain about it. That's a poor reflection on you. Did it catch you by surprise that there were going to be certain things? No, it shouldn't. The rewards are well worth taking the other stuff, which Billy certainly came to grips with.*

Tom Grieve, who played for Billy with the Rangers from 1973 to 1975, had become the general manager of the Rangers during the time in the 1980s that can be viewed as the "hire Billy, fire Billy" Yankee years. He didn't see Billy's hirings and firings in that unusual a light.

▶ **Tom Grieve:** *As far as going back to manage the Yankees all those times, I don't think anybody even thought about that. It was a unique relationship between Billy and George, and even when Billy was managing the Rangers, the Twins, or the Tigers, you knew that he was a Yankee. He had an unbelievable amount of pride of having been a Yankee when the Yankees were a dynasty, and being Mickey Mantle's friend. So you knew, any opportunity he had to be associated with the Yankees, he would do that. I don't think anybody felt less about him going back to the Yankees* *those times. I think everybody understood the relationship he had with Steinbrenner and how much he loved the Yankees.*

But other players and associates who had learned the game from Billy suffered for their manager during those years.

▶ **Mickey Klutts:** *It lessened something for me. I still to this day have a tremendous amount of respect for him, but as he kept going back I lost a little, because I wanted him to be the man that he was always telling me to be, and to stand up for himself. He didn't need to go there. But his Yankee heritage, his Yankee blood, drew him back and back. I don't know—I didn't really care for him to go back there that many times. It made him look bad, and then he started getting a lot of negative press, and he should have gotten positive, good press. People say, "The five-time manager of the Yankees." Well, jeez, what the heck does that mean? I thought it was a circus. Even when he passed away, they didn't mention Billyball too much, and what he did with a bunch of young guys. They mention him and Steinbrenner five times.*

▶ **Mickey Morabito:** *It was frustrating because watching the ups and downs, ins and outs, and everything else, I kind of started feeling that this is not good for Billy right now, you know? But I think that every time that he went back to New York, he probably thought that he was the right guy to save the situation, because of his feeling for the Yankees, the uniform, and the whole deal. Unfortunately, it would last for a while and then something would happen where they'd have to make a change, and then George would want to bring him back again. The way the media treated it, it got to be comical. And it shouldn't have been that way because Billy was serious. He still cared about the Yankees, he still cared about baseball, and deep down he probably thought that he could make this thing work. But the whole yo-yo syndrome there, it just wasn't going to be treated right by the media.*

▶ **Billy Martin, Jr.:** *I would give anything to have had him stay in Oakland. And I'd say that to him, I'd say, "Dad, why do you want to go back there? Put up with all that crap? You own the world right now." And he'd*

say, "Partner, I'm a Yankee." As great as things were for him there in
Oakland, I just don't think he could be truly happy unless he was in pin-
stripes. It's sad in a way. I would just have loved to see what would have
happened had he stayed in Oakland for five years, had he stayed in Texas
for five years. Where he could just go out and mold players and win.

Obviously, Billy gave George Steinbrenner too much leeway over
him after his return to the Bronx from Oakland in 1983. But it was his
own decision, not George's. And during his later stints with the Yankees, he still was doing what he did best—molding young ballplayers.
The experiences Bobby Meacham, Ron Hassey, Dave Righetti, Mike
Pagliarulo, and Buck Showalter each had with Billy took place during
this time frame. Unfortunately, at a very obvious level, Billy wasn't
doing what was best for himself.

Author Paul Stoltz looks at Billy's decision to return to the Yankees
time after time and casts it in the light of someone "Climbing" a
"Mountain":

> "This goes back to the Mountain. I didn't know him person-
> ally, so I can only guess from what is said. It appears Billy
> equated his Mountain or purpose with being the Yankees'
> manager, not inspiring young men to play their greatest base-
> ball. This put him in a vulnerable position, where he could be
> rejected by others, if not outright prevented from his ascent.
> No Mountain, well defined, hinges on one person's opinion or
> actions. This was his mistake. It's tragic. He demonstrated the
> Climber's relentlessness, but on a poorly defined or poorly
> chosen Mountain. This is the difference between a goal and a
> Mountain. A goal has completion. It can be accomplished. A
> purpose—represented by your Mountain—outlasts you. It
> has no summit. You are never 'there.' He had the courage to
> dream and the tenacity to pursue it, which in a way was his
> undoing. Sometimes we beat our heads against an overhang
> until they become a bloody pulp, when it is clear to so many
> around us that it is time to reroute. Relentlessness has a dark
> underbelly if it does not further one's ascent."

The more we see today's players run for the money, shedding their loyalty to a team, to a set of values, and to the characteristics that make life meaningful, we should remember Billy Martin and the love he felt for his team and for winning. His devotion to these dying values made him a memorable leader, and even though the game has changed, Billy's influence is right there, in the Charlie Manuels, Tony LaRussas, Buck Showalters, and Paul Blairs who were exposed to him and who took things from Billy's repertoire and added them to their own.

▶ **Ray Negron:** *That's why I am so excited with the Cleveland Indians right now, because our manager [Charlie Manuel] is a Billy Martin disciple. He's an old school baseball guy, and he put together our coaching staff accordingly. Our first base coach is a guy by the name of Ted Uhlaender, who also played big time for Billy. And he loved Billy Martin. At our meetings, all I hear is, "Billy would do this" and "Billy would do that." That was awesome. It was awesome.*

These men are doing something they believe in with their lives, just as Billy did—and just as Billy taught them.

Notes

1. Roger Nye, *The Patton Mind* (Garden City Park, N.Y.: Avery Publishing Group, 1993), p. 46.
2. Billy Martin and Phil Pepe, *Billyball* (Garden City, N.Y.: Doubleday & Company, 1987), pp. 5–6.
3. Phil Pepe, ". . . And Martin? His Model and Idol is Stengel," *Sporting News*, October 29, 1977.

Chapter 9

Categorizing Billy's Leadership and Assessing His Life

Was Billy a Great Leader?

Columnist and author George Will once wrote of Billy Martin, before the Yankees' rebirth in the mid-1990s, that ". . . [George] Steinbrenner . . . knows so little about baseball that he thought Martin was a winner. Martin wasn't, on the field or off . . . And he was a bad manager."[1] With all due respect to Will, who loves the game of baseball, that statement is simply foolish.

The people who have spoken about Billy Martin throughout this book know a lot more about the man than George Will. And they know a lot more about the game of baseball, too. These men played for Billy, coached for Billy, worked with Billy, and managed Billy. They were around him on a daily basis, through the good times and bad. They know as well as anyone that Billy Martin was far from perfect. But they also know that he was a tremendous leader and had qualities that leaders in all fields should emulate.

▶ **Paul Blair:** *Today's writers, when they want to get headlines, they distort a lot of things that happened with Billy. Billy's the type of guy that just wasn't going to let anybody get the last word in, basically. He stood up for himself. He didn't let nobody run over him, and he got in fights. If a player challenged Billy, he was going to fight—that's all there was to it. So he had a couple fights, but writers wanted to extort that and blow it out of proportion. But basically, Billy was a good guy. He wasn't going to take no junk, now that's for sure, but he was a good-hearted guy, and he really treated us well. Billy was just a helluva manager . . .*

▶ **Tom Grieve:** *When people ask me about Billy Martin, he was without a doubt the best manager I ever played for between the lines. And I played for Whitey Herzog, Ted Williams, Joe Torre, Frank Lucchesi, and Ken Boyer. I mean, I loved the managers that I had. They were all good guys, they were great baseball people, a lot of them were great players, and so it's no slight on any of them. But without a doubt, Billy was the best manager I ever played for.*

Grieve and the others interviewed for this book took part in over 30,000 major league games. George Will played in none. Those interviewed amassed over 21,000 hits in the major leagues, versus Will's zero. They pounded out over 1,700 home runs. Will? None. These men won over 3,000 games as major league managers. Will didn't win any. Could you go out and find players with equal statistics who *didn't* like Billy? Probably. And would they say that he was a bad manager, as Will does? Maybe, though it doesn't seem likely. But that doesn't diminish what the people in this book have had to say.

And yet, there are so many imperfections in the managerial career of Billy Martin, such as his lack of longevity with any one club. Does the fact that Billy didn't stay with one team for 25 years, like his friend Tommy Lasorda, mean anything? Perhaps it just means that he was a different kind of leader than Tommy. Any student of leadership knows that not all situations call for the same type of leader.

For example, when Charlie Finley hired Billy to manage his horrendous A's in 1980, he was fixing to sell the team, and rumors were swirling around the Bay Area that the A's were headed for Colorado or

Florida. Finley had a business problem, and Billy, with his exciting style of leadership, was the answer.

When Billy inspired the Athletics' amazing move from last to second in 1980, it not only made believers out of the players, it made believers out of Bay Area fans. Most important, it made believers out of a Bay Area business powerhouse that kept the team local and infused the organization with working capital. Finley, who had been unable to unload his team for $7 million in 1979, turned the A's over to Levi-Strauss titan Walter Haas and his son-in-law Roy Eisenhardt for $12.7 million in August 1980. Oakland had lost football's Raiders to Los Angeles, but because of Billy, the A's stayed, and by decade's end, they had played in three straight World Series. Billy was more than a manager in Oakland. He was a happening.

▶ **Mickey Morabito:** *You had the national media all the time in New York, but here you come to Oakland where you don't expect it, and all of a sudden you've got the* Time *magazine cover and people you don't expect doing features on Billy. When we first came here, the only paper that covered the Oakland A's on a full-time basis was the* Oakland Tribune. *All of a sudden you've got the* San Francisco Chronicle, *the* San Francisco Examiner, *and the San Jose paper staffing all our home games and even traveling with us for a good part of the season. It all started from nothing and that was all Billy, because Billy was an exciting guy to cover. He was always going to say something, either off-the-wall or whatever. The media was afraid to* not *be around him. He just created an excitement. The media caught on right away and they were all over it. They enjoyed Billy. He was fun to cover.*

Consider the mood around the Oakland Coliseum in early 1981, as described by Ira Miller in *The New York Times*:

> The largest crowd in Oakland baseball history, 50,255, turned out last night for the A's first home opener of the post–Charlie Finley era. It exceeded by 49,602 the turnout for a game exactly two years earlier, in the pre–Billy Martin era . . . Many of last night's fans piled out of vans and campers and set up

charcoal grills for tailgate parties . . . Once inside, the fans gave Martin a standing ovation, and they marveled at the million dollar's worth of improvements to modernize the drab, gray Coliseum. The public address system, for example, which in years past might as well have been broadcasting in a foreign language, played hit music and the A's new Billyball theme song . . . It is an entirely new atmosphere in Oakland . . . season ticket sales this year increased from 75 to 3,000 . . . Steve McCatty says, "Tonight was just incredible. We were so jacked up, there was no way we could lose."[2]

And even in 1982, as the team struggled, there were notable developments. Rickey Henderson set the all-time single season stolen base record, and the team set an all-time attendance record. And as for Oakland's minor league system, Billy noted, "We had seven farm teams and, in my last year there, six of them won league championships and the other one finished second."[3] The A's were an up-and-coming organization. As director of player personnel, Billy helped create a farm system that in a few years fed Mark McGwire, Jose Canseco, Walt Weiss, and Terry Steinbach into Oakland. Certainly that was the Haas organization, too, but Billy was the baseball mind behind the organization's development. There's no reason to say, as George Will does, that Billy was "the quick fix for teams in too much of a hurry to rely on the slow, steady development of young players, the formulation of real baseball prosperity."[4] He was a quick fixer, but that doesn't mean there was no steady development as well.

▶ **Mickey Morabito:** *There was a lot of groundwork laid here. To this day, talk to Roy Eisenhardt and people like that and they'll give Billy a lot of credit. I think there was like that little lull after Billy left, kinda everybody caught their breath here and just went from there. Then they knew they had to go out and get somebody with that type of intensity again, and so in comes Tony [LaRussa], and the whole thing took off again. I think if you talk to the people who were here at the time, there was a lot of good groundwork and a lot of players came into the organization in those years that were important in the early years of Tony's situation here.*

The Charismatic Leader

So how can one give credit to Billy as a tremendous leader, while still acknowledging the fact that he was fired nine times and never managed a club for more than three consecutive seasons? One possible answer comes from work done by Pulitzer Prize–winning writer Garry Wills. In his book *Certain Trumpets: The Call of Leaders*, Wills describes three core types of leadership: traditional, legalistic, and charismatic.

According to Wills, the traditional leader's power is derived from the ceremonial, evokes memories of the past, and essentially is assumed to be secure indefinitely. Potentially stodgy and stagnant, the leadership role is not necessarily earned, and may be more style than substance. In baseball, managers are hired to be fired, and no manager can sit back and relax. However, certain organizations, most notably the O'Malley-era Dodgers managed by Walter Alston and Tommy Lasorda, went decades between managerial changes regardless of the team's placement in the standings. In today's game, Tom Kelly of the Minnesota Twins, who led his club to World Series championships in 1987 and 1991, leads a team, which, at this point, seems to harbor almost no expectations of being competitive. The Twins have had a losing record every season since 1992, and while some fans and executives no doubt ponder ousting Kelly, by no means is he considered wholly responsible for the club's performance.

Legalistic leadership is derived from the ability to politically navigate the various constituencies in and around an organization. In baseball, managers attempt to maintain diplomatic relations with their main followers—the players, but also with the media, the fans, and, most important, the front office. One manager who excelled on each of these fronts throughout his long career was Sparky Anderson. Anderson won three World Championships, but also stayed afloat through offseasons with both the Reds and the Tigers by maintaining an adaptable, pleasant, yet still competitive environment for all parties.

Finally, there is the charismatic leader—the awe-invoking original who gains followers by promising and delivering virtual miracles. He does not rely on political savvy for survival, only performance and the strength of his aura.

Billy is clearly in the charismatic category. As Wills notes, "Charismatic leaders—from Stalin to Sihanouk, from Mao to Fidel—make up a kind of rogues' gallery of recent history."[5] Had he been studying sports figures, Wills surely would have added Billy Martin to his list.

The Early Stage

When the charismatic leader first takes control, he or she is given authority, attention, and a free hand for establishing a new order. The leader is also given great respect. Wills writes, "The charismatic ruler is not merely a king but a founding king . . . Awe is the proper response to charismatic authority . . . The charismatic ruler is original in the most basic sense, originating an entire social order . . . It is complete mastery, outside the trammels of oppressive tradition or compromising legalism."[6] All of Billy Martin's teams fall pretty neatly into Wills's description, especially his A's and Rangers teams, in which young players with horrible records were reinvented as winners in the image of their "founding king." With a Billy Martin social order outside of oppressive tradition, the teams ran amuck on the fields and in the bars across the American League.

As the teams turned around and began to win through Billy's gung-ho managing, the awe from players and fans alike actually increased. During this exciting, electric, and winning phase, Billy could do no wrong. Remember Billy's Miller Lite Beer commercials, featuring punch lines like "I never argue," or "I didn't punch that doggie"? When Billy was riding high, he was an American folk hero, a man with the courage to tell off umpires and bosses or loosen someone's teeth without any concern for the consequences. He was unpredictable, aggressive, brash, *and* successful. He was everything most of us would want to be, if we had the guts.

Wills continues, ". . . all charismatic leaders exist in a glow that fuzzes their image to awed followers . . . Charismatic figures subvert or stand outside the regular forms of authority."[7] The Miller Brewing Company certainly fuzzed Billy's image with its ads, but for the players, that fuzzed glow came from the swagger and the results Billy got for them on the field. Consider these comments from writer Randy Galloway, who covered Billy's Texas Rangers: "The whole thing was magic. The team responded to him like I've never seen a team respond. I don't know what it was, he had something, there was something in his personality."[8] The players themselves concur.

▶ **Toby Harrah:** *For me, I felt like this guy could walk on water. I played for him for two years and didn't miss a ballgame. He was just a pleasure. I mean, I couldn't wait to get out there and play.*

▶ **Tom Grieve:** *He was such an interesting guy to be around that you just enjoyed being around him. I liked listening to him talk. I liked his style.*

The Middle Stage

Yet, as Wills continues, the blissful early stage of the charismatic leader's reign does not continue indefinitely. At some point, another stage begins. "So long as the charismatic leader is performing wonders, few doubt his semi-divine powers. But when conquest yields to stabilization, youth to age, fabulous exploits to everyday routine, how can charisma be 'routinized'? . . . Since this kind of ruler did not rise by traditional or legal agreement, but by the wonders he performed, there can be a swift draining of power from him if he stops performing wonders."[9] And so it was with Billy. In Oakland, after two years of overachieving and managing with a virtually free hand, an agitated Billy began to rebel in 1982 when the Haas family put fiscal restraints on him and the club. And when the team also began losing in 1982, the now–worked-up Billy self-destructed, and without the wins, he was suddenly a lot less charming and heroic.

▶ **Mickey Klutts:** *You know, the only thing that's a true fact about Billy that kind of gets me a little bit, but it is true, is that Billy has worn out his welcome, and that's honestly speaking and that's a fact. He was having trouble with the owners [in Oakland]. I don't know the inner workings, but I'll bet it's just power. But once you start losing, it was hard for him to still demand that power. Hey, you gotta back it up now, and it wasn't happening.*

▶**Mickey Morabito:** *We had kind of built up and overexceeded expectations maybe the first two years, and I think it's the whole combination of things and it just got to the point where it just blew up. And he got to the point where he had made such a challenge to authority that something had to be done on their end. As close as I was to Billy, I told Billy after that, "Billy, you screwed that one up. That could have been a great deal." And it just happened.*

When Billy's teams moved out of the "new" stage and toward routine or poorer performance, the flies in the ointment always began to attract attention. As the awe dissipated, folk hero Billy would begin to be recast as a middle-aged juvenile delinquent. In newspaper articles, the adjectives changed: "Boorish" replaced "brash," "crude" replaced "colorful," and "alcoholic" replaced "unpredictable." In this stage, Billy would be portrayed as a man out of control.

He began to be regarded negatively inside the organization as well. The tough leadership style, when not producing victories, began to be seen as too intense and detrimental to the long-term good of the organization. The now proven ballplayers, once so hungry for direction from Billy, no longer needed or wanted a manager like him watching their every move.

▶**Jackie Brown:** *If he helped me when I was 25 years old, and I become a star, when I get to be 30 years old, now he can't help me no more? And that kind of seems what happened to Billy. And it was that little man's complex, or however you want to say it. People couldn't handle that, and I don't understand why, but I sat and watched it happen. The minute someone would get to be successful, they no longer wanted Billy to holler at them.*

▶**Charlie Manuel:** *I think sometimes, after a year or two, a player's patience will run thin, because all of a sudden he is demanding things of him. And it is a long season. I've always heard this, and it's probably true, too, that for one or two years, the players just absolutely loved Billy.*

But at the same time, he was demanding. He definitely would stay on you if you were not doing things correct. At times, he would grow stubborn and kind of old to you.

As Wills writes, "Charisma inspires people, but also exhausts them, with the unexpected."[10] Again, Billy fits the picture. The players, once so thankful to learn everything they could from Billy, sometimes wearied of the strain, and as a result sometimes they didn't do as much as they might have in better days to keep their skipper clear of trouble.

▶ **Matt Keough:** *We'd be with Billy out someplace, a restaurant or a bar. And why people 6'4", 220 pounds would want to make their legacy on having a fight with Billy Martin, I could never understand. I mean, he wasn't a physically imposing guy. And usually we would try to keep enough people around him where it didn't happen. But as time went on, as the losses started piling up, the injuries started going on, we probably did not do a very good job of protecting Billy. And I think that speaks volumes in Oakland as well as New York. Billy needed to have somebody that was going to watch out for him. And when you're losing, those people kind of have a tendency to walk away, myself included. So, at that part of it, I failed. In my mind, I look back on it, and I say I didn't help him. I was having my own problems. My arm was hurting, I wasn't winning. We weren't doing as well as we should have been doing. So we all had our failings.*

The Leader Moves On

Pretty soon, the miracle worker is on the move again, possibly because the clubs were no longer willing to put up with his ways and style. And so it was with Billy, time after time after time.

▶ **Jackie Moore:** *Billy had the reputation of jump-starting clubs, but also they'll say, "He'll also burn a club out after a few years." But in my opinion, whether you want to call it burnout or what, Billy never let up on what he believed. He never gave in to the system. Others were saying,*

"Oh, we don't have a very good club," or "We won it last year and let's don't do the little things that got us here." But he only knew one way to manage, and that was prepare yourself and do the things it takes to win a game. He expected that every day out of his players and coaches. He wasn't going to change his approach to the way he managed and what he expected out of his ballclub.

▶ **Dave Righetti:** *Let's face it, George [Steinbrenner] was smart in this respect—if he had a quiet manager and a low-key guy and he fired him, he always went to a fiery guy. If he went from Clyde [King] to Billy or [Bob] Lemon to Billy, it was for that butt kicking, and then that only lasts so long, then the players will supposedly wear out from all that and go the other way.*

Note Righetti's use of the word "supposedly." When asked about it, he really didn't think the players were that worn out.

▶ **Dave Righetti:** *I don't think the players—the players that* played*—ever had a problem. In fact, the more he was around them, the bigger the numbers got for the offensive guys, and some pitchers flourished. [Ron] Guidry sure seemed to, and I did, and Shane [Rawley] did when Billy got there too.*

Tom Grieve agreed that Billy's troubles were less with players than with team ownership.

▶ **Tom Grieve:** *It's obvious if you look at his track record that things went good at the beginning, and eventually, and usually pretty quickly, things soured. And it usually wasn't, at least from my experience, his relationship with the players. It was more his relationship with the front office, and I think his lifestyle had a lot to do with that. I mean, he brought a lot of the problems on himself. Those reasons, they're out there, and those are the reasons why he didn't manage the same team for 20 years.*

Garry Wills likens the charismatic leader to a Western gunfighter. Writes Wills, "The gunfighter who has not killed anyone recently is rumored to have lost his speed or nerve or hunger, and challengers begin to move in on him . . . On the run again, hiding as in his outlaw days, he returned to his old skills of deception, guerrilla assault, and 'doing the impossible.' . . . That is the grimmest lesson of charismatic rule. It is always unstable, often short-lived, and at odds with its own foundation. The divinely graced person is supposed to be above failure . . . there is an implicit pledge of infallibility in charisma. The gunfighter has to win every time."[11] Nobody can win every time, but Billy, who dressed in Western clothes and saw himself as a gun-slinging desperado, believed he had to.

▶ **Phil Pepe:** *He couldn't deal with defeat, with failure. It was foreign to him that his team should lose. His team? He's the manager. How could he be losing? They never did before. Just like he had a difficult time admitting to his failures to the press, he had a difficult time admitting to the fact that his team couldn't win.*

In the world of sports, no one wins every time, but Billy needed to win. He had to win. When he couldn't win—when there was absolutely nothing he could do to make things right—he melted down. His positive outlook and his confidence weren't enough. His dugout skills weren't enough. It was time to wait it out. But Billy was not good at waiting it out.

In 1982, there was nothing Billy could do to salvage the A's. His pitching staff began to go down with injuries, and the winning stopped. But because of who he was, and because of the way he had conditioned his players to feel about themselves, he believed that they still could win. And the players did too. The Billyball message had worked *too* well.

▶ **Matt Keough:** *If there was one thing Billy had no grasp of, it's injuries. Then he was in trouble. Where Whitey Herzog would say, "Well, fine,* *we'll wait two years until X, Y, or Z come out of the minor leagues," Billy had nowhere near the patience for that. What we bought into was that we could pitch in the big leagues at 80 percent if we were hurt. That was wrong. To pitch in the big leagues at 100 percent is tough—80 percent, 90 percent, if you're injured, you can forget it, you're going to get your ass kicked. We bought into Billy convincing us that we were so good, we were so athletic, that we could pitch hurt. And we tried to. You can't at that level of competition. The best healthy have trouble competing. The best hurt can't. For that, he was wrong. But did we owe him the chance? I think so. He put his neck out there and got us four-year contracts, showed us how to win, how to be successful, and how to make money. So I tried, [Steve] McCatty tried, [Rick] Langford tried, [Mike] Norris tried, [Brian] Kingman. We all tried.*

▶ **Fred Stanley:** *Billy just himself self-destructed. He was so frustrated with what was going on, and he couldn't fix the ship right then, and he got frustrated with that fact. There weren't a lot of changes to be made because you lose your three starting pitchers, I don't care what organization you're in, you're going to lose.*

Note Stanley's observation that there were not a lot of changes to be made. Billy had built a good team, and just as he had after the 1980 season, he had improved on the 1981 version going into 1982. But with the key injuries to the pitching staff, the club lost its momentum, and Billy lost interest, perhaps largely in part because he suspected that the Yankees job might be looming again.

Did Billy Ruin the Arms of His A's Starting Pitchers?

One of the raps that followed Billy out of Oakland was that Billy had burned out his young pitchers with overuse and too many complete games. To this day, if a pitcher goes too long in an early-season game, broadcasters bring up Billy's famous five starting pitchers—Matt Keough, Brian Kingman, Rick Langford, Steve McCatty, and Mike

Norris—and cite his abuse of their arms. But is it a fair rap to level against him? Did he make the decision to go for short-term results at the expense of the long run—something leaders sometimes elect to do? Many of Billy's players argue that he did not.

▶ **Mickey Morabito:** *I think one of the most unfair raps against Billy was that he abused these pitchers. If you don't walk a guy or you don't strike out a guy, which our pitchers didn't really do a lot of, you don't have to throw three and four pitches. What's wrong with maybe getting a guy to get out on the first or second pitch? Basically, these guys pitched complete games, but they threw 100 to 125 pitches. That is not abusing a pitcher's arm.*

Interestingly, Billy's pitchers and catcher Mike Heath also defend the skipper.

▶ **Matt Keough:** *I got hurt—it had nothing to do with Billy. I slipped on a rainy, muddy night in Baltimore. It was raining, we were trying to get the game in, and I slipped. I think Norris had an impingement. Langford just threw a lot of sliders and eventually they caught up with him, and they were going to catch up with him no matter where he was. So Billy got blamed for it all, but I think that's all b.s., personally. Billy did not hurt us. Brian Kingman got the chance to lose 20 games because he never got skipped in the rotation. We always threw low-pitch counts. He protected us. We had off days in Oakland a lot. We never got bumped up a day early. Everybody says, "Well, Billy broke us and abused us." I would say there's nothing further from the truth.*

▶ **Mike Norris:** *I can only speak for myself, but I'm going to try to speak for the others. Each of us had different arm injuries. That strike-shortened year [1981], after the strike we came back, we did not work out. I speak for myself—I stopped working out. That strike was about 68 days or so. I stopped working out after the first month, so that left about 34 or 35 days without working out. We came back, I started the ballgame against the Baltimore Orioles and went 14 innings, won the*

*ballgame, I think 3–1 or something like that. And from then on, every-
body else did the same things, went out and pitched nine innings. We
just were not in shape, and we went downhill from there. By the end of
the season, everybody's arm was tore up. And we were so cocky that
we were that good, that we'd go out and pitch without working out.*

And as the fall of 1981 turned into the spring of 1982, things didn't
get any better. Still emerging from the frugal Charlie Finley era, the A's
did not have indoor training facilities in Scottsdale, Arizona, and bad
weather made it tough to get in enough work.

▶ **Mike Heath:** *What happened coming out of '82 spring training, we had
a bunch of rain that year, and we didn't have any indoor facilities. So
none of our pitchers could get their work and throwing. So when the
season started, they'd be out there pitching. I'll never forget, Billy'd
come out there and say, "Do you wanna come out of this ballgame?"
And they would say, "No, no, I don't want to come out of this ballgame."
And he'd say, "Well, we can get you somebody in there." And I believe
that these guys weren't in shape simply because of the weather factor,
and they tried to pitch themselves in shape, and I think a lot of them got
hurt that way. And Billy gets the blame for it. I don't buy it.*

As the injuries overcame the staff, the cockiness Billy had instilled in
the pitchers, and had himself, worked against them.

▶ **Matt Keough:** *The biggest problem I had with Billy was when we started
getting hurt, he couldn't accept it. That was the hardest thing, because we
couldn't accept it, and we thought we were good enough to get away with
it. Billy kept running us out there when we shouldn't have gone out there.*

The following table depicts the five A's starters—Keogh, Kingman,
Langford, McCatty, and Norris—and 30 of their peers, sorted by the
highest number of complete games thrown by the pitcher in a year.
(Note that each player did not necessarily amass his greatest number of
innings pitched and his greatest number of complete games in the
same year.)

epe: *His problems were never winning and losing. He always won.
 Billy began to flex his muscles and get a little too self-confident
el that he could start dictating to owners and general managers
n things his way, and it just never worked. I mean, if he messed
 situation in Oakland, where he was the lord and master and he
erything, and he screwed that up, it's his fault, there's no question
 it. He always flexed his muscles. Whenever he got something, he
 wanted more. So he was at fault. He was his own worst enemy. I
magine who would have been able to tolerate all the demands that
ould make, all the power that he wanted. If you own a baseball
you want to have some input, especially today's owner.*

arrah: *He could really be intimidating to you if you're not a base-
an. If you're an owner who has very little baseball background,
s the majority of owners today, a guy like Billy Martin can just
ate you to death. And I think after a while, if you're the head hon-
d the guy under you is really wanting to run the show, sometimes
er to get rid of the guy and bring in somebody else under you
ll listen to what you have to say, even if you don't know what
aying.*

der must play to all constituencies. Dealing successfully with
ve him was something Billy never mastered.

The Hidden Side of Billy Martin

ment of the life of Billy Martin would have to include aspects
 that were often hidden from the public at large. Billy Mar-
yal friend and manager to those he cared about, and he was
iritual man.

A Loyal Friend and Manager

 played with and managed hundreds of players over his life-
if they had been his kind of ballplayer, he was their team-
lifetime. Though it is often obscured by the controversies in
e was a man who did a lot to help people.

**Starting Pitchers, with Career Highs in Innings Pitched and
Complete Games**

Career Highs	High IP	High CGs	Years in Majors	Career Innings
Steve Carlton	346.1	30	24	5,216
Ferguson Jenkins	328.0	30	19	4,499
Catfish Hunter	328.0	30	15	3,448
Mickey Lolich	376.0	29	16	3,639
Gaylord Perry	344.0	29	22	5,351
Rick Langford	290.0	28	11	1,490
Nolan Ryan	333.0	26	27	5,387
Luis Tiant	311.0	25	19	3,485
Jim Palmer	319.0	25	19	3,948
Bert Blyleven	325.0	25	22	4,969
Randy Jones	315.1	25	10	1,931
Mike Norris	284.0	24	10	1,123
Mark Fidrych	250.0	24	7	412
Vida Blue	312.0	24	17	3,344
Dennis Leonard	294.2	21	12	2,187
Tom Seaver	291.0	21	20	4,782
Ron Guidry	273.2	21	14	2,392
Fernando Valenzuela	285.0	20	15	2,669
Matt Keough	250.0	20	9	1,190
Jack Morris	293.2	20	18	3,824
Dave Stieb	288.1	19	15	2,845
Jim Kaat	304.2	19	25	4,528
J. R. Richard	292.0	19	10	1,606
Mario Soto	273.2	18	12	1,730
Dennis Martinez	292.0	18	20	3,748
Steve Rogers	302.0	17	13	2,839
Tommy John	276.0	17	26	4,708
Mike Flanagan	281.1	17	18	2,770
Larry Gura	283.0	16	16	2,046

Steve McCatty	222.0	16	9	1,189
Jim Clancy	266.2	15	15	2,518
Moose Haas	252.0	14	12	1,655
Scott McGregor	260.0	13	13	2,141
Rick Reuschel	260.0	12	19	3,549
Brian Kingman	211.0	10	5	551

It is evident from this table that the A's hurlers did not throw more complete games than aces from other teams, many of whom pitched for Billy Martin at one time or another in their career (including Jenkins, Kaat, Hunter, Guidry, Lolich, and Perry). Only Langford and Norris are even close to the 30 complete games thrown by Hall of Famers Carlton, Hunter, and Jenkins.

▶ **Matt Keough:** *To have four guys have 20 complete games or more, that number sticks out and bothers people. But you look at the innings pitched, I pitched 250. Is that a big number? It's a reasonable number. I mean, when Ryan and those guys pitched 300, no one said a word. When Valenzuela was pitching, when he's down 7–0 and he's still pitching in the eighth inning because [Tommy] Lasorda wouldn't take him out, no one got on Tommy's ass. Why does Billy take the abuse? Because he had* five *great athletes.*

As the table shows, none of the A's pitchers ever threw over 300 innings in a season, whereas Carlton, Jenkins, Hunter, Lolich, Perry, Ryan, Tiant, Palmer, Blyleven, Jones, Blue, Kaat, and Rogers each did. But these guys were the aces of their staffs. They were expected to take the ball and finish what they started. But it's common wisdom that second, third, fourth, and fifth starters don't throw those kinds of innings. Well, there's no reason why they don't, and that's where the Oakland issue gets tricky. Basically, the Oakland team was a team with five aces, like the Orioles of the early 1970s or the Braves of today.

▶ **Matt Keough:** *We [the Tampa Devil Rays] had an argument the other day at our meetings about fifth starters. And one of the older guys said,*

*"There's never been a fifth starter to pitch 200 inni[ng]
one." How 'bout these statistics: 211 innings, 209 [
Those numbers would indicate you had a pretty goo[d
say? Can you name the pitcher? Brian Kingman. An[
20 games. So he was our fifth starter. That tells yc[
was. Today, he'd be worth about $7 or $8 million a[*

Maybe Norris was the ace of the aces in 198[
took over that title in 1981, but for that short pe[
all going out there as an ace, like Hunter or [
primes. It was part of the Billyball culture.

▶ **Mike Norris:** *That's where everybody's mind was
were going nine innings, and we weren't giving
four runs a ballgame, and that was that. And this
to the Keoughs and the McCattys and the Kingm[
and fifth starters. They all had the mentality like*

It can thus be argued convincingly that B[
arms of his A's starting pitchers, although li[
sions, this one will likely continue for years to[

A Great Leader, But a Diffi[

Billy Martin was a great leader, but like General [
Douglas MacArthur, he was not a great emp[
George Steinbrenner or any of the other own[
mately wore out his welcome. This was a flaw [
what made him so good but also, in another [

▶ **Gil McDougald:** *Billy never could fathom the c[
something and being the boss, and being jus[
when you try to tell the boss he don't know h[
hey, I gotta admire Billy, if you call it standin[
thing, but I don't know if that's what you call[
mat, let's put it that way.*

Late in life, Billy recalled, "I guess the one thing that bothers me the most, the one thing about my life I would change if I could . . . I'd like to be remembered as me . . . how I really am . . . I guess I'm destined to be remembered as Billy the Kid in baseball, a quick shooter, a battler. I don't like that. What I would like is to be remembered by the people who know me best."[12] In the following stories, the people who knew Billy best remember him.

▶ **Mickey Morabito:** *Billy was basically a good person. Besides his off-the-field antics and his greatness as a manager, he was a good human being that did things for a lot of people. And if you were a friend of Billy—and I can say this as a friend of his—there was no friend that anybody can have that is more loyal. He's the most loyal guy that I've ever been around to people that are his friends. And I think that that is a very, very key thing, his loyalty to his friends . . . I guess what I'm trying to say is, if you're a friend of Billy Martin, there's no better friend you can have.*

▶ **Gil McDougald:** *He was just a helluva guy. I think of people more as a human being, and I think Billy was a great human being. Billy would give somebody the shirt off his back if they needed it. I tell you, I enjoyed him very much. He was a real super kid. He was a good person. If you were in trouble, he'd do anything he could to help you. What better way can you remember a guy? Hey, he certainly isn't God. He wasn't perfect. But he was a helluva guy.*

Many of the people who knew him best, like Rod Carew or Rickey Henderson or Mickey Rivers, loved him dearly. Yet because Billy didn't publicize his sentimental and loyal sides, he's remembered today mostly by the back-page tabloid treatment that his troubles generated. But he was a good friend. When Mickey Rivers had finally burned his bridges in New York for good late in the 1979 season, it was Billy who paved the way for him to make a new start in Texas.

▶ **Mickey Rivers:** *Look at the time I had to go. I said, "Well, you know, I thought about a time for me. I got to make adjustments. Now I got to try to leave here for a while. Things ain't going good there with the*

family." So I say, "I got to make adjustments. I got to change." Billy set
me up. He said, "Well, I tell you what I'll do. I got a place in Texas. I'll
get you a car. I'll get you a home. You can go to Texas. Would you like
that?" . . . I figured I'd take a chance, I'll take a chance. I went there on
account of Billy. It was Billy's say-so that got me. I'll tell you what he
did, he got me a car, he got me a house, he got me set up. Billy, Jr. was
there . . . So I said, "Boy, I guess that'd be perfect for me. I guess I"ll
go there and take a chance with it." And he said, "Look, you're going to
still do good, no matter where you go at." I said, "Well, man, I'm
leaving New York." But I turned it back around in Texas. I got a cou-
ple hundred hits. I set up the same pattern. I said, "Oh man, Billy
was right."

Rivers was a very popular Ranger, and he enjoyed some great seasons in Arlington, including 1980, when he hit .333 with 210 hits. And
in the off-season, when Billy was around the Arlington area to visit his
son or Mickey Mantle, Rivers was on his mind and part of his life. By
then, Billy wasn't managing Mickey anymore. He wasn't trying to coax
him into giving his best on the field or trying to protect him from
unlucky ponies. He was just looking out for someone he liked, and for
someone who had been a great Yankee for him.

▶ **Mickey Rivers:** *We stayed in touch, because he'd call me. "How you*
doing? How you like the house? How you like the car?" He helped me
out the first couple months till I got adjusted. I said, "I'm kind of get-
ting adjusted down here." It was so quiet; it was a whole lot different
atmosphere. He said, "Yeah, I told you that." He said, "In the off-sea-
son, no problem, we're going to do a lot of things together." I said,
"Look, I like to go fishing." He set me up, we'd go fishing, him and
Mantle and all them guys. That wasn't even a managing standpoint, it
got to be a friend. That's what I liked about it. He didn't leave me hang-
ing out to dry. He watched my back. Every time I needed something,
I'd get on the phone and make a phone call. They're going to find Billy
at the Stadium.

Others players also felt unusually close to Billy.

▶ **Ron Hassey:** *I want to think that my relationship with him was kind of different. Personal. There was times where he would talk to me on the side, maybe on the field, maybe during batting practice, and I always remember that when he got remarried, he sent me an invitation. When I got traded over to the White Sox and came into town, he would call down. When he was announcing, he would call down on the field during practice to see how things were going. He just wanted to say hi, but that was something that I will never forget, because I really never had that type of relationship with a manager. All the negative stuff that you hear about this guy, I did not see any of that. And I just don't know, maybe it was just our personalities clicking together, it made it kind of special for me. I always waited for that phone call. Things like that made it special.*

This was as much the real Billy Martin as any of the headline-making controversy. Wrote sportscaster Howard Cosell in 1986, "Judge Martin by his occasional outburst and you do him a disservice. Judge Martin by the headlines, and you react to a shallow and cheap portrayal of a human being . . . The Billy Martin I have known since the early '50s, since his discharge from the army, is a deeply emotional man, who identifies closely with the people around him, especially people in trouble."[13]

Many of Billy's associates remember stories of when he did just that.

▶ **Mickey Morabito:** *When we were with the Yankees, and we were playing in Minnesota, there was this guy talking to Billy. And I saw Billy peel out some money and hand this guy a couple hundred dollars or whatever. And the guy walked out, and he thanked him. He looked like a janitorial-type person. He was not dressed very well. I didn't know who the hell the guy was, and I went over to Billy and said, "Billy, who was that? Why did you give the guy money? He looked like someone from the cleanup crew." And he said, "You know who that was? That was Zoilo Versalles. He's just really down on his luck right now." He actually was working in an office building doing some kind of janitorial work, I think. But this guy was a World Series hero, one of the great Twins of all time. But I mean, you never saw that written, and he never wanted anybody to know stuff like that.*

The stories of Billy going the extra mile to help his friends go on and on. Another of Billy's kind efforts was for a former Oakland Oaks teammate from the 1940s named Merrill Combs.

▶ **Jackie Moore:** *Merrill Combs was a friend, and back in the old days, you had to have four years of major league service to qualify for the pension. Merrill had three, three and a half years or something, but he was short the half a year to qualify for the pension. So Billy, knowing this, was trying to get him that half a year and brought him up with us [as a coach] in Texas. And he stayed with us for a complete year, not realizing that there was a rule that just four coaches could be on the pension plan, and you couldn't take one coach off if he was still on the club and put another coach on. So he spent the whole year here and found out that he didn't get the half a year. So Billy brought him back the next year, and Merrill stayed and got his time on the pension plan. And it wasn't many years later, unfortunately, that he had cancer and passed away. But at least his family benefited from this, and that's Billy. He was very aware of people and their needs. These are the things you don't hear. You always hear about the marshmallow salesman.*

Billy was charitable when he thought it was the right thing to do. But he was also willing to give somebody a push when that was warranted. When Willie Horton retired from playing after the 1980 season, he went home feeling down and having no idea what the future held for him. It was Martin who shook him up, just as he had shook him up as a player.

▶ **Willie Horton:** *During the time I was retired, I don't know who told Billy that I'm just sitting in the house. He called me. "What the hell you doing?" I said, "Whatcha mean what am I doing? I'm taking it easy." He said, "You ain't called me. You ain't called nobody. You ain't going out. What's wrong? Life ain't over. Life's just beginning, man, what's wrong with you?" Out of all the people that I knew in my life, this man called when I needed him the most. You can have all the people in the world when you're doing good around you, but when I was down, you go through the phase of, "I shouldn't have did this, I shoulda done this."*

You start sitting around. But then you got to accept it and you got to get on in your life. He said, "Well, personally, I'm going to get you into base-ball and get you a job. You got your kids to take care of. That's what you got to do." And he made me recognize that.

As much as Billy was loyal and demanded loyalty in return, he also knew as a leader when to let go. Consider Mickey Morabito, whose career had been greatly influenced by Billy, and who owed Billy a lot.

▶ **Mickey Morabito:** *At one point he wanted me to go back to New York [from Oakland] with him . . . He was putting a little pressure on me to come back. He said, "Now you're going to come back with me if we go to New York, aren't you?" And I would just tell him, "Yeah, Billy, if you want me to, I will"—deep down knowing that if he really wanted me, I probably wouldn't. I did not want to go back to New York at that point, as much as I loved being around him. I really got to enjoy being out here in Oakland. I'll never forget, I was at his house for Christmas, and it was one of those melancholy nights after Christmas dinner, sitting in his liv-ing room. And he said, "You know what, Mickey? You should stay in Oakland. They really like you out here, it's a good situation for you. I think that you'd be better off for your career to stay in Oakland." And that's one of the greatest things. I tell people: Two great things Billy did for me. One is he got me to Oakland, he brought me with him. And prob-ably the second greatest thing, which might sound dumb, is he did not make me go back to New York with him. I really appreciate the fact that he didn't, because I think as a friend he knew that I was better off here, rather than taking me back into that situation there.*

The bottom line is that Billy never forgot the players, executives, and writers who had been loyal to him, and his loyalty to them was for a lifetime—even to Bobby Richardson, the man who took his place as the Yankee second baseman. Richardson and Martin remained friends for many years. Whenever Bobby asked, Martin participated in benefit golf tournaments for and contributed to the college where Richardson became a coach. But for Richardson, there was more. Diehard Yankee fans know that both Billy and Bobby wore uniform #1 when they played for the Yankees. In 1986, #1 was retired by the Yankees in honor of Billy, which meant that no one other than Billy would ever wear the number again. However, Billy took an unusual step granting permission for Richardson to do so, so that today, if you see Bobby Richardson at Old-Timers' Day or a fantasy camp, he'll still be wearing old #1.

▶ **Bobby Richardson:** *When his uniform was retired, he wrote me a letter, and in that letter he said, "I want you to know that as long as you live, you can wear this uniform at Old-Timers' games or wherever you want." And he signed it "Your Friend in God, Billy Martin." I mean, because of that, if I went back to an Old-Timers' game, I could wear the uniform. Now, for instance, [Phil] Rizzuto's #10 was retired, and Tony Kubek, who was broadcasting for the Yankees, couldn't even put on that uniform. It was all because of a letter. He just had a soft heart.*

And finally, Billy could simply be a kind-hearted person, especially if there were children involved.

▶ **Frank Lucchesi:** *A lot of people don't know about what a big heart he had. Billy was for the little guy, in and out of baseball. I think it was Christmas in 1976. He was flying from Dallas–Fort Worth to Oakland, California, and he was sitting in first class. And evidently, some people knew who he was, and this little kid came up to him, about 11 or 12 years old, and asked for his autograph. So Billy says, "Where are you headed, son?" He says, "Well, I'm going to go visit my mom." He's from a broken home. Billy says, "Well, are you bringing your mom a Christmas present?" And the kid put his head down, and he said, "Well, I don't have any money." Billy took out 20 bucks, and he said, "When you get off the plane, you go and take your mom shopping to get her a Christmas present." I loved Billy Martin for some of the reasons that you're hearing. He was just a guy with a big heart.*

Phil Pepe, the writer who saw both the good and the ugly in Billy while covering all of his days in New York, has one very fond recollection of his then–14-year-old son John and Billy, in the days just before the latter passed away.

▶ **Phil Pepe:** *I was going through a divorce, and John was the youngest of four children, like ten years younger than his next oldest sibling, so I was trying to spend a lot more time with him. And every summer, I would try to take a vacation with him. Well, this one year, I said, "I have a great idea, John. Why don't we go up to the Hall of Fame, travel around New York State to a different minor league ballgame every day, and then, we'll go visit Billy Martin in Binghamton." John thought that was a wonderful idea, so I called Billy, and he said, "Oh great! Terrific! When are you going to be here?" And I gave him the date, and everything worked to perfection. Our last stop was to go to Billy's farm and spend an afternoon with him. We get there, and Billy has arranged with a local college kid to come be a companion for my son, to make sure that my son had something to do that was interesting while Billy and I caught up on old times. He had a lake outside on his property, and he had the college kid take my son John fishing. I just thought, "My God, how thoughtful. What a wonderful idea." Most people would say, "The kid'll get along. He'll watch television, or he'll go out and play." But not Billy. My son actually caught a fish, the first time he'd ever caught a fish in his life, and they had a picture taken with my son John holding the fish, and Billy standing by his side. To me, it was such a special thing and told me a lot about the man. Also, while John was out fishing, and Billy and I were talking, Billy was preparing spaghetti sauce. Billy did the cooking himself, and he's going to serve my son a spaghetti dinner. It's completely contrary to everything you've heard about him, but I just thought it was special, and such a considerate and thoughtful thing for him to do.*

A Spiritual Man

For all of his well-documented flaws, Billy Martin also was a very religious man. Billy's faith helped him stay true to his own beliefs and values, even as his many enemies publicly criticized him in the press. Said Billy, "A lot of people mouthed off at me in my lifetime, about my habits. They're wrong and I know it . . . God taught me one thing. In the Bible He says He is the sole and only judge of a man, and that no man should judge another. That is my strength. God is my judge."[14]

▶ **Phil Pepe:** *He was very, very close to his religion, even though you wouldn't think so. Divorced three times, getting into fights and all of that. That was contrary to the teachings of the church. And yet, he went to mass regularly, wore the little cross on his cap. And I guess that came from his upbringing, from his mother and grandmother. But he was very respectful of religion. He often went to church without telling people. He'd just go off to Mass. I don't think he missed. He just didn't like some of the rules, so he made up his own rules.*

▶ **Bobby Richardson:** *He and I sat down and talked about things of the Lord . . . His background was a tough background, but there was a tender heart, and I felt a real relationship with the Lord. See, I grew up in a Southern Baptist Church down here, and basically, my theology is very simple. I feel that at some time in your life, you've got to accept the Lord Jesus as your personal savior, and that as you spend time in His word, as you talk to Him in prayer, and as you tell others about your relationship, that's how you grow in the Lord. And that's what Billy and I were talking about, and he said, "Well, I want you to know, I've done exactly the same thing." He said, "I've accepted Jesus Christ as my savior. Now, maybe I haven't gone to church as much as I should have, and I know I've been drinking a little bit, but my feelings are exactly like yours. I feel like my only hope is in the Lord."*

By being true to himself and ignoring his critics, Billy maintained his identity and self-direction. He defined who he should be and had his own views of right and wrong. He didn't let the press or anybody else dictate who he would be. This is not to say that all of Billy's headstrong ways or behaviors should be emulated. However, the concept of being true to your core beliefs is a fine quality. Billy stuck to his guns throughout most of his career both for better and for worse.

As Billy saw it, only Jesus and God could judge his life, and he encouraged kids to understand this fact. Billy once said, "The most important thing I say to kids is to love your God. That's first. And after that is to be honest—don't lie, tell the truth to yourself and everything else will fall into place."[15] One kid he passed his beliefs on to was his own son, Billy, Jr. As a teenager, Billy, Jr., would spend parts of the summer with his dad, traveling from town to town with his team.

▶ **Billy Martin, Jr.:** *My father went to church on Sunday. He knew where a Catholic Church was in every city. We'd get up, we'd go eat brunch, and we'd go to church. If we'd get there and it was just starting, we'd sit through Mass. If we got there in the middle, we'd stay on. Even if we got there and Mass was over, we'd stay, say our prayers, and leave.*

Billy Martin's Legacy

Sportswriter Thomas Boswell once wrote sadly about Billy, "If he'd only known himself half as well as he knew his game, he might have been the best."[16] But Billy may have known himself better than Boswell thought, and better than Garry Wills with his charismatic gun-fighter analogies could even have written. Back in 1976, Billy said, "Did you ever read Western books? You'll run across a lot of stories about gun-fighters. The gunfighter goes through life having gunfights all the time, everywhere he goes. Somebody is always challenging him. Then one day he is killed and everybody looks at the gunfighter and says, 'So what? There's always another one.' I'm like that gunfighter."[17] Another time, Billy said, "I can't change now. I guess it's like being a gunfighter. Once you start, you do it for life—until somebody comes along and shoots you down."[18] Yes, Billy knew himself well.

Martin was a great leader, but because of the charismatic style of his leadership, he was often forced to pack his bags and move on to another organization. This does not make him a bad manager, any more than a long run with an organization—such as Tommy Lasorda's with the Dodgers—makes someone a great manager. Martin and Lasorda were both great but different managers.

Let us again turn to the observations of Paul Stoltz, who comments, "So many entrepreneurs and leaders have some of Billy's profile—a nontraditional path, childhood adversity, being made fun of or ridiculed, and an uncompromising track record of relentlessness. This is the high AQ (Adversity Quotient, see Chapter 2) Climber profile. These people can really irritate . . . Thank God! Without them, this world would be far less interesting and rich. It is the Climbers who shape whatever game they are in. Once the wounds are healed and the hurt feelings mend, we remember the Climbers most fondly and admiringly for the impact they had and legacy they left."

▶ **Tom Grieve:** *I think the things that made him a great manager then are things that would make any manager a great manager. And let's face it, he managed then successfully and still got fired eight times and still got in fights and still had embarrassing things happen. And if he managed today, all those same things would happen, there's no doubt about it. If he still had the same problems, those things wouldn't change, but having said all that, the things that made him a great manager then are things that would allow anybody to be a great manager today. That part hasn't changed. And the players would love playing for him today just as much as they loved playing for him back then. There's no doubt about that.*

And the players did love playing for him.

▶ **Bobby Meacham:** *I loved playing for him. He was a great manager. He taught me a lot as a player and as an athlete, and that's what managers are supposed to do.*

▶ **Mickey Klutts:** *He just loved what he was doing, he just loved it. He was always at the park at 2 o'clock and didn't want to leave until midnight. And you know, a lot of guys in baseball owe him an awful lot. I certainly do. Every time I put the [World Series] ring on, I think, "He's the man!" And all my friends, and all the guys in my era—he was the man!*

▶ **Mike Pagliarulo:** *The first thing that comes to my mind is I wish he was here. I felt terrible, and I feel terrible now, even just talking. That was a real bad day for me personally [when Billy died]. That's what I think of— I wish he was here. I really miss that. But I do think of him, and I think of all of these things very often . . . I don't know, I'm just telling you this for the first time, but after Billy's accident I went to Minnesota [to play* *for the Twins], and I developed an appreciation for the game more. And whether Billy had something to do with that, I don't know, but I do carry that with me, and I spoke about that when we won the World Series, about some of the teachings and the camaraderie, basically. Which is the part of the game that I miss most, and most players will probably tell you that as well. And with Billy around, there was a lot of that.*

▶ **Ray Negron:** *I was just a little skinny kid, and he just took a liking to me. He gave me his soul. He gave me his heart. This was Billy the Kid, but he was awesome. He was a beautiful person. He was wonderful to me. God knows Billy treated me great. When I got released from baseball, Billy gave me a check to go back to school. He wrote a letter to the bursar, because he knew a letter from him on Yankee stationery would have more of an impact and it would be easier for me to get in. That was Billy. I always enjoyed my one-on-one time with Billy, because it was just me and him at that moment. For the longest time, I just didn't understand why he was so good to me. I would question that a lot. There's no question that Billy and Reggie [Jackson] were my two biggest influences in life, in everything that I do, in how I behave and how I act. My aggressiveness. Everything is Reggie and Billy. When Billy was bad, he could be bad, but when he was good, no one was better, and that's the bottom line.*

▶ **Frank Lucchesi:** *He's a guy that I can never forget. I've had idols in my career, like DiMaggio . . . And in music, Frank Sinatra. Oh man, I'm a Sinatra fan. And I put Billy in the category of guys that I idolized and thought a lot of, although those guys are older.*

▶ **Charlie Silvera:** *I miss him. People say, "What about Billy?" So controversial till he died, and he still is now, and he always will be. He just wanted to win. I think it was just the idea that he was a competitor, and he just had that will to win. And he wanted to be somebody. He wanted to finally be the Yankee manager. I mean, that was his ultimate, and he ended up with that. Billy, he did a great job. Well, they say he couldn't last. He'd win, and then everything would get away from him. He wasn't afraid to challenge people, challenge owners, challenge anybody. He was* *different. He was Billy Martin, and he wanted to succeed. And in a way, he did succeed. And in a way, he wouldn't listen to anybody.*

▶ **Phil Pepe:** *I loved the guy. He really was special, and I'm frustrated and disappointed that not everybody could get to know the Billy Martin that I knew, because a lot of my peers dislike him, and I guess they had their reasons. I have very, very warm feelings about him. It's strange, but as time goes on, you don't think about the negatives. And I miss Billy. I miss the good times. Look, I had a lot of unpleasant memories and experiences with him, but I always think about the good things. I think the one thing that will never leave me is the way he treated my youngest son, because my son is so important to me, and for him to be so impor- tant to Billy is always something special.*

Billy could take an organization and quickly get it moving in the right direction again. And while he may not have lasted at the helm of any club for too many years, he left an impact on his players and the people around the teams that has lasted to this day. He deeply cared for them, and he wanted them to succeed not just for his benefit and the win, but for their own benefit as players and people. There's no doubt that he was their leader.

▶ **George Mitterwald:** *I think he was as good as anybody's ever been, as far as I've seen. Him and Earl Weaver to me were the two best managers in baseball. Billy was the type of guy, he knew what was going on. He was a smart man. He was a lot smarter than anybody will ever give him credit for. He knew how to get the best out of his coaches, his players, and anybody around him. He just had that knack for pushing the right button at the right time to challenge you to just make yourself a little bit better, to make the guy that you're in charge of better for the betterment of the team.*

Perhaps the way Rod Carew, Charlie Manuel, and Mickey Rivers remember Billy tells more about who he was and what he accom- plished than the wins, losses, division titles, and World Series rings.

▶ **Rod Carew:** *The smile on his face, the pat on the fanny, the confidence that he showed in me—I think about all those things. When I made my speech for the Hall of Fame, it was a cloudy day, and all of a sudden, when I got to Billy's name, it started rumbling and there was thunder. I said, "Oh, that's Billy showing that he approves of what's going on today. That he's proud that I got to the highest point of my profession." I'm glad that I was able to talk to you about a man that everyone sees as being a troublemaker. He wasn't totally that kind of person. Underneath he was a very good human being. I would have done anything for that man.*

▶ **Charlie Manuel:** *He would tell me that he was proud of me for what I accomplished playing in Japan. Clete [Boyer] would always tell him how good I was hitting, and he used to tell Clete that I never got a big chance in the big leagues, that people never really saw how good I could play the game. Matter of fact, the last time I saw him, at the winter meetings, he started crying. He told me, "Charlie, I've always pulled for you, man. You know that." And you know what? He meant it. It really kind of made me feel kind of sorrowful. The last time I saw him, that's how I remember him.*

▶ **Mickey Rivers:** *I know one thing, I said, "God bless him." I got to depend on him so much. Every day he'll call me. "How ya feeling? How ya doing?" I'd bring it up to people, I'd say, "Oh man, Billy did this for me. Billy did that for me." I didn't have to worry about nothing, because I know who had my back. He did good things for people. He helped people. It was heart. He helped people in general, whoever. And he did a lot of things for you that even people close to you don't do for you.*

Notes

1. George F. Will, *Bunts* (New York: Scribner, 1999), pp. 215–216.
2. Ira Miller, "Records are Falling for 10–0 A's," *New York Times*, April 18, 1981.
3. Billy Martin and Phil Pepe, *Billyball* (Garden City, N.Y.: Doubleday & Company, 1987), p. 191.
4. Will, p. 215.
5. Garry Wills, *Certain Trumpets: The Call of Leaders* (New York: Simon &

Schuster, 1994), p. 106.

6. Ibid., pp. 103–104.

7. Ibid., p. 106.

8. David Falkner, *The Last Yankee* (New York: Simon & Schuster, 1992), p. 194.

9. Wills, p. 110.

10. Ibid., p. 15.

11. Ibid., p. 110.

12. Martin and Pepe, pp. 270–272.

13. Howard Cosell, "Martin Deserved His Day in the Sun," *New York Daily News,* August 13, 1986.

14. Al Mari and Rick Cerrone, *Baseball Quarterly,* Winter 1977.

15. Dan Morris, "Billy Martin," *Visitor Magazine,* May 13, 1981.

16. Thomas Boswell, *Game Day* (New York: Penguin Books, 1992), p. 353.

17. Maury Allen, *Damn Yankee: The Billy Martin Story* (New York: Times Books, 1980), pp. 299–300.

18. Norman Lewis Smith, *The Return of Billy the Kid* (New York: Coward, McCann & Geoghegan, 1977), p. 213.

The Turnarounds of Billy Martin

The following table shows the turnarounds of teams managed by Billy Martin during his career. In each section, a team's record prior to Billy's arrival is first shown—including wins, losses, winning percentage, and finish—followed by the team's record during one or more seasons we'll call "Billyball" years. The percentage increase in wins under Billy's first full season of leadership is also shown.

Year	Team	Wins	Losses	Percentage	Finish	% Increase in Wins
1968	Minnesota Twins	79	83	.488	7th	
1969	Billyball Twins	97	65	.599	1st	+23%
1970	Detroit Tigers	79	83	.488	4th	
1971	Billyball Tigers	91	71	.562	2nd	+15%
1972	Billyball Tigers	86	70	.551	1st	
1973	Texas Rangers	48	91	.343	N/A	
1973	Billyball Rangers	9	14	.391	6th	
1974	Billyball Rangers	84	76	.525	2nd	+47%
1975	New York Yankees	53	51	.510	N/A	
1975	Billyball Yankees	30	26	.536	3rd	
1976	Billyball Yankees	97	62	.610	1st	+17%

1977	Billyball Yankees	100	62	.617	1st	
1979	New York Yankees	34	31	.523	N/A	
1979	Billyball Yankees	55	40	.579	4th	
1979	Oakland A's	54	108	.333	7th	
1980	Billyball A's	83	79	.512	2nd	+54%
1981	Billyball A's	64	45	.587	1st	
1982	New York Yankees	79	83	.488	5th	
1983	Billyball Yankees	91	71	.562	3rd	+15%
1984	New York Yankees	87	75	.537	3rd	
1985	New York Yankees	6	10	.375	N/A	
1985	Billyball Yankees	91	54	.628	2nd	+11%
1987	New York Yankees	89	73	.549	4th	
1988	Billyball Yankees	40	28	.588	2nd	

Index